Last Rights

To Kathy -
With many thanks to
a dear and lasting friend
and colleague,

Dan

Last Rights

A Catholic Perspective on End-of-Life Decisions

Dolores L. Christie

A SHEED & WARD BOOK

ROWMAN & LITTLEFIELD PUBLISHERS, INC.
Lanham • Boulder • New York • Toronto • Oxford

A SHEED & WARD BOOK

ROWMAN & LITTLEFIELD PUBLISHERS, INC.

Published in the United States of America
by Rowman & Littlefield Publishers, Inc.
A wholly owned subsidary of The Rowman & Littlefield Publishing Group
Inc. 4501 Forbes Boulevard, Suite 200
Lanham, Maryland 20706

PO Box 317
Oxford
OX2 9RU, UK

British Library Cataloguing in Publication Information Available

Library of Congress Cataloging-in-Publication Data

Christie, Dolores L.
    Last rights : a Catholic perspective on end-of-life decisions / Dolores L. Christie.
        p. cm.
    Includes bibliographical references and index.
    ISBN 0-7425-3152-X (alk. paper) — ISBN 0-7425-3153-8 (pbk. : alk. paper)
    1. Terminal care—Religious aspects—Catholic Church. 2. Palliative treatment—
Religious aspects—Catholic Church. 3. Medical ethics—Religious aspects—Catholic
Church. 4. Christian ethics. I. Title.
R726 .C463 2003
261.8'32175—dc22

2003015515

Printed in the United States of America

♾™ The paper used in this publication meets the minimum requirements of American
National Standard for Information Sciences—Permanence of Paper for Printed Library
Materials, ANSI/NISO Z39.48-1992.

DEDICATION

To Bertha, Michael, and Mary
who taught me not only how to live but how to die

To the gaggle of grandchildren
Daniel, Marguerite, Ryan, Joseph, Alexander,
Alexis, Sarah, Christiana, Zoe, and Max
who pledge me life yet to be

Contents

Acknowledgments

The Catholic vision of the human person reminds us of our intrinsic interdependence. Nowhere is this more graphically demonstrated than in the process of bookmaking. Midwifing the literary process were many friends and professional colleagues. My gratitude extends to Robert Heyer, formerly of Sheed and Ward, whose initial interest in the project encouraged me to take fingers to keyboard. More recently the support of Sheed and Ward's Jeremy Langford and his associates now with Rowman & Littlefield have offered the professional help needed to carry the project to completion. Jeremy has shared not only the pain and the possibility of the work but an unorthodox love for J. D. Salinger. Maybe that is why we get along so well.

As the manuscript grew, many readers called me to accuracy and to excellence. I am grateful to the writers' group at John Carroll University and in particular to Thomas Schubeck, S.J., who offered suggestions on additional chapters. Ethicists Allyson Robichaud, Ph.D., and Thomas Shannon, Ph.D., provided the mending kit for two ragged chapters. Neurologist Robert Richardson, M.D., assured the accuracy of medical fine points of the nervous system. Kathleen Whalen Fitzgerald, Ph.D., painstakingly read nearly every chapter. Her meticulous comments were always challenging and courageous and occasionally comforting. General readers will appreciate her efforts at making the prose accessible to those who are not fluent in the foreign language common to academia.

The standout hero of the project is internist and geriatrician Richard Christie, M.D. Dick sacrificed to the god of writers not only professional advice and his personal medical journals but also enduring support. He produced relevant articles, facts and figures, gourmet meals to keep me going, and tissues for the tears when I could not. He read and critiqued every word

I wrote, often twice or three times. To be my partner in life turned out to be a job greater than that for which he had signed on years ago.

Finally, the office and support system provided by John Carroll University and the Catholic Theological Society of America allowed a sacred space to think, to write, and finally to produce what you read in these pages. Thank you all.

Introduction

Topics in bioethics are reported in the news, dissected in professional journals, and discussed in hospital ethics committees. Nevertheless the critical venue for such questions is the real-life cases in which people must make end-of-life decisions for themselves or for someone they love. Religious perspective, life experience, and personal values all contribute to the internal debate that proceeds and often follows such wrenching decisions. "Did I do the right thing when I put Dad in the nursing home? My brothers did not agree with the decision. Mom, looking down from heaven, will never forgive me. And now Dad is dead. I feel so guilty."

End-of-life decisions are not mere scholarly conundra, isolated in the emotional sterility of methodological thought; they are practical questions situated in the exigencies of ordinary lives. To obtain good answers and trustworthy guidance for such vital questions requires more than consultation of a basic text on the principles of bioethics or a quick prayer in the hospital chapel. Principles help to get at the objective evaluation of morality, but they barely scratch the surface of the questions.[1] Prayer finds its resolution after one leaves one's knees. To get a thorough and perhaps even satisfying understanding of difficult issues and to make good decisions, the personal elements of decision-making, the complex facets of the moral subject, the person, including integrity, motivation, psychology, and emotion must be explored.[2] The place of individual rights must be explored not as a rallying cry but in the context of the total situation. One must examine the elements of circumstance. The dialogue partners for this exercise include the decision-makers bringing to bear their unique viewpoints, families with their complicated dynamics, doctors and other health professionals, hospital systems, and even society whose collective focus is the common good.

Every decision has a perspective, rooted in the beliefs of the decision-makers and played out in the unique settings and possibilities of their lives. For the following reasons this book examines end-of-life decisions in the context of the Roman Catholic tradition, a heritage rich in its teaching about the human person, the value of life, and the moral rights and responsibilities inherent to every human being.

First, Catholic thinking offers a concrete vision of the human person, an anthropology through which difficult end-of-life situations can be viewed. Much of contemporary American debate on bioethical issues implies but does not explicate a particular way of looking at human persons and their meaning, what Charles Curran calls "stance."[3] Americans assert that people have rights to health care, but do not establish the source and nature of those rights nor the implications that such an assertion has for other people. They affirm that doctors should not "play God," but rarely specify what that might mean in the face of life's end. Where does human stewardship begin and end; when should human ingenuity step humbly back in the wake of divine jurisdiction?[4] Such questions assume that the universe is involved in some way with a divine entity. Yet this is not the starting place for everyone.

People often are discomforted by such procedures as human cloning and genetic manipulation, but cannot quite articulate why or what it is about human beings that distinguishes them from sheep or fruit flies. They put pets "to sleep," but find it troubling to provide comparable "mercy" for family members. Life is a common experience, death comes to all; but how persons think about end-of-life questions for themselves, their relationship to death and to life itself, and the place of God in this equation influences the important decisions they make. A distinguishing and concrete perspective on the human person, an anthropology such as that offered within Catholic tradition, can serve to anchor and inform difficult decisions and provide a framework in which to think about them.

Second, the vast body of Catholic scholarship about morality, and particularly about medical-moral questions, that has been compiled over several centuries has remained in constant dialogue with technology and science.[5] Historically Catholic scholarship has not reflected a sectarian approach to medical-moral questions, accessible and applicable only to Catholics; rather it has applied "scientific ethical criteria to medical procedures in a manner which enabled them to arrive at universally applicable conclusions based on cause-and-effect analysis."[6] Even the common language used in contemporary bioethical conversation imports the principles and distinctions that have formed the warp and woof of Catholic thinking for centuries: principle of double effect, principle of totality, ordinary and extraordinary means, active and passive distinctions—to mention a few. A quick survey of the literature affirms that end-of-life questions are not new to formal Catholic discourse, but the complex discussion current in the public arena calls for an urgent reexamination.

Third, the Catholic tradition consistently has embraced certain values and principles as the fabric of its belief system and moral teachings, many of which are shared with others. "Christian" or "Catholic" or "gospel" values are embraced well beyond denominational lines; they are not unique. One religious viewpoint does not have an exclusive claim to them. It is perhaps better to describe such values as those qualities which contribute to human growth and development.[7] That is not to deny, however, that they can be found articulated in scripture or in specific Catholic teaching.[8] When terms such as "Christian," "Catholic," and "gospel" are used in this book, we shall try to distinguish what they mean.

Fourth, while readers need not be Catholic to appreciate this book, a "Catholic" perspective on the issues offers a concrete starting point to prompt discussion as a preface to framing opinions and conclusions. A frankly "apologetic" stance, one which defends a Catholic position, need not apologize to a relativistic world; especially if the goal is to promote discussion and good decisions rather than to achieve dominance. To stand clearly in a particular tradition can offer a dialogical starting point in a changing sea of "anything goes." Understanding the stance of another, I can better articulate my own stance, even if it differs. This is a far better place to begin than the indulgent but often uninformed acceptance of any and all positions as competitively valid, a stance which seems to pervade the American scene. My own experience in teaching college courses in philosophy and religious studies on these issues, lecturing extensively, and doing clinical ethics has convinced me of the value of the Catholic tradition and the urgency to connect its insights with the problems of contemporary bioethics.[9] This book explores the critical connections as both a contribution to the literature and a hands-on overview accessible to those who face end-of-life decision-making.

In addition to bringing the Catholic tradition to bear on end-of-life issues in the largest possible context, this book is intended also to help Catholics achieve a better understanding of their own tradition. Many Catholics do not know their own tradition in these matters. Even a formal exposure to Catholic education does not guarantee a grasp of the rich Catholic moral tradition. As someone with twenty years' experience teaching in Catholic colleges I can attest to the poverty of understanding that exists among Catholic students, many of whom ended their study of Catholicism at confirmation. Since serious moral questions about end of life are rarely components of childhood experience, many Catholic adults have no frame of reference from their faith tradition to approach them. Much of what they do have is, in fact, misinformation. Their religious "continuing education" is likely from the evening news, where a clear and accurate presentation of the church's wisdom is seldom found.

Beyond the Catholic discourse is an intracultural conversation that persists on specific life and death issues. Often shedding more heat than light is the American public debate on assisted suicide, removal of life support, and the so-called right to die. A national reluctance to prioritize values or to espouse criteria to judge the efficacy of anyone's positions. Statements such as, "I don't believe in smoking, but you have the right to do so if you wish," stall the conversation. The cultural climate of America provides no adequate forum for dialogue among a cacophony of strongly held religious beliefs. The Hmong woman, whose faith prohibits Caesarean section, is not persuaded by the doctor who insists that she needs that procedure to avoid death. A Christian Scientist refuses a life-saving transfusion rather than risk damnation according to his tradition. The desperate person seeking the aid of Jack Kevorkian to end his life is not particularly concerned that such practice is still illegal in most of the United States. The centenarian in the nursing home resists peg tubes and pills that others—perhaps even the visiting priest—insist are "ordinary means" to extend her life. In what place can such polarized positions be debated?

This book offers a helpful reference for ministers who deal with Catholic patients, for those who do not understand the perspectives of the Catholic tradition and wish to learn more, and for ordinary decision makers for whom these complex issues can be painful and even paralyzing. It aims to provide a user-friendly exploration of some serious topics. Specific issues are examined and practical suggestions for making decisions are offered.

The book is divided into three sections. The first section presents "theory," a context in which to discuss these serious questions. Chapter 1 outlines a "Catholic" approach to the human person, life in its beginnings and in its final hours, and what the approach has to do with its application to decisions. Chapter 2 summarizes the extensive Catholic moral tradition that grounds moral decision making from the objective point of view, that is, a clarification of what is objectively right and good. What is objectively the right thing to do must include not only the values and goals of the individual but the interfacing of that individual with the greater community, that is, the common good. Chapter 3 looks specifically at the decision maker. The primacy of conscience, as set forth in the documents of the Second Vatican Council, is juxtaposed with the bioethical considerations of autonomy, competence, and moral responsibility. Both Catholic tradition and contemporary bioethics insist on respect for the individual personal right to make choices consistent with personal values. The choices of the patient are the preeminent value in medical decision-making. The place and power of emotions, such as guilt, helplessness, and sorrow, are addressed.

The middle section examines more practical questions. Chapter 4 considers the pros and cons of advanced directives, legal statements of patient preferences for treatment and nontreatment should the patient become unable to speak for herself, as part of decision making in light of death. The living will and the durable power of attorney for health care are documents which have been promoted as important both for the sake of autonomous decisions about health care and as safeguards against over- or undertreatment of patients. Chapter 5 deals with futility, the conclusion that further aggressive medical intervention would yield no benefit to the patient, a term that has come to prominence in recent American discussion, where the contrast of good care with good management of money often shapes the debate.

Chapter 6 addresses the specific issues of persistent coma and permanent vegetative state. Chapter 7 looks at the emotion-packed issue of providing artificial feeding and fluids to the dying patient. Chapter 8 confronts suicide, euthanasia, and assisted suicide, placing these questions into the context of a faith perspective and in relationship to the American debate.

The last section of the book addresses the relationship of individual decisions about care to the larger community. Included are discussions about organ donation and hospice intervention. The final chapter focuses specifically on the religious and pastoral dimensions of death. It examines the place of suffering and religious rituals as part of human need.

The book is structured so that it can be read as a whole or in parts. Cross-references link related passages throughout the text. The glossary at the end is meant to help those unfamiliar with technical medical and ethical terms, while avoiding clutter within the text. The appendices and bibliography provide resources for further study as well as some helpful tools to smooth the transitions at life's end. Whether read in parts or as a whole, this book provides a helpful resource for individuals faced with the difficult task of making end-of-life decisions and for those whose work it is to help them decide.

NOTES

1. There is increasing recognition concerning the need to supplement a principle-based approach to bioethics with other insights. See Edmund D. Pellegrino, "The Metamorphosis of Medical Ethics: A 30-Year Retrospective," *Journal of the American Medical Society* 269, no. 9 (March 3, 1993): 1158–62.

2. This "new" idea is being expressed as well in a broader arena than the Catholic tradition. See Bette-Jane Crigger, "Where Do Moral Decisions Come From?" *Hastings Center Report* 26, no. 1 (January/February 1996): 33.

3. Many Christian authors have struggled to address what elements comprise a "Christian" starting point. Curran seems to me to have been the most successful in defining what it might be. See the most recent and brief treatment of Curran's appoach in Charles E. Curran, *The Catholic Moral Tradition* (Washington, D.C.: Georgetown Univeristy Press, 1999), 33–34.

4. Courtney Campbell takes up this question. See "Religious Ethics and Assisted Suicide in a Pluralistic Society," *Kennedy Institute of Ethics* 2, no. 3 (1992): 253–57. I have discussed his ideas in "Relativizing the Absolute: Belief and Bioethics in the Foxholes of Technology," in *Notes from a Narrow Ridge: Religion and Bioethics*, ed. Dena S. Davis and Laurie Zoloth (Hagerstown, Md.: University Publishing Group, 1999), 101–102.

5. See David F. Kelly, *The Emergence of Roman Catholic Ethics in North America* (New York: Edwin Mellen Press, 1979).

6. Kelly, *Emergence*, 5.

7. This more basic perspective is common to the natural law method that has historically been characteristic of Catholic moral theology. Unfortunately an unnuanced representation of natural law has rendered this theory as a quaint vestigial of the past. Misunderstood, it has been marginalized as a useful approach to moral thinking, especially in philosophy.

8. See, for example, the enclyclical letter, *The Gospel of Life* (Boston: St. Paul's Books and Media, 1995), in which John Paul II outlines the ecclesial position on the value of life and its implications.

9. The call for a systematic rendering of religious perspectives as applied to specific bioethical concerns is increasing, not only in the life-and-death issues discussed in this book but in issues raised by new technology. See Mark J. Hanson, "Religious Voices in Biotechnology: The Case of Gene Patenting," *Hastings Center Report Special Supplement* 27, no. 6 (November/December 1997): 1–19.

Chapter One

A Catholic View of the Human Person

What has the church said about life, its beginnings and its endings? Is there a particular approach to defining human beings that is distinctively Catholic? Could such a Catholic vision help people better understand life itself and make better decisions on end-of-life issues?

Often the decisions people make are influenced by some deeper values they cherish, what might be called "systems of meaning." How a person envisions the existence or not of an afterlife, whether she believes that she is responsible for her decisions or that God is, what she images the human being to be—these core beliefs will inform moral decisions, particularly the crucial decisions concerning the end of life. The orthodox Jew who sees death as the ultimate and final end might exercise a greater effort to preserve biological life than a mainstream Methodist who expects to live on in eternity, whatever becomes of the body. Someone who follows Enlightenment thought, using human reason as the key criterion for decision-making, might choose different medical interventions from the person who believes that God is master of the world and expects humanity to be stewards of divine creation.[1] Whether someone calls the product of conception a "baby" or a "mass of cells" has a distinct bearing on what he thinks about it and how he might treat it.

Many of the elements that inform moral decisions are never brought to a conscious level. They remain buried deep beneath the surface of human consciousness, much like a vast iceberg invisible beneath the horizon of our psyche. Slogans such as "right to life" or "right to die" seem to give reasons for chosen actions, but they are only loud assertions, shaky statements largely without a logic to support them. Such statements represent merely the tip of the moral iceberg which informs what people do and why they do it. To assess the influence of deeply held beliefs on decision-making is a critical part of the process, as important as it is for a ship's captain to be aware of an iceberg's vast mass under the water and not look only at the icy protrusion that cuts the water's surface.

This chapter will examine the specific attitudes and positions that the Catholic church holds about the value of life and about the human person. While these beliefs are not necessarily unique to Catholic thought, they are clearly delineated in the tradition. What is the meaning of human personhood and ultimately of human life? What has this attitude to do with how one makes end-of-life decisions? Let us examine these questions in turn.

THE TRADITION ON LIFE

Throughout the centuries, the Judaeo-Christian tradition has supported the value of life, especially human life. The creation stories of Genesis single out human beings as the epitome of God's creative work. Only when all the rest of the world is complete are human beings made, after the likeness of the divine (Gen. 1:26). It is God's own handiwork that fashions humanity from the mud of the earth and places the best of all creatures in a world designed for human use (Gen. 1:7–8,15). In the Catholic tradition human life has always held a special place, a place of awe and respect.

The murder of Abel, the younger son of Adam and Eve, by his jealous brother is severely punished by God. The taking of the life of another is not to be permitted. Cain is punished by banishment and alienation from the soil (Gen. 4:12). But this primordial killer is spared a punitive death: "If anyone kills Cain, says God, Cain shall be avenged sevenfold" (Gen. 4:15). Even the life of a murderer is sacred.

In later biblical accounts we see a tectonic shift away from human sacrifice in the community of those covenanted with God. Ancient peoples believed that God demanded the sacrifice of human life as part of religious practice. This belief was shared even by those who followed Yahweh, including the patriarch, Abraham. He was prepared to kill his precious heir, his "only one" (Gen. 22:2), whom Abraham loved. But the people whom God shepherded would do things differently. Human life was not to be destroyed, even as a sacrifice for God. From the moment Abraham laid aside his knife to spare Isaac, innocent human life has been given a privileged place in human thinking.

When we shift focus to the Christian scripture, we notice that what gives Jesus credibility with the people is his power to heal, to cast out demons, to bring people who are dead to life. His "ministry" affirms the goodness of human life and the importance not only of bodily health but of psychological and spiritual well-being. His "new teaching" (Mark 1:28) had less to do with intellectual dogma than with his ability to cure and to banish the "unclean" spirits which disrupt human equanimity. Ultimately the shocking message of Jesus is one of "eternal life" to those who eat his flesh and drink his blood (John 6:54). The bodily life of human beings is important, but it becomes relativized in the context of the "life" offered to believers in the community of love that is the font of Christian hope.

As Christianity spread and set deep roots in Western culture, the shared attitude of respect for life and expectation of afterlife was not routinely questioned. Little "official" teaching can be found to support what was an assumed and commonly shared vision.[2] It is not until Pius XII (1950s) that we begin to see more specific Catholic teaching on life issues.[3] Vatican II affirmed the importance of human life and personhood but did not concentrate in detail on life issues.

In recent years the Catholic church has taken a strong stand in favor of a "consistent ethic of life," drawing from the term popularized by Joseph Cardinal Bernardin.[4] Bernardin's writings stress the continuum of human life from the moment of conception until life's end. "Those who defend the right to life of the weakest among us must be equally visible in support of the quality of life of the powerless among us,"[5] says Bernardin. The "consistency" he calls for has to do with how we view abortion, the care of the weak, the administration of capital punishment, and anything that deals with *quality* of life. Bernardin calls for public policy that affects taxes, welfare, nutrition, and health care. Certainly in a society which has been accused of having a "culture of death," where such figures as Dr. Jack Kevorkian have brought assisted suicide to an arena that borders on the commercial, it has become increasingly urgent to stand strongly in favor of the value of human life in all its forms. Pope John Paul II responds to this need in his characterization of Christians as the "people of life and the people for life."[6] Modern Catholic teaching has rejected any unequal treatment of human life, affirming the preciousness of all humanity from the first cries of birth to the final amen of death.

What then does it mean to assert that life has value? There are situations in which any material value—and life is a material value—*may* and sometimes *must* give way to a higher value.[7] A clear example is the voluntary death of Jesus, a figure lauded throughout history because he sacrificed his life for those he loved. The tradition asserts that life may sometimes be replaced or overridden by another more important consideration.[8] Such prioritization must be kept in mind when difficult end-of-life decisions must be made.

Further, since life and its exigencies are not totally under the control of our will, whims, and wishes—nor even that of modern medical technology and the professionals who administer it—there are times when life's end must be recognized and accepted. There are ethical criteria to determine how and when this ought to happen. We shall examine them later in the book. The tradition that calls itself "Catholic" has always recognized both human stewardship over human life and the real need to give way to divine stewardship in appropriate instances. How to assess the situations in which this might occur will be examined further.

THE HUMAN PERSON

Appreciation of the human person in every aspect is key to everything else we are about to discuss. We begin with the essential connection between humanity and God as affirmed in the Christian tradition. The doctrine of the incarnation, that God came concretely into history enfleshed in Jesus, is arguably the cardinal Christian belief. The incarnation is central in establishing criteria for moral action. The contemporary expression of the meaning and implication of this doctrine for Catholics flows from Vatican II's groundbreaking document on the church in the modern world, *Gaudium et Spes*. The document details the essential connection between the belief that God became human and the humanity in which God dwells. It is this belief that roots what might be termed a Catholic or Christian anthropology, that is, the characteristics, context, and customs of human beings through a frankly faith-based lens. The categories established by Louis Janssens, formerly professor of moral theology at the Catholic University of Leuven, Belgium, and adviser to many who attended Vatican II, in his influential work which preceded the council will be a major source for this discussion, since they present a systematic approach to the ideas found in the council document.

First, located in the doctrine of the incarnation, *Gaudium et Spes* affirms that the human person is made in the image and likeness of God. Even before the birth of Jesus the pastoral language of Genesis 2 details God's intimate involvement with the creation of humanity: God forms with God's own hands the first human being and animates this awesome creature with the very breath of the divine (Gen. 2:7). Human beings, the psalmist tells us, are made "a little less than the angels" (Ps. 8:6). Such an assertion speaks to the intrinsic value of the human being and to human life on Earth as well as ultimate human destiny. To look into the eyes of a human being is to see a reflection of the divine. God is the origin, the axis, and the terminus of human existence. Human beings have what Janssens calls a divine "spark." This intimate and essential connection to the divine should influence how persons think about themselves and about others. It is this same *imago dei* that shapes what might be called a Catholic theory of human rights, the basis from which the demand for just treatment of persons flows.

Recognition of this intrinsic human dignity evokes an attitude of awe and respect for each human being, particularly for those who are vulnerable ("Whatever you did for one of these least brothers of mine, you did for me" [Matt. 25:40]). Few persons are as vulnerable as those who look immanently into the face of death, more so if they have been weakened in a battle with a debilitating illness. The idea of human dignity has implications not only for how to treat an individual who is sick, but for such modern concerns as universal health care, particularly in the light of statistics that 40 million Americans are currently uninsured for medical care.

Second, human beings are embodied spirits. Flesh and spirit combine, not in a dualistic opposition, but in an inseparable reality. John's gospel puts it most graphically when it affirms that the divine Word *became*—not merely *took on*—flesh (the Greek word is *sarx*, or "meat"). The body of Jesus is not a sham or some troublesome redundancy. It is an integral part of who Jesus Christ was and is. Without a fleshy body, there would be no Jesus Christ. The glorified Christ appears not as a ghost but in bodily form. The same is true for the rest of us. Human beings are not mere spirits, noncorporeal realities trapped in time awaiting a resurrection free from a limiting material body. Nor are they mere biological entities, carbon-based puzzles to be analyzed, prodded, and probed toward improvement until they reach some optimal form and function.

For many the relationship with the body is a discomforting one: some dislike the package, disdain its functions, and/or spend much time and money trying to make it better. Modern preoccupation with vitamin supplements, Viagra, physical fitness, and plastic surgery testify to this phenomenon. Human beings do not readily accept and embrace the material aspect of humanness as good and as integral to who they are. People often do not embrace the body as an intrinsic part of their selves. Rather, they seek to control its functions, its size and shape, and its destiny. This attitude becomes magnified when people face illness or death, both of which represent the ultimate betrayal by the alien bodies they were doomed to inhabit but inclined to disdain. As Elisabeth Kubler-Ross said in her landmark book, *On Death and Dying*, denial attempts to change what is inevitable, or anger may characterize behavior as persons stand before death. Most of the 200 dying patients whom she interviewed reacted to their terminal diagnosis in this way.[9]

By contrast the Catholic tradition affirms that the body is good—God saw what God had made and said it was good. Goodness of the body is an essential component of the reality and the uniqueness of each individual. It is precisely through the body that human beings achieve their ultimate destiny. To put it clearly in the religious context of Catholicism: the body is the only vehicle through which the person reaches the gates of heaven or hell. Human beings must deal in a realistic but hopeful manner with the body and its movement toward death. Such an attitude is not only essential near death but should be cultivated throughout life. To focus too narrowly on either the bodily or the spiritual aspect of the human being is to fall outside the middle road of what is Catholic.

In a period of history that disavows the spiritual dimension of humanity and concentrates on the material, a painful conundrum for medical decisions arises. This problem is especially acute for decisions about end of life. Human beings are flesh, their existence in the known world is bound by limits common to all organic matter. Life, tied intimately to human bodiliness, is a finite good which cannot be sustained forever. That is why it is newsworthy when a person lives to celebrate a centenary birthday, and why insurance tables are created to calculate the odds of anyone surviving beyond a certain mathematically defined age. As medical specialists struggle to keep the mortal coil of human stuff wrapped tightly around the person who is dying— which in a sense is every person, it is good to balance optimism about the organic with realism about its outcome. In the history of human existence, no empirical evidence exists that anyone has ever avoided death. If the fundamental material-physical dimension of the person is recognized and accepted, a different approach to life's end can and should be envisioned. These ideas will be explored further.

Human beings are likewise intrinsically spiritual. Christian belief points to a reality that consists of much more than disposable and interchangeable tissue. Patients are not merely the "acute fulminant liver in bed two," "the cardiac case scheduled for surgery," or "the peg tube in the day room." Human beings are more than a sum of their pieces and parts. Even the Frankenstein monster was portrayed as having feelings. The spiritual dimension of humanity may be intimately bound to the biological, but it is a real and nonnegotiable part of humanity. It is interesting that recently in the scientific world there have been studies to investigate the connections between prayer and health. Even science does not eschew the reality and importance of the spiritual.

Because of their spiritual dimension persons have a meaning, purpose, and final destination that transcends bodily life, what Charles Curran calls their "resurrection destiny."[10] Whatever medicine is able to accomplish, its endeavors must always be tempered and even relativized by such a perspective. Awe for persons means more than the celebration in an intensive care unit that certain organs can be functionally maintained. Modern medicine has many examples of such activity,[11] which underplay or deny the essential spiritual aspect of human personhood.

Third, Catholic tradition sees human beings as *naturally* attracted to good, the ultimate expression of that good being God. This position represents a notable difference between Catholic thinking and some other Christian traditions, which view human beings as so corrupted by sin that they cannot of themselves recognize the good that is before them. Such a negative anthropology may form the basis of an approach to medical decision-making that favors paternalism. It would dictate that if the patient is unable to recognize good when it presents itself in the form of a medically recommended treatment—the doctor's assessment of what is best for a patient's body—that patient should be urged if not forced to accept that good. The difficulty is exacerbated in situations where choices against such treatment are likely to end in death.

But Catholic anthropology affirms that people by their nature are "capable of knowing and loving [the] creator," says *Gaudium et Spes*.[12] They have "a law written by God" which is "the very dignity of [persons]."[13] To speak of resurrection destiny is to see each human life as moving through individual decisions toward God or away from God. Every moral choice a person makes either advances the journey toward God or sets it back. What this means in medical decision-making is that the choices individuals make as they follow the dictates of their own consciences, *even if the conclusions disagree* with the recommendation of medical personnel and/or the wishes of friends and family, should be respected. All persons have an intrinsic right, even a duty, to follow the decisions of the deliberation of conscience.

An anthropology that asserts that human beings are good and can perceive good when it stands in their path of choices should result in a certain trust in the decisions people make, even if these decisions would not be our own.[14] In the anxiety of the hospital room, it might be well to remember this notion. Sometimes the patient's version of what is the good may differ from that of the doctor's. "Yes, doctor, I want you to stop treating my baby aggressively. It's time to let her go. She has had three surgeries during the last four months and is not really any better for it. You tell me that she will always be dependent on feeding tubes and will never live a normal human life." If God has created this parent with an inherent ability to recognize a concrete good when it is before her and to choose it, others should respect that ability and its choices—even though the decisions might not represent what they would do. Those in charge of the technological interventions may not always honor such choices, however: "But Mrs. Jones, I can't just stand by and let you kill your innocent child. That's what will happen if you don't allow us to perform this surgery this time." People of goodwill and human-worthy values may have different conclusions about the same scenario. Such a statement does not yet serve to assign a moral judgment as to the rightness or wrongness of either conclusion. Nor does it mean to say that every opinion has the same moral value.

Catholic anthropology demands both human responsibility toward decision-making and respect even of dubious decisions people may make, since it affirms that persons have the God-given "wiring" to make good decisions. Catholic anthropology affirms the primacy of individual conscience and its choices. It is essentially different from the anthropology of such thinkers as Karl Barth or in such modern novels as William Golding's *Lord of the Flies*, where it is only God's direct intervention—in the case of Barth—or the rules of civilized society—in the case of Golding—that protect humanity from seeking its own destruction.

This stance has many implications. Later we shall discuss the Catholic meaning of conscience in greater detail, and how this intersects with the notion of autonomy as it is perceived in American thinking. We shall discuss why this view of the human person demands that the advance directives of persons should be respected and honored, even in cases where they are not executed on the proper form. While protection and implementation of one's wishes under the law are available in the United States, such protection is framed in a legal rather than an anthropological perspective.

Tension often characterizes disagreements among the patient/person, family members, and the attending medical personnel about treatment options. A real affirmation that an individual patient's decisions are to be trusted, since he is the one most qualified to understand what is good for him, helps alleviate tension and confusion in decision-making. This is acutely true in the face of death. As a person enters the process of dying, the last thing needed is anxiety over disagreements on treatment. Dying is a once-in-a-lifetime event, one which demands the full attention of the individual and of those in attendance. An appreciation that even God does not violate the choices a person makes may help relieve the anxiety that accompany it.

Gaudium et Spes asserts that human beings are created to be free. Freedom in the sense used in Catholic moral theology is not an isolated entity, but rather has its basis in the resurrection destiny discussed above. Freedom is always conceived as striving for the good. "The morality of acts is defined by the relationship of [human] freedom with the authentic good," as John Paul II has observed.[15] Janssens points out that this has to do both with the liberty to choose one's final goal and the ability to make incremental choices about how to get to that ultimate goal.[16] The person is most free when he or she moves toward the good with no external nor internal constraints.

Freedom of conscience as articulated in the Catholic tradition is a very different thing from the notion of freedom as it is usually characterized, or perhaps caricatured, in the United States. Americans often view freedom almost as the license to do whatever pleases the individual, with no normative reference or standard for evaluating the choices against anything but personal beliefs, preferences, and feelings. I should be "free to be me," in the words of a popular 1960s Marlo Thomas song. Such uncritiqued and unbridled freedom may embrace many objects: buying a big car or getting a face lift, building a hate fence or painting one's house orange. Each of these examples may form the basis of free expression of a person's personality but without normative measure for the external value of the objects of choice.

Such a sense of freedom may imply an entitlement to any and all kinds of medical intervention to prolong and save an individual's life, whatever the cost. Freedom in such a situation is only an illusion, however. Often this illusion of entitlement is played out on the front pages of the newspaper as families plead in the public forum for the right to funds for exotic or experimental treatments that (usually an adjective similar to "hard-hearted" or "money-grubbing" is appended or at least implied to elicit support for the cause) insurance companies will not authorize because they are experimental or their value is perceived to be minimal. The emotional stakes go up if the needy patient happens to be a charming and vulnerable child. Not stated but accepted tacitly and without challenge is that the American way of freedom embodies a right to whatever the individual needs or wants without an articulated responsibility for whose task it is to make that happen. The notion of rights in medical matters as viewed through the filter of Catholic tradition will be treated more fully in chapter 9.

Freedom is not an attribute that attends every moral choice to the same degree, however. Human ability to choose freely depends not only on knowing the object of the choice, but on the psychological and physical states that accompany the process of choosing. In its moral teaching the church has spoken about impediments to freedom which impact on individual human choices. There are circumstances or conditions which render free choice less possible and even sometimes impossible. An IQ of 160 enables a student to get a better score on the SATs than an IQ of 50. The brighter student has more "freedom" to achieve success than the less intelligent one.

The freedom necessary to think clearly and to act appropriately can be compromised by the influence of drugs or alcohol. A habitual smoker is not as free as a first time smoker to quit cigarettes. Such things are examples of diminished autonomy, but not the only examples. Diminished autonomy can often be the by-product of illness itself or of its accompanying anxiety and must be addressed in relationship to human freedom to make decisions about health and treatment. The next chapter will explore these ideas in greater detail.

Bioethics textbooks speak about human freedom and autonomy as among the grounding principles of medical ethics, but they are universally unclear as to the foundations of these principles in a specific anthropological stance. In an American context freedom is often expressed in terms of "rights," without a clear notion of what "rights language" implies, what kind of rights are being asserted, or where they get their authority in anything but a legal sense.

As understood by the Catholic tradition, freedom is never exercised in a vacuum. It inevitably works within the limits imposed by a real situation. In medicine, choices may be constricted by the medical condition and prognosis of the patient, the material limits of health care resources, and the prioritized values of the decision-maker. Freedom is also circumscribed by the needs of others, called in the tradition of the common good. Individual freedom to swing one's fist ceases at the margin of the other's nose. Individual choice is limited by the needs of others.

Fifth, connected with the notion of freedom and free choice is the idea, expressed in Vatican II, that the human person is a unique and, in a sense, an "unfinished" entity. Each person has a personal one-of-a-kind history based on a set of experiences that differentiates her from every other person. As a teacher of bioethics I have heard strong differences of opinion among students, often nursing students, about what to do in response to a case presented in class. When examined more closely, the disagreements are seen as rooted in the divergent and often unique experiences of the students. One insists that tube feeding for nursing home patients is a terrible thing. When questioned as to why he holds this strong belief, the student might say, "I work in a nursing home. I see these old and frail people, none of whom wants that feeding tube. They are nearly vegetables, simply existing because someone insists on pouring in nutrition to keep them going. Many times the site of the tube becomes infected and the person dies anyway. I sure wouldn't want a loved one of mine to end up in such a state." Another student, strong in her belief that tube feeding is a good thing, talks about her grandmother who gained several healthy years because she was artificially fed. The dipolar perspectives flow from the unique experience of the individuals. *Gaudium et Spes* articulates this reality when it speaks of the uniqueness of each human being. Every human being is "an unsolved puzzle,"[17] even to himself. This uniqueness will influence the decisions that each person makes, rendering them different for different persons. Different does not necessarily translate that one decision is right and the other is wrong.

Sixth, one of the most basic characteristics of humanity is limitedness. Much as I might want to play in the NBA, the fact that I am well over fifty years old and well under six feet tall ("vertically challenged" at just over five feet) limits my potential to achieve that goal. God clearly is not calling me to the athletic life typified by the legendary Michael Jordan. Likewise, if my son is asked by a doctor whether to continue to treat his infant who has several congenital anomalies which will perhaps require many surgeries, he is limited in his ability to make a good decision by the technical information given him by the health care professionals. Even health care professionals can only quote the statistical odds; they cannot know with certainly what they will mean for this particular patient. Will the treatments, though painful, result is some real quality of life for the child? We cannot know, for sure, what the future will hold. We can only take the information of probabilities and make the best choices we can here and now. All of us can resonate with the enlightenment of hindsight after making decisions under the limits of the real situation: "If only we had known." But we did not and, in fact, could not have known. Real-life decisions are always decisions based on the limited knowledge that is available when the decision must be made. The gravity of this truism is most acutely felt in decisions about life and death. There is never a decision that has all the knowledge that might be needed to make it perfectly.

None of us knows exactly when or how we will die. We can take medication, exercise and eat properly; however, our limitedness, specified by our genes and influenced by the odds of chance occurrences, precludes a certain knowledge or control over our ultimate destiny. Even in the trivial decisions of ordering a meal in a new restaurant we cannot be sure that the dish will live up to what is alluringly described in the menu.

What the tradition calls "original sin" also creates a condition of limitedness for human persons. While we human beings are perceived as essentially good, the evil that affects us—the metaphor of Adam and Eve's sin—limits both our vision of and our striving toward the good. The human person "has inclinations toward evil too, and is engulfed by manifold ills which cannot come" from God.[18] This is a sobering thought in an otherwise optimistic anthropology. It reminds us that it is foolhardy to make decisions in the solitary vacuum of only our own insights. It reminds us that our limitedness may sometimes result in decisions that are not the best, but that the best decisions are not always known or possible to us in the reality of time and space.

Seventh, human persons are beings in process. Both collectively, through cultural and technological advances, and individually, through the unique experiences of each human sojourner through life, persons learn and grow and develop. What someone knows today is more than that person knew yesterday, and tomorrow will bring more knowledge and insight. Is not this process at the root of what is often unreasonable hope that technology might advance to find a cure tomorrow for the disease that is killing someone today?

This continuum of process affects human ability to make decisions at the cultural and societal level—such as the time lapse before a cure for a particular disease is found—and at the individual level. A culture or society cannot be morally responsible for what it does not yet know. If Abraham thought that God required human sacrifice of innocent children—an assumption of the culture of his time—he could not be held morally responsible for taking

Isaac's life. Any mother will regret mistakes she made as a novice parent that she no longer makes with her more recent children. My own daughter, recently the mother of her second child, commented on how much easier it was to care for and to nurse baby number two. Even with her skills as a family practice doctor, the experience of caring for the first child was needed to do better with the second. The firstborn is like the first pancake of the batch—not at all perfect. The children in a family often talk about being raised in different family cultures. There is much truth in such statements. Hindsight is a wonderful source of moral wisdom, but one which is not accessible when needed in the here and now.

More specifically, the things that persons value and how they make decisions will change as they move through their life cycle. The cherished dolls and prized baseball cards of youth become forgotten in the blush of adolescent love, which in turn gives way to concerns of mortgage, family maintenance, and IRAs. The eighty-year-old sees far more value in being able to get his body to move at all than to master all the new dance moves essential to the eighteen-year-old. For this reason a cautionary tale must be told regarding medical decision-making. Those nearing life's end may be, in their own unique process, in a very different place from those around the bedside. Perhaps it is a sense of prioritizing the important values differently; perhaps it is only the yearning to be done with the fight to live through repeated interventions and ready to accept the inevitable process of dying. While it is common belief that this distinction is one of the old versus the young, it is sometimes the wisdom of youth trapped in a cancerous body that is ready to end the fight. This disparity of values is true for family and friends of a dying person, of course, but it applies to caregivers as well. The twenty-five-year-old nurse or the doctor eager and fresh from residency have no experience of what it means to be ninety, in constant pain, and without the companionship of one's friends and family long dead. The family of a very sick teenager may not understand her need to be done with treatments and hospitals. They avert their eyes from the face of death that she already knows in detail and embraces as friend.

Eighth, a Catholic anthropology locates human persons as essentially connected to one another. We do not exist independently; no one can in fact be human without others. This is not merely a pious illusion or the sappy conclusion of a Broadway tune: "People who need people are the luckiest people in the world." It is a fundamental condition of humanity, as constituted in the Catholic tradition. We are related collectively to each other, to God, to the universe, and even to ourselves. Without our relationships there is no humanity. Exotic stories of children raised by wolves, isolated from human contact, testify to lack of language and lack of connectedness that results. Even monkeys nursed through bottles suspended from chicken wire were found to be negatively affected by the absence of real warmth and contact with their mothers.

What are the implications of saying that human beings are connected? When we realize that we are related, we accept certain obligations to one another. These obligations demand that in decision-making each person takes into consideration what the impact of his or her decision are on the "others" in the equation. Marie has been told by her doctor that, due to a blood transfusion several years ago she has a terminal liver disease. A transplant could save her life. This news is a terrible shock to the forty-year-old Marie. Very quickly she tells the doctor to go ahead with plans for transplant. "Put me on that list. Not only do I have my life to live—many dreams are still unfulfilled—but I have three children who count on me for financial and emotional support. My relationship to them and their dependence on me make it important that I say "yes" to the treatment offered. To die now would not only deprive me but would be very hard on my family." Marie's decision-making process embraces the best of the anthropology of connectedness to others. Marie has considered not only the possible consequences to herself but how her death would impact her family.

Might the moral implications change if the scenario given above is altered slightly? Here is Maisie, seventy-five. She has raised her family and her retirement is secure. Age is not a criterion for exclusion from the liver transplant list, however. With a transplant it is likely that she will live a few more years, perhaps in pretty good health. At first glance this would appear to be an easy decision. We want to say, "Go for it, Maisie! Get the transplant." After all, insurance will pay for it and Maisie certainly has as much "right" to that organ as anyone else. She is a good citizen and deserves all the benefits that good health care can offer. Looking more deeply, however, Maisie assesses the limited number of organs available for the many patients who may need them to survive. She decides to forgo being put on the list. The reasoning: "I have lived a happy and complete life. Others who may need a new liver have not been so lucky. Let them go first." Her reasoning is based in the common good, which takes into account an understanding that any decisions she makes will affect not only her but the whole set of people who made need transplants to survive. It is a decision grounded in the idea that each person is essentially related to and thereby morally responsible to every other person.

Human persons and their decision may never be conceived in isolated or static terms. They must be viewed from all aspects, to get a complete picture of the moral implications. Louis Janssens used a phrase to describe this: "the human person, adequately considered." His term, adequate, is meant to convey both the multivalent reality that is the human being and the incompleteness of our vision at any one point in time: look at all aspects ("adequate") but know that the vision is incomplete (as against "perfect"). Without this multivalenced approach—adequate—the person making decisions at the end of life is short-changed.

KEY ELEMENTS IN A CATHOLIC WORLDVIEW

A treatment of a Catholic anthropology would not be complete without the mention of two additional and important elements. As noted earlier, much of what is specified as "Catholic" is not antithetical to or necessarily different from other belief systems. The major Western religions, believing as they do in a personal God, affirm that human persons have a relationship to that God; and that respect is due humanity. Eastern traditions, while not sharing a focused interest in a personal God, also see value in respect for persons. What category of human beings "counts" as deserving such respect may differ. A disparate ethnicity (ancient and modern "ethnic cleansing" testifies to this gap), a different age or biology (unborn humanity or adults of diverse castes or color may not hold the same rights in some traditions), or a different religion or value structure (the bombing of the World Trade Center as a godly act multiplies examples set by the Israelites in their wars against foreign tribes) delimit those protected by religious perspectives of human rights.

Besides highlighting the special value of the human person, Catholic tradition places a strong emphasis first, on the common good and second, on a belief in an afterlife. What have these to do with the topic of end of life? First, let us examine the common good.

Catholic tradition makes a distinction between the common good and the principle of utility. Utility has as its moral goal the production of the greatest good (or pleasure) for the greatest number of people. The Achilles' heel of this perspective is that allows little concern for the rights of and results for the minority. It is exemplified in a marketplace mentality, a willingness to sacrifice the few for the many and, often, for the money. If a certain formula of medical care will benefit the majority, a utilitarian morality is comfortable with having a percentage of the population whose medical care is not paid for. It may be cost effective, morally acceptable by a utilitarian standard, to limit reimbursed care to those without a preexisting tendency toward diabetes or who carry the gene for breast cancer. Since it might be expensive to test for these conditions or to treat them, and since only a minority of persons are likely to get these diseases, the majority would not benefit from such coverage. Utility would demand that insurance payments get, as they say, "the best bang for the buck." This would leave people with diabetes or breast cancer without medical insurance coverage. In the United States, many health care plans offered by companies exclude coverage for certain conditions, leaving desperate people scrambling for options for care.[19] Many Americans have no health insurance at all, another instance of the principle of utility at work.

Common good ethics, on the other hand, may not exclude minorities. By definition, a common good stance requires that the benefits derived must be available to all. At its root is the philosophical conviction that each person has equal worth and therefore a right to share in the benefits that derive from a certain policy or good. Not just the worthy, the rich, or those who do not have certain diseases should qualify for paid health care, but if such care is legislated it should not discriminate.

If someone's house is razed to put through the highway, all drivers—even the person whose house is gone—will benefit from the highway. It would be immoral, according to the common good, to have this highway accessible to only those who drive Mercedes. That might be justified underutility—those who drive Mercedes are in the majority and/or pay more taxes—but never under the common good, which seeks to offer at least a portion of the benefit to everyone—even those who have a ten-year-old "junker" and don't make enough to pay taxes.

The final element in what we have called a Catholic worldview is that of resurrection destiny, the belief in an afterlife or a heaven. This element must be kept in mind in making decisions, since it relativizes anything that is done. A balance of what we can do and what we cannot do is essential to a Catholic perspective on moral decision-making. Our decisions, especially those connected to the end of life, should be based on thoughtful and informed consideration, but they do not need to be omniscience or perfect ones. Ultimately it is only God whose "worldview" is complete and whose providence makes up for that which our humanity cannot program or predict with certainty. Resurrection destiny is the hope of Christian life, where tears will be wiped away and imperfect choices will be made right. The promise is embodied in the image of Ezekiel's dry bones and in the triumphant, "He is risen." It reassures and reminds us that we are neither completely in control nor completely responsible for the decisions we make in the limited horizons of earthly life.

MAKING CONNECTIONS FOR BETTER DECISIONS

Finally, we must consider how a peculiarly Catholic view of the human person contributes to decision-making. Most people will make decisions based on how they feel, especially when those decisions must be made quickly and with little time for discernment. Crises, such as those which occurs at the end of life, have an impact on the quality of decisions and on how decisions are made. Stress compromises decision-making.

A more thoughtful and perhaps more efficacious approach includes a reflection *before* a crisis occurs as to the principles that underline one's choices. All of us who might eventually deal with such emotionally charged decisions as those which accompany life's end and those who may be in a position to help others make such decisions will benefit from such methodology. A Catholic approach includes a consideration not only of the freedom of choice each person has, but how choices line up with objective values, the needs and expectations of others, and the common good. This approach reverences not only the values espoused in the Catholic tradition but appreciates the unique character of every person and the unique hierarchy of values which each holds. It realizes the incompleteness and inadequacy of any human decision-making. In opposition to the guilt that often accompanies imperfect decisions characteristic of real life, it respects the inability of any decision-maker to know all and to have complete freedom of choice in the exigencies and urgencies of time and space. Finally, it acknowledges the sovereignty of God both within the person and in the overall providence of life and life thereafter. Decisions made from such a context serve the objective moral order established by God and the current and ultimately wellbeing of the persons whose lives are affected by them.

QUESTIONS FOR DISCUSSION

1. Is there a distinctive Catholic position on life?
2. What elements make up a Catholic vision of the human person?
3. What are the key elements in a Catholic worldview?

NOTES

1. This idea is the key one in the dialogue between the American approach to the questions we will discuss here and the approach taken from Catholic tradition.

2. A concise history of Church teaching on euthanasia and suicide can be found in Michael Manning, *Euthanasia and Physician-Assisted Suicide: Killing or Caring?* (New York: Paulist Press, 1998), 16–25.

3. Pius XII spoke forcefully on issues from artificial birth control to eugenic population control. He affirmed the right of persons to reject interventions that posed undue burdens. See Manning, *Euthanasia*, 20–21, and Kevin D. O'Rourke and Phillip Boyle, *Medical Ethics: Sources of Catholic Teachings*, 2nd ed. (Washington, D.C.: Georgetown University Press, 1993), which contains excerpts from a number of church documents focussing on respect for life and end-of-life issues.

4. His addresses can be read in *Consistent Ethic of Life* (Kansas City, Mo.: Sheed & Ward, 1988). The book also contains the collected papers from a symposium held in Chicago in 1987.

5. Quoted in O'Rourke and Boyle, *Medical Ethics*, 289.

6. John Paul II, *The Gospel of Life* (Boston: St. Paul Books and Media, 1999), 92.

7. In the field of ethics, values are generally divided into two catoegories: *formal values*, which have to do with the character of persons (e.g., honesty, love, courage)

and *material values*, which designate certain desirable objects among which persons may choose (money, food, etc.). Those values which are described as "formal" are unlimited. I can be honest with you and still remain honest with another; my love for my spouse does not keep me from loving my children. Material values, on the other hand, are limited values. Generally my choosing one of them limits my option to choose another. If, for example, I choose to amass money, I may do so at the expense of another value.

Life is a limited value. A human person, or any being with life, has only a certain span of years in which to exist. Perhaps one will even sacrifice one's life for another value, say the life of another or the pursuit of money.

8. *Absolute values* is the name given to values that must always be honored and can never be set aside, even for very good reason. "I must always tell the truth, even if it costs lives," might be an example of truth as an absolute value. To say that life is not an absolute value is not the same as affirming that human life is trivial or should be considered expendable for modest reasons. The current debate about the use of human embryos for various "good" projects may shed some light here.

9. Elisabeth Kubler-Ross, *On Death and Dying* (New York: MacMillan, 1969), 38.

10. *Gaudium et Spes*, 22, urges humanity to "hasten forward to resurrection in the strength which comes from hope."

11. See, for example, the case recounted in Lawrence J. Schneiderman and Nancy S. Jecker, *Wrong Medicine* (Baltimore: The Johns Hopkins University Press, 1995), 134, in which a long white line of specialists were each pleased with the response of a patient's systems to specific treatment. Dialysis kept the kidneys functioning, constant attention kept the heart beating regularly, other systems were kept going, but the patient was little more than a prisoner of the intensive care unit with little hope of parole. "Our job is to keep her alive," was the response of the physicians.

12. *Gaudium et Spes*, 12.

13. *Gaudium et Spes, 16.*

14. Chapter 2 will consider the nuances of this statement. That a choice is *my* choice is a necessary but insufficient criterion for judging moral rightness.

15. John Paul II, *Veritatis Splendor* (Washington, D.C.: United States Catholic Conference, 1993), 72.

16. See Dolores L. Christie, *Adequately Considered: An American Perspective on Louis Janssens' Personalist Morals* (Louvain, Belgium: Peeters Press, 1990), 44.

17. *Gaudium et Spes*, 21.

18. *Gaudium et Spes*, 13.

19. Some fear that cost effectiveness may prompt medical professionals to deny certain kinds of treatment to dying persons, naming it "futile," because it is costly. (See Gregory E. Pence, *Recreating Medicine: Ethical Issues at the Frontiers of Medicine* [Lanham, Md.: Rowman & Littlefield Publishers, 2000], 163.) Pence suggests that the term "futility" may mask the more onerous "rationing." My experience is that this is not the case. Rather, professionals may be more likely to overtreat at the end of life both in response to family anxiety and to avoid the possibility of suit.

Chapter Two

The Catholic Moral Tradition: Objective Elements

How can someone know what the right and the good responsible actions are, especially when one is forced to make medical decisions for oneself or for a loved one? When all the choices seem bad, what should be done? What does the tradition offer to help make decisions in difficult situations?

Calculation of what is objectively the right thing to do must include not only the values and goals of the individual but the intersection of the individual good with the good of the greater community, what is called "the common good." Determination of the morally good includes an assessment of certain qualities of the person. The discussion in this chapter will be limited to the objective criteria for moral assessment; the next chapter will consider the subjective criteria, which reside in the person and may affect the moral quality of a given action.

Those who stand in the stream of Catholic moral theology that has nourished the contemporary field of bioethics can be rightly proud. Twenty centuries of thinking about moral matters by Catholicism has provided a valuable font for decision-making, one that is useful not only to Catholics but to anyone who wishes to make good decisions. Using this rich source, we look at the distinctions between rightness and goodness and how the person's intention enters into the moral equation. Objective criteria—what we do and why we do it—are the elements which comprise the external standards for judging morality.

Among the tools for decision-making is the principle of double effect. This principle underlies a number of terms used frequently in bioethics, such as "ordinary and extraordinary," "intended and foreseen," "greater good and lesser evil," and "proportionate and disproportionate," but ultimately all these terms are variations on the basic theme articulated in the classic "double effect."

Finally we will consider the concept of the common good, so long a part of Catholic tradition, particularly in its social teachings. For some readers this chapter will be a refresher course.

THE OBJECTIVE ASPECT OF MORAL EVALUATION

The Catholic moral tradition determines the rightness or wrongness, goodness or badness of an action by assessing two perspectives. The first aspect has to do with certain *objective* components of the act itself, those elements which exist on the horizon of possible choices for the person in a real situation. The objective component has to do with values, those things or qualities that *in themselves* have worth and are considered appropriate for human pursuit. Values are distinct from the person's ability to act freely and knowingly and do not, by themselves, determine the morality of a given action. Yet they are an essential part of that calculation.[1] Values embodied in an individual action include both the action and the intention behind it: what is done (caring for a sick daughter) and what I wish to do (enhance the sick person's well-being). Values embodied in the person's character may have to do with motivation, the "why" of the action (he took care of her because of his great love; he took care of her because he wished to inherit her money).[2]

To achieve a morally right action, someone must choose what is called an objective good, something that embodies a value or values for persons. A morally right action also includes a more elusive good, one which characterizes the person herself. Both these elements, however, are objective. They comprise a standard not changed by such variables as the physical, emotional, or psychological state of the person.

A subset of the first kind of objective goods, nonmoral values, includes what can be called *material values,* illustrated by such disparate things as life and lemon meringue pie. Among the objective category of *formal or moral values* are included the qualities of human personhood such as virtues and certain motivation.[3] They are designated *formal or moral value*s because they define desirable qualities which can be found within the character of the person. They are illustrated by such traits as freedom and fearlessness. These values and others like them form a horizon of things possible to human choice.

"Choose life" is a slogan which urges an individual to select a good and turn it from the theoretical to the real. "Eat Mrs. Smith's pies" reminds us of the comfort of sweet things and suggests that we choose those manufactured by a particular company. "Be free" has rallied oppressed groups from the time of Sparticus to Martin Luther King Jr. "Be not afraid" has emboldened ancient Israelites as well as modern Israelis. Notice that the examples given derive from two different components of the moral act.

The first examples (life and pie) have to do with material things which exist in reality. Material goods are always limited goods. Such goods are often in competition for our choice, since grasping one often requires the letting go of another: if one wants to maintain a long life and is diabetic, for example, it is better not to choose pie—even Mrs. Smith's. If one fills one's stomach with pie, there is no room left for that marvelous broccoli leftover from last night's dinner.

The second examples (freedom and courage) have to do with the character of the person—not what the person *does* but how the person *is*. One cannot go to the grocery store or the organ donation bank and get a year's supply of freedom and courage. Nor does someone ever have to choose one of these (moral or formal) values over the other, as is the case with material values. Moral values coexist with others in varying amounts within the character of the person. Catholic tradition cherishes both kinds of values and looks for their realization in the choices that people make. Both are essential in the calculation of the moral quality of a given action.

At the end of life the set of material values or goods available as alternatives is often more limited than in other circumstances. At the bedside of a severely impaired newborn there are no real choices of grade school soccer over football, cooking classes instead of piano lessons, public school or private. There will never be the troubling choice of lemon pie over broccoli. The real choices facing the distraught parents may be limited to continuation of treatment, removal of life support, or a surgery involving a minimal expected benefit. All the possibilities in this scenario seem to embody bad things rather than good. If a wife is told that her husband is brain dead because of an irreversible oxygen deprivation, the options for medical choice are likewise very narrow. The scope of the moral arena in concrete situations is precisely the scope of the real. Human moral choices are limited in the concrete by what is concretely possible.

Kevin Wildes, a Jesuit priest who has written extensively on bioethics, notes,

> In one sense, bioethics is a confrontation with the limits of human life. Clearly, in spite of our increasing technological capabilities, the practice of medicine daily confronts the limits of human existence. Human beings die; they get sick; they suffer. . . . Bioethics is a confrontation with the limits of human knowledge about what is right and wrong in making decisions for life and at the end of life.[4]

Both examples given above describe selection among material values. All choices having to do with life or health are concerned with the material; they are choices among values that are limited by time and space. Regrettably, we cannot have it all in the material world.

Given the Catholic understanding of the human person as capable of knowing the good when it stands before her, a preference for "good" things is hard-wired in human nature. Both the objective reality of what is chosen (the actual "what"

I intend to accomplish) and the motivation for choosing that reality ("why" I do it) must be "good" to render the action moral. It is an objectively good thing to give money to the hospital in my city. Certainly the institution's chief executive would concur, as would anyone who believed in the value of health care and who knew how much it costs. Both what I do and what I intend—to donate the funds—are good. But what if I give the money as a bribe, to influence the hospital to fire a doctor I dislike or to assure that my family and I would not only be treated there but treated royally? Such an action, good in itself, is compromised by what motivates me: hatred or envy or selfishness. This motivation, an objective moral component of the act, is evil. The action, though producing a tangible good (actualizing a material value), cannot be separated from the character trait or disposition which moves it. The motivation in this case renders an ostensibly "good" moral act to be, for me, an immoral one. The Catholic tradition has always found these two aspects, *what* is done (the object) and *why* it is done (the motivation), inseparable in judging moral rightness and wrongness in the concrete instance. Both are objective criteria for the determination of what is a moral action.

What does it mean to affirm that an action is "good" and appropriate as an object of moral choice? Catholics believe that there are certain realities which are of objective value in themselves, what might be called "human worthy," and which should serve as the basis and content for moral selection. Church teaching has long championed an objective moral order: the God of Genesis saw what divinity had created and asserted, "It is good." These words express a dispassionate objective statement about the intrinsic worth of what has been made. These "good" things are not defined by the preferences and whim of the individual—I specify what works for me as my good; your good may be something entirely different—but are fixed as objectively good by what they are in themselves and how they enhance human persons.[5] Further, what is good for human persons in general and in their relationships constitutes the gold standard held up by *Gaudium et Spes* against which rightness or wrongness are judged. Other goods are judged in relationship to this standard.

Relativism, the notion that everyone chooses arbitrarily his or her own good and that there is no universal standard for judging that good, has been consistently rejected in Catholic teaching and practice.[6] Catholics are not free to hold that death is as good as life or smoking is of equal value to a carrot salad. Simply because I choose to believe such statements are true and to act freely upon them does not make them true. I may tell myself that this ice cream sundae contains all the food groups (chocolate, dairy, and nuts) and that it satisfies my nutritional requirements for the day. As the waitress brings my dessert, she may insist that nothing has calories after 9 P.M. We both laugh, knowing that what we say is not the truth. The point is that *naming* an entity does not in itself define its reality. Our assertion of a calorie-free zone for sundaes does not make it so. The sundae's reality is not a function of our take on it. Reality and its intrinsic goodness or badness exist outside the subjective perceptions of those who view it.

In sharp contrast to this idea, American culture tends to favor individual choice as the standard of what is and should be valued. There is a collective American reluctance to judge as wrong what another holds as important or valuable. We are a pluralistic nation which endorses a creed of diverse personally defined values. As a culture we are tolerant of almost any value choices, so long as they don't block the pathway of another's choice.

When conflict occurs it is civil law, rather than any universal objective order or divine law, which circumscribes our actions. This is Enlightenment individualistic thinking taken to its logical conclusion. It is embodied in such assertions as, "I may not believe abortion is right for me, but who am I to criticize your proabortion stance? If you think it is right for you, that is fine. It is your choice. I have no business telling you what is right and wrong. Your values underpin and validate moral action, since they are yours." "You may believe that my wish to take my life is wrong, but who are you tell me what is right and wrong?" The key is found in the statement: "for me" or "for you." Rightness or wrongness in America tends to be defined largely as a function of personal choice, independent of objective validation.

One of the most clear examples of this thinking is found in recent end-of-life legislation; which has been written, as Daniel Callahan notes, "to remove medical and legal obstacles, then to allow us to shape a death of our own, with our own meaning."[7] Callahan sees that in America such legislation "too easily mistakes the limited purpose of the law for the broader and deeper demands of morality." Regarding "right-to-die" laws, some hold that it is morally right (since it is legal) to get a physician to help one die in Oregon but not in Ohio. It is this contemporary relativism, grounded in what Catholic tradition views as a misunderstanding of human freedom, that is criticized strongly by John Paul II in his encyclical *Veritatis Splendor.*[8] By Catholic standards "It's my choice" is not an adequate justification of rightness or wrongness. My "choice" in and of itself does not define the reality of value or of the good. Similarly, to deem an action *legal* is not the same as saying it is objectively moral. In both cases what is missing is an assessment of the value, the objective worth of the object of my choice.

From a Catholic perspective there are some things that are always right or wrong, outside the scope of personal choice. One may not directly choose to end one's life, since such an action goes directly against the basic good of life.[9] Life has intrinsic value, outside the domain of how we choose to think about it. It is also accurate to say that life's value has limits, since it is a material value subject to the exigencies of time and space. There is an objective but limited reality to the value of life. Its opposite, death, is a disvalue. While a direct choice against life is *legally possible*, among the free choices available to an individual; it is not a morally right choice. The strong ecclesial prohibitions against murder and suicide codify this affirmation that human life is (objectively) good and as such should be honored and protected. It is not the codification that renders these actions wrong but rather the intrinsic badness of them, since both murder and suicide by definition act directly against an objective good. Codification merely states what is already true.

In real life the issues are often not that simple. Sometimes when I choose to do a good, the means I must employ to arrive at that good may embody something which could be characterized as "evil." If I defend my spouse and house from a raging and crazed murderer, that is a good. Perhaps the only means I can use to protect my spouse is to shoot the intruder. No one would deny that killing *in itself* is a bad thing. To intend to kill directly an innocent person (action in itself) to get his money (motive), for example, is always a wrong action. It is only in the aiming at good—saving my family (motive)—that I may use such an evil—shooting the intruder (action in itself)—as a means.

In medicine almost any action is a complex admixture of some good—cure and health—and some bad—surgery, side effects, and so forth. At the end of life many factors intersect to muddy the clarity of rightness and wrongness. That is the reason the quality of decision-making, the sober examination of values (the possible good embodied in *what* might be done), intention (what I *wish to do*), motivation (*why* I do what I do), and available choices (what can be done), is essential. Right decisions are the fruit of a good decision-making process. Some of the factors which contribute to this process will be addressed more completely in later chapters. Here we wish only to consider the tradition on objective morality that informs concrete decisions.

The above examples embody what in the Catholic tradition has been named *the principle of double effect*. Arguably, this principle is at the heart of all medical-moral decision-making. Let us look more closely at this very important contribution from Catholic moral theology.

THE PRINCIPLE OF DOUBLE EFFECT

The "what" that I choose to do clearly is not always an uncomplicated choice of a good. Often, maybe always,[10] my choosing to do something good implicates me in a choice of an appropriate means to get there—the "how" I do it. I choose to pound a nail into my bedroom wall to hang a picture. The "means" I use is a hammer. Although the nail may be driven into the wood using other means—

since I am in the bedroom it may be quicker to grab a shoe to do the job—it may not work as efficiently. To achieve a good end, it makes sense to choose the most appropriate means to get there. In an ideal world we would always choose an uncluttered objectively good means to get to objectively good ends. It is the end that "justifies" the means that I employ, that is to say: What I wish to accomplish determines what will constitute the best means to get there. It does *not* mean that anything I wish to accomplish (good or bad) can justify the use of an *evil* means to get there. This distinction is often quoted and more often misunderstood. The hammer is good. Pounding in a nail to hold up the picture of my loved one is good for me. Using the one to accomplish the other is good and justifiable. While it is not an *evil* means, I likely cannot justify using the shoe, since it is not the *best* means to my end nor is it likely to be good for the shoe.

In medicine the end (the good I wish to do), the health and well-being of the body and the person, is generally achieved by means which are not benign. Surgery, chemotherapy, physical therapy after an injury, or pills are not *good* in themselves. We raise the objection, "But these things *are* good. They cure disease and help us live longer healthier lives." Not so. Even pills which control blood pressure or relieve the symptoms of asthma have certain side effects which are not good *in themselves*—the definition of value. This is why drug companies continue to research alternatives with fewer side effects, or for our purposes here what we would call "evil" effects.

The moral test for intrinsic "good" or "bad," as the words are used here, is whether the thing is ever embraced for its own sake, not simply as a means to an end. Would we take chemotherapy, surgery, or even aspirin just because we were bored? Would we choose to have our bodies invaded and parts removed *except* as an effective way to cure cancer or regain mobility? Such treatments are perhaps the only avenue by which to achieve health. Their use is *justified* only because they are the most appropriate, albeit not perfect, means to an end. They are, in fact, what the Catholic tradition would term *evil* means to a *good* end.[11] The use of the word "evil" here is not meant to convey a moral judgment but rather to name the negative components inherent in the moral equation.[12]

Enter the *principle of double effect*. This principle was developed to be applied in cases such as those enumerated above, where the situation presented has bound into it an outcome with one or more effects and the plural effects are not all good. It is the principle underlying the so-called just war theory. To use the principle, certain criteria must be met:

In an action with more than one effect (probably all actions) and in which the plural effects are not all good, certain criteria must be met:[13]

1. The person may not do morally something:
   —that is intrinsically evil[14]

—with a bad intention

—in such a manner that the good effect occurs *directly* as a result of a morally evil action (moral evil as means to a good)

2. There must be a "proportionate reason" to tolerate the evil effect[15]
    —as a means which is part of the overall action, that is,
    —the value one is willing to sacrifice must be at least commensurate
    —with the value that one wishes to protect.

To examine the first part: I may never, for example, murder someone (an intrinsically evil action, since it includes both material and formal (moral) evil, that is, killing (what I wish to do = intention) and malicious reason for doing it (why I want to do it = motive) even in a case where great good will come. No matter what good I wish to do, an evil or bad intention renders that action as morally bad *for me*. In bioethics this idea is well illustrated in the case used by James Rachels in a well-known article exploring whether doing something or doing nothing are different moral entities.[16] Rachels gives an account of Smith and Jones, both of whom will gain an inheritance upon the death of a six-year-old cousin. Smith purposely drowns the child in the bath, arranging the scene to appear to be an accident. In contrast Jones comes upon the child taking a bath. He stands by as the child slips, hits her head, and goes under the water. Jones does not intervene but watches while the child dies. Rachels, rightly, sees no moral difference in the two actions. He argued that the actions are not different morally simply because one is "active" and one is "passive." Both Smith and Jones wish the child to be dead (malicious intention, although Rachels does not develop this point). One actually kills, the other merely lets death occur. In fact, the morality turns on both the intention (wanting the child dead) and the nature of the evil itself (death) rather than whether the agent actually *does* something. It is not altered because one did something and one merely stood by and let it happen. Both Smith and Jones are responsible morally for the child's death, an *evil* in itself. Both *intend* the death. Both are *motivated* by the hope of personal gain. The Catholic tradition insists on the examination of the total moral picture of a given event to assess its moral quality. (1)What is the outcome or consequence (in this case, a death)? (2) What is the aim or intention of the moral agent (in this case, intending the death of the child)? (3) Why did the moral agent act or not act (in this case, to receive an inheritance)?

Our choices—what we wish to happen—are generally accompanied by some way of getting to them, technically the means to the end. We wish to go to San Francisco. The means we choose may be car, airplane, or train. Three possible ways to reach our goal are presented. Any one of these is an acceptable means. There is nothing especially good or bad about the range of possible methods of transportation: train, car, or airplane. One of us may suffer from carsickness, however, or have a fear of flying. Another might quibble about cost or the amount of time it takes to get there by one or the other. A third might favor a short trip over the opportunity to see leisurely the beautiful country. None of these means of travel is a particularly bad way to reach California. In making plans the several possibilities must be weighed against the benefits they bring. While we do not reflect consciously on the process of our decision-making most of the time, it is this process which is operative below the surface of consciousness in the morally charged decisions that we make.

Perhaps more in medical decisions than in others, to seek the good is difficult, compromised as it is by the "evil" that necessarily must come along. I choose to look younger by removal of a few wrinkles and bags on my face. An efficacious means to accomplish that end is plastic surgery. In this scenario, however, I must understand that plastic surgery carries with it some degree of risk, some "evil." The anesthetic may cause problems, the cutting into my flesh is not in itself a good thing, surgery is not a foolproof procedure, since it carries a small risk of infection as well as the possible slipping of the surgeon's knife. These are potential "evils" connected with a "good" choice. They will be found in the range of possible or unavoidable "effects" along with my new, more beautiful face: there will be a scar; there will be time lost from other pursuits as I recover. In the judgment made to go ahead with surgery, however, the "evil" effects are weighed and seen as proportionate to (lesser than) the "good" effect of the new look.

Consider going into the hospital. From the moment we arrive, "evil" is part of the process. Clothes are removed, familiar surroundings are replaced with sterile, technological equipment, the body may be violated with needles, toxic chemicals, or even the violence of electrical shock.

If these intrusions were in a setting other than a hospital, we would be outraged at what was happening: they are indeed "evil." Yet all of these and more are tolerated as "means" to an "end," the restoration to health and well-being. No one would choose any of these intrusions *except* as a means. They would never be chosen for their own sake. Nevertheless we embrace them when they are the appropriate means to the good end we seek.

The key objective components in the *principle of double effect* are the primary consequence which is the aim of the person (the *telos* or end), and which is good in itself (health), and the secondary (accepted but not intended) consequence which is used as a means. The appropriate means carries with it the least amount of evil. Note that the "evil" in the means becomes part of the end result (the object), part of the consequences of the action. If we aim at pain control in the dying person, the medicine given likely is in part "evil." It has side effects or consequences on the body, perhaps making the person groggy or constipated or given to hallucinations. The aim is pain control. The best medicine to get there (means) has consequences that are not wanted, but which are accepted as part of the path to pain relief.[17] The bad consequences are tolerated, because they are less evil than the good they bring. Using a means with some bad consequences is permissible morally only if this proportion is met.

This principle is the basic for most, if not all, moral decision-making. Certainly it is essential in the medical setting at the end of life. This idea of proportion or double effect is implied in such terms as "ordinary and extraordinary means" or "intended and foreseen consequences." "Ordinary means" is a phrase used to define those means with relatively benign side effects, and/or whose cost-benefit ratio (proportion) shows a greater good over evil. A person is morally obligated, according to Catholic tradition, to employ ordinary means in moral action. If someone has a small malignant mole which can be removed in the doctor's office and is paid for by insurance, it would likely be objectively morally wrong for him to forgo this procedure. To perform surgery on a newborn to correct a defect in the heart which, left untreated, would lead to death is an easy choice. In both cases the good outweighs the evil. Placing a young car accident victim on life support while the bodily functions adjust and return to normal from the trauma may save a life. The Catholic moral tradition affirms that one is morally responsible to elect an end which can be effected through such "ordinary means," those whose benefit is rather clear and whose "cost" is not overwhelming. The term "ordinary means" is prominent in church documents.[18] It has been a consistent term in Catholic medical ethics, if sometimes misunderstood.[19]

Much of the misunderstanding revolves around the generic notion of ordinary means and its application. The calculation of "ordinary" is always case specific: what is ordinary in the sense that it is commonly available may be extraordinary (and therefore not morally obligatory) in certain cases.[20] It may be ordinary to cure pneumonia with a common antibiotic. A young person presenting with such an infection should certainly be given the medicine to effect a cure. Nevertheless the same treatment might be deemed "extraordinary" and therefore not morally obligatory in the case of an elderly person with a painful terminal cancer who contracts the disease. The antibiotic would certainly cure the infection, it is cheap and available—certainly "ordinary in the medical sense; but it is disproportionate in the specific case.

Wildes makes the point: "What may be an ordinary (common) medical procedure may nonetheless be extraordinary to a patient."[21] All assessments of what are ordinary and what are extraordinary interventions are case-specific. Part of the confusion in decision-making in concrete cases is precisely this: all calculi of proportion (what is ordinary and/or extraordinary) *must be applied to the specific situation.*

The distinction between ordinary and extraordinary is one of the most confusing points of Catholic tradition. Again and again articles and even official documents speak about "ordinary means" as if they are some universal set of treatments about which everyone agrees and which can be applied universally to all cases. "Well, it's easy and cheap to place a feeding tube, do this surgery, keep your child on a ventilator. All of these are certainly 'ordinary,' so how can you refuse them?"

Not only medical personnel but also Catholic teachers espouse this position, even though it is not official Catholic teaching nor does it reflect the consistent tradition. The Pennsylvania and Florida bishops, for example, published strong opinions in favor of artificial nutrition and hydration for patients in a persistent vegetative state. In his strongly worded critique of these pronouncements, Richard McCormick has affirmed that the documents "fairly droop with authoritative accents" which "could easily mislead people into thinking that what the bishops say is 'the teaching of the Catholic Church.' It is not."[22] This opinion is not only that of Father McCormick, but is echoed in the *Directives* and represents the consistent Catholic tradition of making the distinction between what are general guidelines and their application to specific cases.

Extraordinary means are those which constitute what Wildes terms "a moral impossibility for human beings in general (absolute norm) or for a particular person (relative norm)."[23] No one is obligated to a treatment which always carries with it unbearable and enduring pain or is so expensive that a person would have to resort to poverty to afford it (absolute norm). Some people may be morally excused from consenting to treatments that, *for them,* in their unique individuality, are judged to be too burdensome (relative norm). Wildes cites the example of a person who would personally find it too repugnant to live with the mutilation connected with amputation. The person's subjective assessment of the relative burden would be morally sufficient to consider the means "extraordinary."

An example of a case brought to a hospital ethics committee on which I serve comes to mind. An elderly scientist, who lived alone, refused a life-saving surgery to remove a gangrenous leg. He believed strongly that life without his leg would not be worth living. Although he did not wish to die nor did he attempt in any way to end his life, he was unwilling to consent to treatment that would leave him without a limb. Since he had no one to help him, the amputation itself likely would have rendered him unable to carry on the tasks of daily living by himself. With no relatives or friends, and independence so important to him, likely his assessment of the situation was correct. For this patient a simple (ordinary) amputation became disproportionate in light of his judgment (extraordinary).

Intended and foreseen consequences have to do with the reality that, in achieving a favorable medical outcome, there will always be regrettable but unavoidable side effects: the scar from surgery, the burning stomach that may accompany ingestion of aspirin to alleviate a headache, or the unavoidable death hastened by the removal of invasive life support or the slowing of respiration caused by radical pain control. While a favorable consequence is the aim of the action, the person making the choice knows that other effects will come along. While not *intended,* these effects are in fact *caused* by the means chosen and implemented and can be *foreseen.* The key morally is to assess their proportionate evil in relationship to the proportionate good intended. The evil foreseen and caused should be proportionately less than the good intended.

All these terms boil down to finding a good result by means of a proportionate and appropriate means, and the acceptance that some bad stuff comes along in the mix. Louis Janssens has noted that reflective human persons always make such an acknowledgment with regret; knowing that they have been participant in the creation of real, if unavoidable, evil in the world. The person who removes the breathing tube from a dying person, knowing that the technology is merely prolonging the process of death, does so with deep sorrow and regret that it cannot be otherwise. The limits of human existence inevitably wash up on the shores of death.

THE COMMON GOOD

Often marginalized in medical decision-making is the foundational Catholic principle of the *common good.* As the *Directives* note: "The dialogue between medical science and the Christian faith has for its primary purpose the common good of all human persons."[24] What exactly is meant by this concept? Pope John Paul II has reflected on the idea in his writings. He speaks about it as a derivation of the *"I-thou"* dimension of the human condition.[25] Vatican II defines human beings as essentially communal. We do not exist and prosper in isolation from each other. Communality is an essential component of being human. Therefore it follows than in their moral considerations and action that the human communal dimension must be taken into account.

Pope John Paul II has noted that this ontological reality has "also a normative [and thus ethical] meaning."[26] What this means is that the good of each person is tied to the good of all persons, placing responsibility on each person to consider others' well-being and advancement in his or her decision-making. The concept of the common good differs from the "bottom line" or utilitarian calculus, which estimates the greatest return for the greatest number of people and which neglects the return for the minority. Common good seeks to distribute something to everyone, even if doing so diminishes the benefit to some in the group. In common good practice those "some" may not get a large benefit, but they will share with all the others in what is given. In utility the "some" may derive a large benefit, but the minority will receive nothing. Common good thinking ties the good of each individual to the good of the community. The person is both a unique individual and a social being. Both aspects are important considerations in moral decisions. Utility demands no particular respect for the individual, except as that individual is part of the head count of the majority.[27] Voters put into office a candidate whose platform serves their interests. The candidate with the most votes wins. The interests of the minority voters are not an important part of the calculus, nor are they necessarily considered when the candidate later helps to frame favorable legislation.

How does this theory play out in practice, particularly in decision-making at life's end? Persons who make decisions for themselves medically must begin to think beyond the individualistic mores of the American culture, "I got mine; yours is your problem." They must begin to consider the consequences of individual action and choice upon other people. Institutions should formulate policy based on this principle.[28] Adequate consideration in medical moral decision-making must take into account the effects of the decision on family and associates of course, but it should include the implications of decisions for the care team and the community at large. What does this decision mean for those around the patient? What impact has it on the health care profession? Are there implications for the community as to cost of health care, use of limited technology, or the investment of the emotional capital of others? Parents who cling to the impossible hope that a severely compromised newborn will become whole and healthy and demand that "everything" be done will not get the results they seek. They will place the daily nursing care personnel in a difficult position both professionally and emotionally and compromise the common good by consuming care that is, in this particular case, futile.

A doctor I know talks about a case of a tiny infant whose physicians were in conflict as to what treatment plan to follow. Some of the care team wanted to treat aggressively. The sad prospect of the death of one so young and innocent was a resultant option, even in the face of poor prognosis. Without consideration of the short- and long-term effects on many people, including not only the family but the community in general, some of the care team would opt for a legacy of long-term care with impact not only for family members but for society in general should family resources be insufficient. That option brings with it no promise, no hope, that the fragile life with ever become a functioning person. The decision to treat, while understandable at the emotional level, carries with it neither proportion nor consideration of the common good.

Moral decisions that include notions of the common good are in radical opposition to American individuality and squarely within the mainstream of the best of Catholic tradition. Decisions which consider only the needs and wants of the individual and are blinded to other considerations are not consistent with Catholic thinking. Richard McCormick has graphically stated the individualist position, "Damn the effect on the family and friends. Damn the effect on the medical and nursing profession. Damn the effect on society. Damn any consideration that qualifies autonomy."[29] Defiantly and narrowly autonomous decisions do no justice to the human person considered in all aspects, a person in community. They do not reflect the best of the Catholic tradition.

THE PRINCIPLE OF TOTALITY

Another principle which has been developed as a part of Catholic tradition is the *principle of totality*. One does not read much about this principle today.[30] It was developed in the past to explore and subsequently to endorse the morality of certain surgeries which removed diseased parts of a person (the amputation of a limb, for example) and, by extension, those procedures which removed healthy parts of a person's body (a kidney to be donated by a healthy person to someone whose kidneys no longer functioned).

The principle, while developed for other reasons, may find an application to end-of-life issues. "Totality" refers to the idea that certain aspects of bodily integrity may be licitly and morally sacrificed to serve the total person. As Pope Pius XII noted in 1952, "the part exists for the whole . . . the good of the part remains subordinate to the good of the whole."[31] The central idea is that no constitutive *part* of the person is dominant over the whole person, the integrated and enduring person. One may and sometimes even should sacrifice a part for the whole—the gangrenous leg is removed to protect the person's life—and for the other—the kidney can be excised to give life to another. The principle illustrates the enduring Catholic anthropology of the importance of person over biological parts and the essential connectedness or responsibility that persons have to one another.

Application to end-of-life issues demands looking at this principle backwards. If the important (essential) entity is the person and the person's connection to others, keeping alive the parts when the person is gone and, further, consuming limited resources that might serve others to do so is a violation of a basic conclusion of Catholic tradition. As concrete issues are addressed later in the book, the reader should keep this principle in mind.

CONCLUSION

In consideration of the objective aspect of the moral act the values at stake must be viewed in the context of proportion and of the common good. Both these principles ground moral decision-making in the context of Catholic tradition and promise better decisions than otherwise. Good decisions take time and may be more difficult than those which exist only on the pages of philosophy texts or official church pronouncements. They are messy human events where sincere and tentative feet moving resolutely toward the good often get very dirty as they slog forward in the mud of the real. Good decision-making will result in good decisions. Good decisions likely are morally right ones.

QUESTIONS FOR DISCUSSION

1. What is needed to have a morally right action?
2. Is a relativistic stance congruent with a Catholic position on morality? Why or why not?
3. Differentiate between something that is good in itself and something that would not make a morally good choice.
4. Explain the principle of double effect and show how it is used in medical decision-making.
5. Distinguish between ordinary and extraordinary means as they apply specifically to medical decisions.

NOTES

1. Philosophers consistently use the term "nonmoral" to describe those values that embody the useful (a hammer is good to drive a nail), or are judged to have intrinsic worth (knowledge is good; democracy is good), or are contributory to another good (fences make good neighbors). Other kinds of values, the kind that may distinguish the person's character or personality (he is patient; she is just), or describe persons of a particular group (the third-graders always share; they are good citizens) are called "moral" values. A complete discussion of values and their nuances can be found in William Frankena, *Ethics* (Englewood Cliffs, N.J.: Prentice-Hall, 1963), 63–77. The limited presentation here is intended only to set the stage for application to end-of-life issues.

2. Notice that the *same* action could have been done with totally different motivation. Such difference can change the moral character of that action.

3. See Frankena's expansion of these ideas, *Ethics*, 48.

4. Kevin W. Wildes, *Moral Aquaintances: Methodology in Bioethics* (Notre Dame, Ind.: University of Notre Dame Press, 2000), 182.

5. In the contemporary world of diversity and historical consciousness, it is essential to nuance such a statement. Catholic moral theology can no longer espouse a static notion of the good, fixed in nature for all time. Although what is of value is not a totally subjective determination, values are embodied in the experience of the community and that of each individual person. Further, and based in that varied experience, values will be ranked differently by different communities and individuals. They are discovered and embraced over the span of a community's or individual's unique temporal experience. The particularity of both community and person affect how objective values are appropriated by a culture and in individual decision-making. For further discussion see Kevin Wildes, *Moral Aquaintances*, 127–28; and Louis Janssens, "Ontic Good and Evil: Premoral Values and Disvalues," *Louvain Studies* 12 (1987): 62–82.

6. See *Veritatis Splendor*, 48. Note that the pope takes a different methodological approach to premoral goods than I do. I do not believe, however, that there is a basic disagreement in principle from the position expressed in the encyclical. Both the pope and I affirm the existence of an objective moral order and the limits of freedom in morally good acts to the choice of objective good.

7. Daniel Callahan, *The Troubled Dream of Life: Living With Mortality* (New York: Simon & Schuster, 1993), 16.

8. See John Paul II, *Veritatis Splendor*, 48, 84, for example.

9. The notion of "basic goods" is more clearly outlined in Germain Grisez's (1983) work. See *The Way of the Lord Jesus*, 123–24.

10. Peter Knauer, in a groundbreaking article, calls it the "fundamental principle of all morality." See Peter Knauer, "The Hermeneutic Function of the Principle of Double Effect," in *Readings in Moral Theology, No. 1: Moral Norms and Catholic Tradition*, ed. Charles E. Curran and Richard A. McCormick (New York: Paulist Press, 1979), 1.

11. Never does Catholic teaching or tradition sanction a morally evil means even for the best of ends: one could not, for example, murder a group of people whose vote stood in the way of building a magnificent medical center to serve the poor. *Morally* evil means render the entire action morally wrong. In such a case the end cannot justify the means.

12. Catholic moralists have used a variety of terms to describe the concept: physical evil (Thomas Aquinas/Peter Knauer), ontic evil (Louis Janssens), nonmoral evil (Bruno Schueller), premoral evil (Joseph Fuchs/Richard McCormick). The concept is the same: some realities, while not in themselves good (floods, fire, bacteria, for example) are sometimes chosen as an appropriate means for what they can achieve (irrigation, stripping a field of diseased plants, human digestion), although in themselves they represent evil. A further discussion can be found in Richard M. Gula, *Reason Informed By Faith: Foundations of Catholic Morality* (New York: Paulist Press, 1989), 269–70; and in Knauer, "The Hermeneutic Function," 18–21.

13. For comparison and additional resources from the Catholic tradition on the principle, see Christie (1990), *Adequately Considered*, 120.

14. When the Catholic tradition speaks of "intrinsic evil" it refers to a nexus of action/intention/motive that can never be considered morally good, no matter what the circumstances. Some moralists have argued that the category is a tautology, so narrowly defining both the material and formal components of the action that there is obviously no question that such actions are morally wrong. For further discussion, see Timothy E. O'Connell, *Principles for a Catholic Morality*, revised edition (New York: Harper & Row, 1990), 187–96.

15. It would not be morally permissible, for example, to cut off a healthy limb just to have something to do (evil as an end), but it would be morally permissible to cut off that same limb if doing so would restore a person to health by eliminating a cancer.

16. This article, a classic, can be found in a number of bioethics textbooks. A reprint may be found in Thomas A. Mappes and Jane S. Zembaty, *Biomedical Ethics*, 3rd ed., (New York: McGraw-Hill, 1991), 367–70; and in Kenneth R. Overberg, *Mercy or Murder* (Kansas City, Mo.: Sheed & Ward, 1993), 23–32.

17. The belief that heavy doses of pain medication tend to hasten death, because they slow breathing, has been disproved in clinical studies.

18. National Conference of Catholic Bishops, *Ethical and Religious Directives for Catholic Health Care Services* (Washington, D.C.: United States Catholic Conference, 1995), 56: "A person has a moral obligation to use ordinary or proportionate means of preserving his or her life."

19. An excellent clarification is found in Kevin O'Rourke, "Evolution of Church Teaching on Prolonging Life," *Health Progress* 69, no. 1 (January/February 1988): 28–35.

20. The *Directives* are very clear on this point, 56: "Proportionate means are those that *in the judgement of the patient* offer a reasonable hope of benefit and do not entail an excessive burden or impose excessive expense on the family or the community" [emphasis mine]. This directive does not stand only on its own as a statement of the Catholic bishops of the United States, but quotes the Congregation for the Doctrine of the Faith, "Declaration on Euthanasia," part IV (1980).

21. Kevin W. Wildes, "Ordinary and Extraordinary Means and the Quality of Life," *Theological Studies* 57, no. 3 (1996): 505.

22. See Richard A. McCormick, "'Moral Considerations' Ill Considered," *America* 166, no. 9 (March 14, 1992): 210–14. McCormick does a careful analysis of the distinction between general teaching statements by the magisterium and thier application to specific cases and contexts.

23. Wildes, "Ordinary and Extraordinary," 503.

24. *Directives*, "General Introduction."

25. Karol Wojtyla, "The Person: Subject and Community, " in *Person and Comunity: Selected Essays*, trans. Theresa Sandok, *Catholic Thought from Lublin,* vol. 4, ed. Andrew N. Woznicki (New York: Peter Lang, 1993), 248.

26. Wojtyla, "The Person," 249.

27. Pope John Paul rightly criticizes utilitarianism as judging the morality of actions "without any reference to [the person's] true ultimate end" *(Veritatis Splendor*, 74). Consideration of the dignity of persons lies outside the scope of utility's concern.

28. *Directives, 9.*

29. Richard A. McCormick, "Bioethics: A Moral Vacuum?" *America* 180, no. 15 (May 1, 1999): 9.

30. A cursory survey of current textbooks both in fundamental Catholic morality and in bioethics revealed little mention of this principle. For the interested reader excerpts of pertinent Catholic teaching on the principle can be found in Kevin D. O'Rourke and Philip Boyle, *Medical Ethics: Sources of Catholic Teaching*, 2nd ed. (Washington, D.C.: Georgetown University Press), 325–28. See also David Bohr, *Catholic Moral Tradition* (Huntington, Ill.: Our Sunday Visitor, 1999), 227–28, which presents a contemporary conservative view of Catholic moral teaching.

31. Pope Pius XII, "The Intangibility of the Human Person," quoted in O'Rourke and Boyle, *Medical Ethics: Sources,* 327.

Chapter Three

The Decision-Maker and the Tradition

What is autonomy and what compromises it? How does a person's conscience function and how does illness affect it? Don't Catholics have to listen to the church rather than make their own decisions at life's end?

An old TV commercial portrayed the headache-producing conflict between a woman and her mother, arguing over how something would be done. "I'd rather do it myself, mother," says the younger woman. This petulant response captures the essence of autonomy: "I'd rather do it myself."

Moral decision-making is based on two elements: the objective, *what* is chosen and *why* it is chosen, and the subjective, how *free and knowledgeable* the choosing person is. To make good, consistent, self-creating decisions someone needs to have freedom (autonomy) and sufficient information about the possible choices to understand the consequences and implications of the decision (knowledge). It is the state of the person, not only her motivation but her ability to think and to choose, which is pivotal to this discussion. These concepts have been addressed in both the contemporary bioethics literature and the tradition of Catholic moral theology.

The concept of autonomy, the power to make choices on one's own, is very much at the center of contemporary bioethical discourse, particularly in cases of serious illness or impending death. In America autonomy has become the trump card of bioethics. Thomas Murray, director of the Hastings Center (a nonprofit organization that carries out educational and research programs in medicine, health care, technology, and the environment), has observed that it is used, as "a kind of universal solvent" to wipe away the strong paternalism that previously characterized American medicine.[1] At the service of autonomy hospitals distribute brochures detailing patients' rights, families threaten

suit to keep dying mothers on expensive machines, newspapers feature stories of insurance denial for seriously ill children in need of transplants. Consent forms and permission slips proliferate at all levels of medical and other
areas of civil life. Autonomy is also at the heart of Catholic moral teaching.
It is the prerequisite for the healthy exercise of conscience, at the root of what
it means to be human. It will be the purpose of this chapter to examine autonomy, its implications when competence is in question, its connections to
conscience, and finally some implications for decision-making. The linkage
of language and concepts from the Catholic perspective will be made to contemporary understandings of the concept as treated in the general bioethics
literature.

THE MEANING OF AUTONOMY

Catholic moral theology has consistently taught that personal decisions of
conscience lie at the root of the moral project. Vatican II reaffirmed this tenet
in the vision of the human person developed in *Gaudium et Spes.*[2] Human
persons by their natural makeup have the tools for good decision-making: the
ability to recognize the good when it is presented to them and to choose the
good they see. These ideas have been treated in some detail in chapter 1. In
many ways the Catholic vision of the human person is similar to the Enlightenment or libertarian notion of individual rational freedom. This value roots
American independence and its system of personal rights. Freedom to make
choices congruent to one's values is exercised in the context of the knowledge
appropriate to the decision at hand is autonomy in its best form.

The bioethics literature is full of material on autonomy. It is called "self-
governance or self-determination."[3] *Self-determination* demands that the person is *able* to make a decision and to act on that decision. If a person is totally paralyzed, he cannot exercise the "freedom" to open a pill bottle and
take aspirin to cure his headache.[4] If a person is comatose, she is not free to
choose her daily routine or the direction in which her bed will face.

Not only does freedom demand a real *possibility* of acting, to be truly free
there must exist real *choice*. It is decidedly more than self-determination.
When a physician says to a patient, "This treatment is your only option,"
the doctor is effectively *denying* freedom to the patient rather than promot-
ing it. Even when treatment options are limited, a patient should always be
made to understand the option of simply saying, "No." Refusal of treatment
is a legitimate option and a valid exercise of freedom. If there is only one
"choice" available there is no real choice. Without true choice there is no
moral activity.

It is also an exercise of moral freedom to defer the implementation of one's decision-making responsibility to someone else. In certain families, the custom may be that some decisions are always made by the husband or by an eldest son. When out to lunch with some married friends, I have observed that the wife always begins her decision-making about what to eat by asking her husband what *he* wants. If he cannot decide between two entrees, she often orders one of *his* choices rather than exercise a strong personal preference. This family "rule" might extend to decision-making for all members of the family. In some cultures, the decisions which might be necessary at the end of life are never made by the individual but are made collectively by the family or a designated family member.

While both the American embrace of freedom and the Catholic insistence on self-creation for each person favor that moral decisions be made by the person involved, a lifetime of deference or a culture that does not prize individual choice can and must be respected. Sometimes the most free decisions are those we cede to others.[5] When persons marry, they freely choose to give themselves to their partners for a lifetime. In medical decision-making, to demand that habit patterns and years of acting in a certain way be changed ("Mrs. Smith, you *must* make your own decision about having chemotherapy") is to manipulate the very freedom one is trying to preserve. In the name of autonomy (and perhaps to promote the choice he wanted) a doctor in a local hospital had all family members removed from the hospital room of an elderly patient to force her to make her own decision and not rely on the family's opinions. Such an action is a violation of respect for cultural family-based decision-making and of the patient's values.

Autonomy consists of *effective deliberation*. First, this means that a person exercising autonomy should be offered certain necessary information that can serve as a prerequisite and ultimately the grist of decision-making. One cannot decide about something without the facts pertinent to that decision. The information necessary to make an informed choice can be described as meeting the "reasonable person standard": the person who needs to make a decision should be given the amount of information needed by a theoretical "reasonable person" to make a decision.[6]

The idea behind this standard is that someone on the one hand should be presented with sufficient pertinent facts to fold into the process and on the other hand not be burdened by a laundry basket of information that may or may not have bearing on making a good decision. Sometimes too much information, which may not have bearing on the results of one's decision, impedes rather than helps the process. As I read the small print of possible side effects for a given medication that my doctor has prescribed, I am bombarded with a list of things that could happen to me if and when I swallow the pills.

Most of these potential side effects happen to only one in a million patients. Do I really need all this information to make an informed decision about whether to take this medicine? Knowledgeable medical personnel should provide needed information to patients and them apply it to the particular situation under consideration. While resuscitation is considered by some to be a useful tool to restore the beating of a heart, for example, it may not be statistically useful for a particular case. And beyond the statistics, it may not have reasonable use for this irreversibly brain-damaged young person.

A patient or a patient's surrogate has both the right and the responsibility to obtain information for decision-making. If the patient or surrogate is not able to articulate questions or if severe illness or other impediment makes it difficult to do so, a pastoral caregiver or other patient advocate could be a helpful addition to the moral process. Hospitals have ethics committees whose members are usually available to help in such matters. The expertise of these committees is generally made available to patients, family members, medical and pastoral personnel—anyone who thinks that a "consult" would enhance good decisions. Anyone other than the patient or the designated surrogate does not have decision-making responsibility but acts only as a help toward making the process a good process. Committees or persons other than the patient, however, are not the decision-makers. Ideally the patient who is affected by the choice should decide. The goal of the process is to make the decision-maker a free and knowledgeable agent, a human person who has the potential for moral action.

Second, in order to deliberate effectively, the decision-makers must have a sense of their own personal goals and aspirations for the future, the ability to prioritize and change or discard these goals, and must be given the particular information necessary for an understanding of the implications of the particular decision under consideration. "What do *I* want for my life and health? Is living longer important, or would I rather live a shorter time without tubes and treatment and in my own home? Even though I might refuse this treatment, do I respect my family's wish that I continue because my love for them supercedes my own wishes?" It is this kernel of personal identity that ultimately charts the direction for achieving personal life goals. This idea will be developed more completely below in the section on conscience.

Catholic and secular bioethical perspectives concur in their affirmation of autonomy's importance. Essential ingredients of autonomy are *freedom* and *knowledge*, both integral to the nature of the human person. It is the recognition of inherent human dignity and right to self-determination that undergirds contemporary proliferation of patients' rights documents, development of laws on advanced directives, and insistence on informed consent.

THE LIMITS OF AUTONOMY

The exercise of autonomy appears simple. As a marketing slogan for a sports equipment company states, "Just do it!" Such facility is rarely the case in the real circumstance. A real person never acts with total freedom or total knowledge. As Catholic anthropology emphasizes, human beings are limited in time and space. Where I am in a particular historical context, how much time I have to gather information, where I am in my own span of life—all affect freedom and knowledge. Someone living in the nineteenth century, for example, was not "free" to choose penicillin as a treatment for a bacterial infection. If a person has to decide right now about resuscitation, intubation, or other treatments that may or may not be useful, she does not have the leisure to read about these treatments and consider all the odds. If a person eighty-nine years old, it is likely too late for him to be free to take beginner lessons in downhill skiing. Limits circumscribe every situation of decision-making.

In the Catholic tradition the factors that limit either freedom or knowledge are called "impediments." It is important to distinguish between "ideal autonomy" and "actual autonomy,"[7] or "diminished capacity." Diminished capacity compromises the potential for decision-making, what is termed "competence." Impediments to total competence accompany virtually any decision-making event, and the *actual* state of autonomy is not the same as the ideal. Diminished capacity generally refers to a situation in which the overall ability for a patient to make decisions is seriously compromised. A person with diminished capacity may not be able to understand the facts about a particular medical procedure or may not be able to process them effectively enough to make an adequate decision. Sometimes the question of diminished capacity is not raised until or unless the patient disagrees with the physician's recommendation for course of treatment. Whatever the name or the situation, however, the condition has implications for individual decisions and the moral evaluation of an action.

What circumscribes or limits human freedom? First, there are physical conditions or disease which may impair this freedom. A person may lack the maturity needed to have a set of goals or a vision for her life. The anencephalic infant, dying even in the throes of being born, will never possess a self-identity or a plan detailing how she wishes to shape her unique human life. She will never become a person in the true sense of the word. Any decisions made for her will be those of her parents.

Small children have not yet developed a moral identity, although they may and should be encouraged to make choices within their capacity ("Do you want to wear your blue shirt or your striped shirt today?"), they likely cannot process the sophisticated information needed to make decisions about medical care ("Do you want to have a small bowel transplant which will commit you to taking medicine for the rest of your life?" "Do you wish to have a surgical procedure on your sexual organs, since your genitals do not clearly define your sex?") nor do they yet possess a true "self" ("Tell me what values guide your life." "What gives your life meaning?"). Rather, who they will become is shadowed beneath the values and goals of their parents until they grow beyond its reach. Sometimes the cloud is thick and enduring. Children have a limited potential for free choice, but its maturity resides somewhere in the future.[8]

Persons who formerly were capable or morally competent to decide for themselves may lose temporarily or permanently the ability to remember who they are, to interact, or to adjust their life patterns and trajectory to new moral dilemmas. The young man unconscious from a motorcycle collision has in common with the elderly woman with Alzheimer's disease a suspension of the inherent freedom to choose and to work out an identity. In the first case that ability may return; in the second the diminution is progressive and possibly permanent.

Other physical conditions are less dramatic but may likewise affect a person's ability to think clearly and to make good decisions. If one is tired or in pain, if drugs or alcohol have dulled or impaired the senses, the ability to make decisions is compromised. Habit or addiction may infect the ability of a person to act freely. A smoker may be told by her physician that quitting is imperative if she wants to live. She may even have tried to quit but finds it difficult or impossible to do so. In the hospital for chronic lung disease she pulls her IV pole with her outside the hospital building in the dead of winter so she can enjoy one more cigarette. Is this activity morally blameworthy? Perhaps, but likely the freedom to stop smoking is severely attenuated by years of habit and probably by physical addiction.

The Catholic moral tradition affirms that as freedom is diminished by physical or emotional condition, by habit or addiction, so is moral responsibility.[9] I cannot be held accountable for that which I am unable to do. If I have been up for several nights with a sick grandchild, I need not feel guilty for taking a nap today instead of scrubbing the floor or editing the draft of the final chapter of my book. If my teenage son borrows someone's motorcycle and has a serious accident while I am out of town, I cannot take the blame for his injuries. This idea of mitigated responsibility is helpful in ameliorating not only the judgments we place on others for bad habits or bad actions but also the harshness with which we often judge ourselves. Such an indulgent attitude does not diminish the values or rules that are not honored in a particular situation, but it recognizes the reality of insurmountable limits that are part of the human condition. The Catholic tradition is more realistic and perhaps more forgiving than we ourselves may be. In the painful and often accusatory environment that may pollute the air of the deathbed room, it is a moral imperative to suspend judgment and to forgive what cannot be undone.

Beyond the physical and biological perimeters to freedom are some more subtle limits. Especially in the foreign and relatively toxic situation of medical decision-making, psychological or emotional factors may compromise decision-making. Fear, anxiety, guilt, and even anger accompany such events, distracting the mental processes like children clinging to parents on the first day of school. "What if my spouse were to die, how would I cope? I have never balanced the checkbook. Who will help me with the children? What will I do all alone? Maybe if I had called the paramedics sooner or had given him a better diet or made him stop smoking, this would not have happened. It's my fault!" Or, "How could he do this to me? Just when life was becoming easy and we could spend some time traveling, he had to go and have a heart attack." While the reactions in these scenarios could be criticized as irrational, they represent the frequent and real attitudes and feelings of those destined to stand across the scrimmage line from death. And death is holding the ball.

For those who face death and for those who survive them, feelings at the end of life are mixed. They may be peaceful or agitated; sanguine or gloomy. People may say what they think or what they think others want to hear. An elderly woman with a terminal illness abides by her children's wishes for treatment, "Okay, kids, I will agree to the aggressive treatment you want me to have." In her own mind she is thinking, "I know it is futile and I really don't want it, but the family's comfort level is more important to me than my own wishes. If it were only me deciding, I would never undergo the treatment that is being proposed." A retired oncologist signed on for experimental chemotherapy to treat his own deadly cancer. The always optimistic physician believed: "Maybe this time I can win the battle." Another man, anticipating relief from a long period of care for his wife suffering from Alzheimer's disease, secretly hopes that maybe she *will* die. Such "terrible" thoughts are painful, but graphically real. The "medicine" the man might reach for to blunt the pain is to demand more and more aggressive treatment for her. He is reluctant to face his ambivalent and not so positive feelings, so they are denied as he opts for the irrational in the form of the ineffective. A young woman whispers to her husband that it is okay for him to let go as he clings to life by a thread only for her sake; having made peace with her wishes, the man dies soon afterward.

Finally, there are elements of the social and cultural context of medical decision-making that may inhibit freedom. The effect of the power differential that exists between patient and professional is a real and pernicious catalyst in the medical decision-making situation. This disparity is likely present in every situation, especially in the critical hospital arena. Consider the scene: doctor, carrying an arsenal of knowledge and authority, the starched white coat, an army of colleagues and assistants; patient, unschooled in medicine, uniformed in hospital gown, surrounded by foreign technological gadgets, and in pain. The remarkable stage play "W;t" describes such a context. The main character, a cancer patient undergoing therapy, describes the recurring encounter with medical personnel:

> I have been asked "How are you feeling today?" while I was throwing up into a plastic washbasin. I have been asked as I was emerging from a four-hour operation with a tube in every orifice. . . . I am waiting for the moment when someone asks me this question and I am dead.[10]

Clearly the experience of this cancer patient reveals how difficult decision-making can be for the patient, especially in the wrong context. The patient feels physically terrible, vulnerable, stripped of modesty, normalcy, and authority as a person. This is an all too common scene at the threshold of death, when decisions are not only important but vital. How does one question medical judgment or even begin to wrest some degree of control or freedom in such a context? And is having control the same thing as autonomy? The effect of power differences may become even more pronounced in situations of differential gender, race, or economic vulnerability.

A variety of feelings can influence and sometimes even paralyze decision-making. This is true both for the patient who may be competent to decide for himself as well as for those who may be the default decision-makers when the patient is unable to voice his own choices. The cacophony compromises a process that in the quiet of reason would be simple and clear. Feelings, particularly those which remain buried and unexpressed, may act as impediments to the freedom necessary to good decision-making. Much of the medical treatment demanded at life's end—particularly by surrogates—is a function of unresolved and often unspoken negative feelings. Many of the flowers that arrive at the funeral home are testimony to regret, to feelings and deeds unspoken until it is too late. We make up for what we think should have been said or done earlier in life's relationships by electing the irrational in the present. Unfortunately it is often too little, too late. Such hidden agenda, particularly if not recognized, acts as a severe impediment to good decisions. Further, they may compromise good end-of-life care.

Catholic tradition has long recognized impediments to freedom and knowledge as fellow travelers in the moral journey which, precisely because they limit decision-making ability, lessen or sometimes completely destroy moral responsibility in a given situation. A person cannot be morally responsible for what he cannot know or do. A person who is impaired does not have the same moral acuity as someone who is totally free.

Family members, caregivers, pastoral care personnel, and others can help by encouraging everyone to express the feelings and emotions stirring beneath the surface. Empathic dialogue enhances moral freedom. Asking a caregiver a compassionate and direct question, for example, may uncover what's really going on and promote better decision-making. "Are you feeling conflicted about your spouse's impending death? Maybe that's why you want the doctors to 'do everything,' when they have already told you that the medical possibilities have been exhausted. Certainly you are afraid. That is understandable. Let's try to look at what your spouse would have wanted you to do and make the decision based on that rather than the understandable fear you are feeling."

To summarize: the Catholic tradition, like the contemporary bioethics literature, recognizes both the standing of persons to make decisions for themselves and the real possibility that some people are not competent to do so. Physical, psychological, and emotional forces are always at work to limit and in some cases to destroy a person's ability to make good decisions. When the ability to decide is compromised, the moral responsibility of one's decisions is attenuated. These factors are important in the consideration of the subjective aspects of moral decision-making, that is, the things that have to do with the moral judgment of goodness and badness. We shall now look more directly at the issue of competence.

COMPETENCE: A PREREQUISITE TO AUTONOMY

Competence plays an integral part in the understanding of autonomy. Consequently we will address the following questions: (1) What is competence, and particularly how is the term applied in medical decision-making and consent to treatment; (2) How is competence determined; and (3) Who determines the competence of a person?

First, we must consider what competence is. It is essential to distinguish between competence as a term used to determine one's ability to make choices about one's medical treatment and its use as a legal term. Competence as a legal entity usually is an adjudication of a person's ability to perform effectively the tasks of daily living. The competent person remembers to brush his teeth, pay his bills, and most of the time can locate his car keys when needed. A person who forgets where they are, does not attend to normal bodily care, or has significant other signs of loss of memory may be judged to be legally incompetent. A process is initiated to establish the person's status, and a guardian is appointed to oversee the normal decisions that the person can no longer make.

A legal judgment of incompetence, however, is not identical with the capacity for decision-making in medical situations. Even a persistently demented person under guardianship may have the ability to understand here and now the choices and risks involved in a proposed procedure or treatment. Doctors attest from experience and ethicists agree, "[D]decision-making should not be equated with the legal standard of competence and its specific goals and criteria. Medical determinations of varying degrees of incapacity may coexist with the legal presumption of competence or even a court determination of partial incompetence."[11] Someone unable to balance a checkbook or find the way home from the park may still be able to process the data and exercise the freedom to make decisions about medical care. This statement is not a universal endorsement of the ability of demented persons to make good decisions, but it should remain a cautionary admonition. Caregivers need to consider seriously the possibility that patients could participate in the decision-making process. As Joseph Welie and his coeditor observe, "[P]atients, except for the unconscious, are seldom incompetent globally. A demented patient may not be able to decide between three different medications, but [may be] quite able to decide between three methods of administration."[12] Sometimes it is the physical appearance of a person that suggests that he is incapable of making decisions. It must be remembered that a person, perhaps frail, weak, and dying—dressed sparsely in a hospital gown and adorned only with a wrist band and various medical paraphernalia—is not rendered incompetent by her condition or demeanor. It is probably better to err in the direction that respects the essential human dignity and right of persons to chart their own life path than to override these important considerations.

Second, we must differentiate clearly between the criteria that determine and define competence (present *before* the decision) and those which characterize the quality of the decision (present as a *result* of the decision). Competence is determined on the presence here and now of the skills (freedom and the ability to comprehend to some degree the implications and consequences of possible choices). The authors quoted above suggest that the more important question that must be asked is "what it *means* to be able to make decisions that foster one's own health," rather than "what it *means* to be competent."[13] Decision-making capacity is determined by the person's ability to comprehend the relevant facts and their implications and to have and be able freely to weigh available choices.

Third, the *specific decision* a person makes and its perceived reasonableness to others are not the criteria by which competence to decide should be judged. *How* and *what* one decides is a very personal matter. It is dependent on the individual ranking of values of this person and how the decision relates to them. The patient's *awareness* of her values is at issue, rather than the values she holds.[14] It is the patient's ability to understand the information presented, rather than what she does with such information that must be assessed. This point is revisited in the chapter on advance directives (chapter 4).

Determination of these conditions is not the purview of the psychiatrist but of those at the bedside, those who know the patient. Since the assessment of decision-making capacity is not one of psychiatric disease or mental state but rather one of whether the person can process information, understand choices, and choose among them; those who know the person and how she usually behaves and chooses are better equipped to do make this judgment. Even professional psychiatrists are reluctant to assume the mantle of "gatekeeper" for such adjudications.

A final comment on competence: when and if a person is declared incompetent to make decisions for himself in medical matters, such a state does not suspend or set aside any written or orally expressed preferences that may have preceded this declaration. If a person has executed a living will, or if he has stated clearly that he would never want specific interventions (resuscitation, artificial feeding, etc.), those choices are *still valid* when and if the person subsequently becomes incompetent. Confusion about this point sometimes leads to medical treatments that patients have expressly eschewed and would never have wanted. Recently I received a call about a hospitalized nursing home patient. Should a feeding tube be placed? Her surrogate decision-maker was having trouble deciding. Nevertheless the right decision was clear; the patient had clearly stated in an advance directive years ago when she was competent and repeated in her yearly visit with medical director of the nursing home that she never would want "extraordinary measures," which for her included artificial feeding. The job of the surrogate was to honor her wishes. There seems little point in expressing in advance one's wishes should she become incompetent, if no one pays attention to them. More will be said about this matter in chapter 4.

What has the bioethical notion of competence to do with Catholic tradition? As the factors that limit moral responsibility increase, a person moves further and further from what is called "competence" in medical jargon. Yet since awe for the human person is paramount in Catholic thinking, it is wrong to dismiss too quickly a person's ability to participate in decision-making. Every effort should be made to bring the person into the process of deciding. After all, it is the body and life of *this* person that is ultimately affected by the decisions that will be made. It is this person's self-creation that is at stake.

THE ROLE OF CONSCIENCE IN AUTONOMOUS CHOICE

Finally we look specifically at the Catholic understanding of conscience and its application to the decision-making process in medical matters. Conscience, is "the judgment of the practical intellect deciding, from general principles of faith and reason, the goodness or badness of a way of acting that a person now faces."[15] What exactly does this mean? Catholics believe that persons are able to make judgments about the rightness or wrongness of actions from tools they possess as part of who they are. By their nature, human beings can know the good. This general disposition is given content from their personal experience and from the collected wisdom which they inherit from past experience, particularly from their faith tradition. The "judgment of the practical intellect" is an end product which applies the content of the developing moral identity of persons to the real situation before them. Everyone spends a lifetime building this identity, learning from personal experience and from the wisdom of the past. This wisdom derives from family, friends, institutions such as the church or the social structures to which everyone is exposed. When faced with concrete decisions, a person already has a store of knowledge and choices from which to view and to decide the question here and now as well as the tools to apply them.

Yet, because persons are unique both in experience and what they incorporate from the religious and social culture around them, each will come to the place of decision with a different perspective. One person values family, another values independence, still another sees financial security as the most important value. What one's moral identity ranks as most important will determine in large measure how one chooses here and now, how one exercises in the practical situation one's conscience. Individual moral identity becomes the unique rudder which guides each moral decision.The functioning of this core reality, the sorting and ranking of values based on past personal and collective wisdom and experience, is often not brought to a conscious level. It lies beneath what is decided. Sometimes it may be helpful to dig into it to see what people really want.

Let us apply this idea to a real situation in medical decision-making. Mary appears to be near death. All her life she has valued family and other's opinions—particularly those of her husband, Leo—over her own. Rarely has she made an important decision without consultation with him. In fact, she generally subordinates her wishes to his. Now she is facing a decision as to whether to allow the doctors to treat aggressively a life-threatening cancer, the recurrence of a tumor that had been treated previously. Her moral identity, her personal frame of reference and set of values is clear: whatever the family and particularly Leo want is what she will do. A doctor, a family friend who is not the treating physician, believes that further treatment is not indicated but will only bring her added pain and stress during her final days. The attending physician recommends treatment, but is unable to guarantee a positive outcome. Mary does not decide. She looks to Leo. He is so grief-stricken that he, too, seems unable to decide. Finally the grown daughters, in consultation with the family friend doctor, opt for no further treatment. Leo is not comfortable with their choice, so he agrees to have Mary undergo extensive therapy. Clearly the values held by each family member are different, and therefore their consequent choices are different: Mary values deferring her opinion; Leo values Mary's continued life, at whatever cost; her daughters value a pain-free end to her suffering, since treatment seems futile. Every person has a different moral identity causing each to view the case from a unique perspective. Each will offer a different solution to the dilemma. Is one answer morally right and the others morally wrong? The answer is "no."

A cautionary note: decisions are not considered morally right *only* on the basis of diversity and/or because they are embraced by individuals as their own. It is not morally acceptable to choose evil (disvalue) directly, even if it is valued as part of the moral identity of a person. Simply because the moral identity of a thief values taking what does not belong to him, such action is not morally right. In the scenario above, all the possible solutions are morally acceptable. Persons seek to actualize something that is of worth *to them*, be it respect for another's viewpoint, health, or end to suffering.[16]

The primacy of conscience is affirmed by Vatican II in *Gaudium et Spes* as an important element of decision-making. It is the teaching of the church that the individual decisions of conscience are inviolable. They are personal, private, even sacred decisions to be judged finally in the sacred space between God and the individual. While this aspect of Catholic thinking has generally taken a backseat to the articulation of objective moral teaching, it is a very important expression of human development and moral judgment.

"Primacy of conscience" does not mean that people have license to do whatever they please. Conscience is a much more nuanced activity. The word itself, from its Latin root, means "with science" or "with knowledge." Conscience is bound to gain knowledge about what is good and to select only the good it perceives. Catholics and all human beings are called to make the best decisions possible in the limited and real circumstances in which they find themselves. They are challenged to exercise the widest range of freedom and knowledge *as applied to real choices of the good.* To disconnect these two essential elements, the subjective and the objective, is to impoverish the moral person and the moral life.

Catholic teaching takes seriously not only the objective good but also the internal disposition of the subject, how free or how knowing the person is. Even a gravely morally flawed act can be dismissed as not blameworthy if the person lacks freedom and/or knowledge. Such a position does not diminish nor trivialize any real evil that has occurred (the objective aspect of moral action), but ultimately what counts is the disposition of the person (the subjective component), not the act *by itself.* The subject is responsible, insofar as she is able, to choose freely those possible things that embody the most good possible in messy situations. The subject is responsible for finding out the pertinent information that a reasonable person would need to do this. In the tense and urgent context of end-of-life decision-making, this is a heroic task. The exercise of conscience, particularly in the difficult context of death and dying, requires great strength. As a good friend of mine put it, "It is a robust, sweaty, 'between the eyes' struggle." For those who profess a Catholic vision of the human person and embrace the moral tradition that has developed over centuries, moral actions are constructed by the free and knowing choice of the good. Often the choices of good persons are compromised by unavoidable evil. The ability to choose freely and knowledgeably likely is compromised by the limits imposed by the very humanness that allows that choice. In medical matters, such actions are never easy.

QUESTIONS FOR DISCUSSION

1. What two elements comprise the moral act?
2. What are the things that enhance and those that inhibit autonomous moral choice?
3. Is competence the same thing as decision-making capacity in deciding medical issues? Explain your answer.
4. Does "primacy of conscience" mean that whatever I choose freely is morally right? Explain your answer.

NOTES

1. Thomas H. Murray, "Individualism and Community: The Contested Terrain of Autonomy," *Hastings Center Report* 24, no. 3 (May–June 1994): 32.
2. See *Gaudium et Spes*, particularly 16.
3. Mappes and DeGrazia, *Biomedical Ethics*, 25. Their exposition is the basis of the material to follow.
4. Parenthetically, the concept of freedom = moral rightness (discussed in the previous chapter) is key to understanding the movement in American law to co-opt assistance with suicide. It is certainly not the understanding of moral rightness from the Catholic perspective. The connections will be discussed in chapter 8.
5. Every death is always outside one's personal control. The Catholic belief in God's dominion over both life and death reminds humanity of this fact.
6. The "reasonable person standard," a legal concept, is not meant as a measure of whether the decision the person makes is itself a reasonable decision. Often persons, given the same data, will differ on what they perceive to be good decision.
7. See for example, Wim J. M. Dekkers, "Autonomy and Dependence: Chronic Physical Illness and Decision-Making, *Medicine, Health Care and Philosophy*" 4, no. 2 (2001): 188.
8. A helpful framework for decision-making with children can be found in D. M. Foreman, "The Family Rule: A Framework for Obtaining Ethical Consent for Med-

ical Interventions from Children," *Journal of Medical Ethics* 25, no. 6 (December 1999): 491–96.

9. Students in my classes often disagree, feeling that such statements let people off the moral hook. The Catholic tradition is clear about the mitigation of moral responsibility by impediments to freedom and knowledge.

10. Margaret Edson, "W;t" (New York: Faber and Faber, 1999), 5.

11. Dekkers, "Autonomy and Dependence," 191. He refers to a 1989 article by D. M. High.

12. Joseph V. M. Welie and Sander P. K. Welie, "Is Incompetence the Exception or the Rule?" *Medicine, Health Care and Philosophy* 4, no. 2 (2001): 125.

13. Joseph V. M. Welie and Sander P. K. Welie, "Patient Decision-Making Competence: Outlines of a Conceptual Analysis," *Medicine, Health Care and Philosophy* 4, no. 2 (2001): 127. The authors offer a helpful list of criteria for this determination, 133–35.

14. Welie and Welie, "Patient Decision-Making," 133.

15. John A. Hardon, *Modern Catholic Dictionary* (Garden City, N.J.: Doubleday and Company, 1980), 126.

16. If a fourth possible solution were added—giving a lethal injection, for example—that solution would be outside the set of morally acceptable actions. Why? From the Catholic perspective, to intend and to act directly to kill someone—even for a benevolent reason—is morally wrong. This is true even in the face of one's preferred stance that euthanasia is a great idea. It is an action directed precisely against a basic good. Part of the moral identity of persons trained in the Catholic tradition will be the fundamental aversion to such actions. Again, the American moral scene demonstrates less definity on this matter. Consistent Catholic teaching, however, is very sure. One of the complicating factors is the lack of clarity by many Catholics about distinctions among church teaching, civil law, and common beliefs of the culture.

Chapter Four

Making Plans before Dying

What are advance directives? When should they be written? Why should I bother with them? Doesn't my being Catholic make it wrong for me to stop life-saving treatment?

The last quarter century has seen legislative initiatives designed to return control of end-of-life choices to patients.[1] The national 1991 Patient Self-Determination Act (PSDA) directed states to enact laws allowing and encouraging persons to specify in writing the kinds of intervention they would or would not wish, should they become incapable of speaking for themselves. This law has received mixed reviews. Some have seen it as an efficacious step toward planning for the inevitable. Others have felt that the legislation merely adds an unnecessary legal layer to the relationship between patients and physicians. Some have suggested that even when people execute living wills or other forms of advance directives, no one pays attention to them in the very situations they are designed to ease.

There has been considerable confusion as to how this law and its implications relate to Catholic prolife teaching. How-to pamphlets, flyers, and seminars on the formation of advance directives abound. This chapter describes advance directives, when to make them, and their moral and legal usefulness. It will explore the connections between such preplanning and the Catholic tradition.

WHAT ADVANCE DIRECTIVES ARE

Many years ago my father was baby-sitting my oldest son. They were driving past an expanse of uninterrupted, well-trimmed lawns. Mike asked Dad what the place was. "It's a golf course, Mike." They were actually passing a city cemetery, but until the day death forced him to do so, my dad could not face the reality underlined by this field planted with head stones.

Denial of death is a common posture, especially for Americans. Ernest Becker has noted how impossible it is "to live a whole lifetime with the fate of death haunting one's dreams."[2] Human beings constantly do whatever it takes, he says, to deny and to avoid thinking about death. In the same vein Schneiderman and Jecker observe, "The fact [that human beings resist death] is so self-evident that we consider it unnatural—pathological—when a person seeks to die."[3] Such denial and resistance may contribute to deferring decisions connected with dying, often until it is too late to have reasonable control over its surrounding events. It is natural to put off odious tasks: computing taxes, sorting the piles of paper on the desk, taking out the garbage—all sorts of things are left undone until they become acutely urgent. For many, anything connected with death is placed at the very end of a to-do list. Although it is absolutely inevitable, it is likewise exquisitely avoidable. Yet most people want their deaths to be an extension of how they have lived, the final chapter in their life story, full of the values and goals that have shaped their lives.

Diane Meier, a physician noted for her work in palliative care, notes the disparity between the ideal scenarios people have about their death and what really happens.[4] She cites research that shows most people want to end their lives in a familiar environment, with pain and other symptoms of their illness controlled. Most express strong antipathy toward aggressive technological interventions that merely prolong the dying process. People want to use their final precious days to strengthen relationships with those they love, not to inflict burdens on them. Yet research indicates that just the opposite occurs, notes Meier. Most people die in hospitals (53 percent) or nursing homes (24 percent). Less than one-fourth of dying persons die where they would choose.

Americans passionately espouse the right of individuals to pursue their personal life goals. A right to life, a right to die, a right to privacy—all are mantras that influence the American culture. Nevertheless the right of persons to determine the course of their final days is a fairly new concept. "Patient rights" represents a recent renovation to the citadel of medical ethics, largely in response to landmark cases such as Cruzan and Quinlan, and more recently Finn,[5] in which patients' families were challenged in their attempts to stop interventions that they believed were contrary to the wishes of their loved ones. These cases are only a small sampling of the controversy over end-of-life treatment decisions occurring every day in American hospitals.

The Patient Self-Determination Act (PSDA), emerging from such controversies, articulates and protects the legal rights of persons to participate in their health care decision-making. The act applies to hospitals and nursing homes, as well as home health care agencies, HMOs, and hospice programs. It specifies that all facilities accepting government monies for health care (Medicare and Medicaid) must provide patients with a statement of their rights as patients and determine whether they have executed legal documents (advance directives) outlining their health care preferences should they become unable to speak for themselves. If a patient has advance directives, that fact must be noted in some way in the patient's medical chart. If the person wants to express his care preferences in a legal and written way, but does not have advance directives, the facility is required to facilitate the implementation of such documents.

By law the health care provider must disclose specific policies peculiar to its facility. Prospective residents must be informed, when a nursing home does not provide resuscitation or feeding tubes, so they have the option of choosing a facility whose policies are compatible with their values and wishes. Someone whose advance directive indicates that she would want artificial feeding should not enter a facility that eschews such intervention. Each state has the responsibility of incorporating the national PSDA into its own laws.

Advance directives are commonly expressed in two types of legal documents.[6] The first is the living will, a clear statement of an individual's treatment preferences for end-of-life care. This document can be as extensive and specific as the person wishes. Living wills state whether a dying person wants life support measures, such as machines to maintain breathing or artificial nutrition and hydration. They need not be limited to these prescriptions, but may give other instructions for care or which reflect personal values. Christian Scientists, for example, may indicate that they do not want chemical intervention as part of their medical care. Jehovah's Witnesses may specify that no blood products be administered to them, no matter how serious the condition. As legal documents, living wills have standing only when the patient becomes terminal[7] and *only* if the patient cannot speak for herself.

Living wills are meant to be the voice of the voiceless patient, articulating preferences that the person no longer can verbalize. Any consent or withholding of consent for treatment by a patient who is conscious and capable of speaking for herself, *even and perhaps especially those decisions which may conflict with the terms of the living will*, takes precedence over a previous written statement such as a living will.

The second type of document, known as a Durable Power of Attorney for Health Care (DPAHC),[8] formally designates a surrogate. This is a person charged to make decisions for another who is temporarily or permanently unable to voice his own choices for care. Unlike the living will, the DPAHC becomes active at any time the patient cannot speak for himself. It is not necessary that a terminal condition be present. Besides naming a decision-maker, the DPAHC can indicate the patient's preference regarding specific treatments such as resuscitation and artificial feeding. State laws may limit the scope of what decisions a surrogate may make for another.[9]

A recent trend has been to effect documents which would be legally binding in venues other than a particular facility (the so-called portable DNR) as well as to specify particular additional care the patient might want.[10] This expansion responds to a loophole in the law that might deny the person the right to avoid certain treatments because their living will was from another venue (a different state, a nursing home from which the patient has been transferred, etc.).

Since the implementation of the PSDA very few Americans have taken advantage of this opportunity to chart their own medical course. More than a decade later no more than 25 percent of the general population had advance directives. Even those with diagnosed terminal disease such as cancer or AIDS showed little interest in executing such documents.[11] Studies show that even when advance directives are present, the care patients receive is inconsistent with their specific directives in half the cases.[12] There may be a number of reasons why this is the case. Some of these will be treated below.

WHEN TO MAKE PLANS

There are three circumstances in which directives are usually prepared. The first is when a person is in good health. A healthy person, unencumbered with the emotional and physical baggage that illness often brings, can understand potential choices and their implications. A healthy person is more likely to experience herself as a whole "self." Persons in pain are focused on the discomfort itself and are less likely to see themselves as an integrated whole. A healthy person may be more in tune with the needs and values of others, since illness often causes not only physical but emotional withdrawal from the social dimension of life. A time of good health provides an excellent opportunity to consider the context of one's dying. Second, some people are motivated to execute advance directives when faced with a diagnosis of terminal illness. Finally, admission to an intensive care unit presses the issue to urgency. Patients and families are forced to ponder the face of death and the choices this proximity demands.

People have the potential for the best decision-making (1) when they can exercise freedom and (2) when they have the knowledge necessary to inform that freedom. Healthy persons' mental and spiritual state allow them to understand and to process the knowledge needed to make an informed decision. Pain, anxiety over an illness, even a general feeling of disruption, act as impediments to the exercise of freedom. Even mundane tasks such as balancing a checkbook can be compromised by fatigue or a bad toothache. Those with physical and psychological well-being have the tools to make better decisions than those without this equilibrium. Crisis, depression, and illness produce stressors that distract and limit the natural abilities to think clearly and to act freely.

One physician I know makes it a point to discuss patients' treatment wishes well before they become unable to voice their preferences. This discussion is part of an early get-to-know-you appointment, lessening the potential for patient anxiety: "Why are you asking me about these things, doctor? Am I really sick and you just haven't told me?" If patients wish, written documents can be prepared. At the very least, the physician will gain insight into patient values and preferences. In an ordinary office visit, with no pressing issues or fear of impending death, patients can ask questions about side effects of treatment, their benefits and burdens, and how they might fit in with an overall plan for health care. Contrary to the myth that, if issues surrounding death are discussed prematurely, people will be put off or frightened; evidence indicates that such discussions are well received by patients.[13]

Discussion profitably begins with a listing of a patient's values. A number of resources have been developed to help people do this.[14] Whatever specific treatment may be warranted, the essential task is to learn about this unique individual. What brings joy and satisfaction? What makes life worth living? What goals in life still lay ahead in the horizon of future's hope? Are there things the person wishes she had done or said? Is there a fence left to mend? Is there a story to tell as a legacy to the next generation? Such questions may motivate people to do things they really want to do but may not yet have articulated, even to themselves.

The Catholic concept of purgatory certainly represents an accommodation to the realization that we don't always complete the tasks of this life before we die. At the very least, such a conversation brings to a conscious level the hopes and dreams all persons keep within themselves. Regret for things unresolved may contribute to the pain experienced on the deathbed. Thoughtful advance planning helps avoid that possibility.

Eventually this conversation may turn to the specifics of end-of-life care. Is a long life, even one that is pain filled or limited in its scope, more important than a shorter life lived to the fullest? The aging actor, Kirk Douglas, was interviewed after having had a stroke. He considers the limits of his current situation an acceptable price to pay for continued life. Many activities still bring him meaning, including the reception of a lifetime achievement award shortly after his stroke. Originally, weighed down with the discouragement of his seemingly hopeless condition, he had attempted suicide. While certainly not endorsed in the Catholic tradition as an acceptable moral choice, suicide is commonly entertained as a solution to severe pain or a feeling of hopelessness. Douglas's attempt to end his life failed. As he began to see the scope of his continued existence beyond the prison of his bodily limitations, the actor reentered the drama of living. It is interesting to note that he deeply embraced his Jewish roots and faith.

By contrast, Bertha, seventy-three, was unwilling to engage life after her husband of thirty-three years died. She continued to dream about him, remembering especially the times they went dancing. After breaking a hip she stopped participating in most social activities and eventually stopped eating. She judged her life to be over. From her lifelong Catholic perspective her only perceived community was in the future, in heaven with her husband. She died peacefully and apparently with no regrets.

The advance directives for these people might look very different. Kirk Douglas might opt for a "do everything medically possible" scenario: "Yes, even life after a stroke is a life worth living." Bertha clearly would choose an opposite course: "Don't you put in a feeding tube! Can't you see that without my husband, life is not worth living for me?" The important thing is that persons have the right, perhaps even the responsibility, to chart their own course of dying.[15] It is the last act in the drama of their living. It is important for the production that every person to play out his part authentically to the final curtain. The total play and the other players depend on it.

To think about end of life before it is imminent allows time to explore preferences through discussion with family and friends. Nancy Cruzan, a young woman when she was irretrievably injured in a car accident, had told her family that she never would want to live a vegetative life. Knowing her feelings allowed the family to let her go, without the burden of guessing what she would have wanted.[16] A conversation begun with a professional, perhaps a doctor or pastoral care person, may lead to richer reflection and discussion with family and friends. And even if no advance directives result from such conversations, understanding is improved.

A practical and morally compelling reason for articulating one's values and preferences is to alleviate the burden to family or friends. The essential relatedness of persons and the resultant responsibility to the common good demand that others be considered when I make a moral decision. As David Kelly notes, "The Catholic tradition is clearly open to the possibility that a treatment may rightly be forgone in order to help others with the resources saved."[17] Helga Wanglie's ventilator[18] may have been her choice, but it was a choice that did not consider the limited availability of such technologies for others who might benefit from it nor the prolonged suffering for her family. Wanglie's story represents a worst-case example of American "independence" run amuck: autonomy allows doing whatever pleases me. The Catholic perspective reminds us, however, that "we are not isolated individuals, that we have obligations to others, even to unnamed others in vague far-away groups."[19] Our moral decision-making is never in a vacuum, but always in the context of our relationship to others.

Nothing is more painful than a family—even a small family—with disparate ideas of what should be done for a critically ill loved one. There is inevitably the out-of-state son or sister who has differing ideas about what treatment is appropriate. Unpleasant disagreements can be avoided if the person whose body is at issue has made preferences clear. Sometimes a formal "values profile" may help, especially when a considered intervention does not fit neatly into the categories of the living will document. A person may be emphatic that she does not wish to be resuscitated, but an understanding of her values and intentions in making such a statement may allow a nuanced interpretation: resuscitation in the operating room during a routine procedure with likely full restoration to previous function would be acceptable.[20] Restoration to a life of severely limited function is not.

An example of good preplanning is found in a young married couple who faced the death of the husband from AIDS. The pair had worked closely with the family physician to determine what would be done as the illness progressed. All agreed that when death approached, no aggressive treatment would be attempted. The patient would be supported by comfort measures only.

The patient developed an infection that required assistance to breathe. The doctor and the couple agreed to place the patient on a ventilator, to allow the body time to heal. As the infection cleared, several attempts were made to wean him. None were successful. It became clear that this time the patient would not improve enough to live independently of the ventilator.

Two possible courses of action presented themselves: (1) the ventilator could be continued; life—albeit one of limited quality—would go on; and (2) the ventilator could be removed, and dying would proceed. Since the couple had discussed such scenarios—common with AIDS patients—the decision was simple. Certainly no one wished the man to die, but medical opinion confirmed that no amount of time on the ventilator would bring him back to health. It was removed. Doing this altered the course of treatment: pain control and comfort care became the focus of the care plan. The man died with dignity and with family and medical team on the same page. No one, including the patient, directly intended his death. Yet the trajectory was unavoidable. The shift in care allowed those involved to do what they were actually able to do.

Preparing advance directives early allows someone the time and thoughtful deliberation to appoint a surrogate, often a family member, one who knows and understands the sick person's values and treatment goals. Sometimes a surrogate from outside the family is a better choice than a family member, since he or she does not carry the emotional baggage that pervades even the best of family systems. Consider, for example, the last illness of a partnered gay person. Unresolved issues with family surface. A lifetime gay partner is marginalized from decision-making because of the status of legal next of kin. Awkwardness and the pain of deciding who should decide things in such an instance may well be minimized by careful and clear advance planning. The lifetime partner of a gay person can be named as the legal DPAHC. Doing so gives that partner legal standing to make health care and treatment decisions ahead of any "next of kin."

In the end there are two essential criteria for choosing a surrogate. First, the person chosen should have a clear knowledge and understanding of the values and life goals of the patient, so as to make decisions similar to those the patient himself would make. Second, the surrogate must have a spirit of generosity, courage, and detachment, so as to carry out what the patient wants even against the surrogate's own sensitivities and emotional bias. There was a daughter who insisted, against previously stated patient wishes, that her mother be resuscitated. The expected outcome in the case was bleak. The doctor tried to change her mind, asking, "Would you want us to do this to you?" She answered, "Oh no, never, but it's my mother. I can't just let her die." Sometimes people make decisions directed by emotion rather than the wishes of the loved one in mind. A good surrogate should not be swayed by his emotional preferences but by the direction previously indicated by the patient and/or good medical advice.

Advance directives are often prepared when a serious illness is discovered or a terminal diagnosis is made. Many people do not find themselves ready even to think about death until an unexpected encounter with their mortality brings it to the forefront. Some would argue that it is only when people are faced with real illness and real possibilities that advance planning has meaning. Serious illness offers an opportunity to plan—still without urgency—for the inevitable. There is a clearer appreciation of the real situation that must be faced. Death is not imminent, but the problems associated with sickness are.

A video used to teach nursing students about ethical challenges in their work portrayed the story of a man diagnosed with Lou Gehrig's disease (amyotrophic lateral sclerosis). He and his wife—both in their late forties—thoughtfully considered what they wanted done or not done as the disease progressed. They agreed that aggressive treatment was not what they wanted: no feeding tubes, no extraordinary intervention. They decided to move to the country, the bucolic setting more conducive to the enjoyment of their remaining time together. They calculated the move to limit accessibility to unwanted technology. They spent their days on long walks in the woods in preparation for the time when the illness would dominate their destiny and would narrow their world of free choice. A living will and durable power of attorney were prepared, which specified the minimal intervention he wanted. Unfortunately an automobile accident sent the man into a local hospital with broken bones and other complications not associated with his illness. The hospital stay was an extended one. Significant interventions resolved the injuries from the accident, but his ALS continued to progress. The patient lost his ability to speak and to breathe on his own. Only his living will testified to his wishes, which did not include the use of a respirator. Advance planning allowed this man to die as he and his wife had planned, over the strong objections of medical personnel.

Diagnosis of a serious or terminal condition can serve as a wake-up call to the reality of mortality and to the need to make plans while one can. It could be argued that this situation is perhaps a better time for planning than when one is healthy, since the reality is more immediate and the possibilities can be anticipated more accurately. Respect for autonomy leaves the decision whether to plan and when to plan to the patient.

Perhaps the most frequent time advance directives are used is with a patient whose condition is already precarious and even close to death, likely in the intensive care unit. The urgency of the situation may undermine autonomy and comprehensive decision-making. Medical personnel, concerned both with patient preferences and the potential for suit, urge patients and families to execute documents indicating their treatment preferences. Patients and families are brought face-to-face with real choices, not hypothetical ones. My child is dying; my mother will not leave the intensive care unit; my husband has less than a 5 percent chance of living more than a week. Decisions must be made. Now! The knee-jerk reaction: "Do everything, doctor." Such a statement buys into the optimism so effective on prime time television medical shows. Doctor Cantfail, the good guy in white, rides into the ICU brandishing all the necessary technology and tools to vanquish the evil axis of disability, disease, and death.

The intensive care situation requires more carefully thought out strategies than the other two scenarios, strategies that can promote good decision-making in an adverse situation. First, those involved must attend to language. All must have a shared understanding of what is being requested when patients' families buy into the drama of "Do everything, doctor." What is "everything": antibiotics, blood, ventilators, PEG (feeding) tubes, aortic balloons? Rarely does anyone unpack the loaded imperative in order to get to its meaning.

"Everything" can include sophisticated interventions to stabilize falling blood pressure by chemical injections or such primitive techniques as shocking the heart muscle to make it beat properly. The chest cavity can be opened surgically to allow manipulation of the heart, and tubes can be inserted to provide everything from oxygen to nourishment. How much "everything" is needed to maintain a functioning heart, lungs, or brain? Will more of "everything" restore the patient to the previous level of function? What are the risks? Will "everything" bring the cure I desperately hope for? These questions must be addressed in the intensive care unit, because the primary medical and moral focus of an intensive care team is—and should be—aggressive intervention. The tools are available. Blood flow can be maintained, blood pressure and respiration can be monitored and adjusted to keep fragile life afloat on the angry sea of deadly illness.

Physicians and other health care professionals, even with extensive knowledge of the minimal likelihood of success and multiple risk factors, may fall into the same traps patients and families do. They may initiate the conversation about advance directives by asking, "Do you want us to do everything?" This question, unnuanced by the facts about futile medical intervention, likely represents a genuine concern of professionals to bolster the hope of patients and loved ones against the perceived despair of death. Sometimes health care professionals may be attempting to avoid their own confrontation with the denied inevitability of death, which represents a failure of the medical mandate to heal. It is important to recognize the multiple factors, many beneath the surface of consciousness, that influence behavior in the intense context of intensive care.

If "do everything" is one possibility, is the alternative that the care team will "do nothing"? This is often what families fear and why they agree to aggressive treatment. Some patients are afraid that if they specify "do not resuscitate" in living wills they will be neglected as they die. Others are terrified that "do nothing" will result in loved ones' not being given water and thereby doomed to die of thirst. Families certainly do not wish their dying loved one to be abandoned in a foreign environment. American distaste for death renders it an acutely foreign landscape. Is there a middle ground, where interventions for cure are replaced with interventions that care? Can a medical "care plan," the term usually employed to speak about how the patient will be treated medically, mean more than aggressive and often ineffective intervention?

Let us consider a model. Let us consider a continuum from total medical intervention, which ideally hopes for cure, to a stance of do nothing. What that latter statement really means, especially in the intensive care setting, is that technological intervention will no longer achieve its goal. It should not mean that nothing can or will be done for the patient. Between the two extremes of the continuum there are a number of possible interventions. The focus of attention must change from a model of cure and biological maintenance to one of intensive care of dying and its process. The primary goal in discussing advance directives in intensive care is to clarify the point on the continuum occupied by this particular patient, their real choices, and the potential risks and benefits associated with them. Some questions may help clarify this place.

First, in what way is this aggressive medical intervention beneficial to this particular patient? This question includes both the general inquiry into the patient's condition—is she terminal—and any specific interventions that may be under consideration. Once the possible interventions are laid out, the benefits that are expected from each should be articulated. A longer life? An easier death? A few more days or hours to live are not necessarily a good, especially in cases where the assault and discomfort to the patient by the intervention itself is severe.

Biological maintenance is not the same as human living. As the "Ethical and Religious Directives for Catholic Health Care Services" emphasize, "The well-being of the whole person must be taken into account in deciding about any therapeutic intervention or use of technology."[21] The "care" plan must address the initiation of do not resuscitate orders and the implementation of other interventions. It must address how the handling of the case fits in with the life goals of the dying patient. It must address the relief of pain and other symptoms as well as the promotion of comfort and control due the dignity of persons.[22] Certainly in caring for the dying we should "do everything," but the meaning of that imperative must be expanded in the face of impotent technology to mean aggressive attention to the humane elements of the event.

As decisions are made for end-of-life treatment, nonmedical benefits may come into play. It may become clear that further aggressive treatment could be better described as "battery" than as "benefit." Nevertheless the dying person may have "unfinished business" which would argue for continued medical sustenance. Even a few extra days of life may allow time for proper closure. The nephew in a distant state may be the only one with whom the dying person has not made peace. A few days on life support, although medically futile in the long run, might allow this to be accomplished. I have often said that I don't want to die until my house is clean. It would not be out of the question that I would wish to live a few extra days to allow some industrious cleaning company to accomplish that final, if frivolous, goal.

Second, is the burden of the treatment greater than any benefit it may provide. Medical intervention inevitably carries burdens with its benefits. Even the insignificant aspirin, while highly beneficial to relieve pain and to help prevent stroke, has the potential side effect of stomach upset. Life-saving interventions may be helpful, but one must assess whether the cost is too great. This assessment is always case, or more accurately stated, person, specific.

What may be too burdensome for one person to bear may appear a fair price for another. Once it is decided that the benefit is not commensurate to the burden in this particular case, one can be free to concentrate on interventions that *will* be of benefit.

Third, respect for a dying person in the final hours of life argues preferentially in favor of interventions that preserve and promote that person's dignity and comfort—a very Catholic value. No reason exists for anyone to die without good pain and symptom control. Comfort measures—a warm blanket, a quiet space, the hand of a trusted friend—should not be foregone in favor of a futile intensive care protocol. A friend has told me that his ideal death includes the taste of chocolate on his tongue. Such a simple request, but so much more humane than the taste of plastic from body-preserving tubing. The dignity of human persons demands the consideration and preservation of what it means to be human. Respect, pain control, comfort, and the proximity of those one loves are among the proper "four last things" that should ornament the bedside of the dying.

As the focus of attention moves from critical care to critical caring, the consideration of benefit and burden and of case-specific promotion of dignity is essential. In recent years the new field of palliative medicine has developed to address these issues. It has become more and more clear that no one needs to die in pain or without the support that befits human living and dying.

THE DIFFICULTIES ADVANCE DIRECTIVES POSE

Advance directives are not an unmixed blessing. The bioethics literature has many articles not only questioning the efficacy of directives but detailing the problems that are raised precisely because we have them. Here we shall address some of these problems.

The first problem has been raised by Rebecca Dresser and others: is it possible to make decisions for the future?[23] Is it not as likely that what I want now may not be what I want when a crisis occurs? Can what I say now be guaranteed to be what I mean later? There is evidence that some people do change their minds about what they specified in living wills when they *can* speak for themselves.[24] Although it is true that people may change their minds over time about certain things—marriage partner, career choice, hair color—it can be argued that the trajectory of a person's core values likely will remain the same as they move through life. Empirical studies have demonstrated that a "change of mind" is more likely the result of changed circumstances or more accurate perceptions of the implications of particular treatments. I state vehemently that I would never want to be on a respirator. Later, I get an infection in my lungs that makes it impossible to breathe adequately on my own. The doctor tells me that a short time on the machine will allow my body time to heal. "Of course, give me the treatment," I say. "My advance directives *meant* that I wouldn't want to be on a respirator *if I could not be cured from an underlying condition.* I would never want to live the remainder of my life hooked to a machine."

The second problem usually arises when a person is no longer able to speak for himself and those around him are called to honor or not to honor his wishes. If Dresser is correct, this is a very serious concern. "My husband said he would never have wanted to be intubated or fed artificially, but he is only forty. He could not possibly have meant that for now. It probably was a directive that he would want only if he were old and finished with his life." In such a situation it is important not so much to follow the letter of the directive but to put the directive in the context of the present situation. Such attention to the real circumstances of a situation demands asking the same questions posed above, which get to the real possibilities for return to the former state of life and health that interventions imply.

The dilemma of whether to honor a person's advance directive raises further areas of concern. What is the legal standing of the actual document? Is it written on the proper form? Are all the legal loopholes addressed? Fearing legal reprisals, institutions may refuse to honor documents that do not fulfill the letter of their state statutes or those prescribed by their own institutions. Families may see the medical treatment road map of a loved one impeded by legal boulders. Such challenges may be used to mask an unwillingness of the medical personnel to forgo treatment they believe to serve the medical best interest of the patient.

Those who insist on legal impeccability have missed the point. The only pertinent question is whether the document—in whatever form—is a valid representation of the wishes of the person who can no longer speak for herself. Ultimately the moral legitimacy of honoring one's requests is more important than the legal form. Documents are meant to confirm the wishes of patients, setting down in writing the directions that they are no longer able to speak. The precise task of the medical team is to carry out the known wishes of persons. *Legal* confirmation of those wishes is a secondary issue.

From the point of view of Catholic tradition, the *moral* stance of the patient's wishes to refuse treatment or intervention takes precedence over the legal standing of a particular document. As O'Rourke put it, "Court decisions and state laws may recognize and structure our decision-making rights, but they do not create these rights."[25] The right of persons to chart their own course is an inherent right which cannot be denied by legislation. Only those actions which harm the common good should fall under the shadow of law.

By contrast, neither laws nor the moral right of patients to make end-of-life decisions for themselves can force the participation of someone into engaging in unreasonable or immoral actions, *even when specified on a proper form*.[26]

The implementation of the written directive is sometimes complicated and even compromised by the fact that only a doctor may write a "do not resuscitate" order. Whatever the living will *says* in this regard must be supported by the written order of a physician. This is a startling departure from standard medical practice. For almost all treatments, the consent of the patient must be obtained before any intervention takes place. I sign a consent form for surgery or to have tests performed, indicating that I understand risks and benefits and am willing to have certain things done for and to me. The *only* medical procedure that is initiated *without* my express consent is resuscitation. Without my expressed prohibition and a doctor's order, it likely will be performed if deemed medically necessary. The default position, unlike all others, is for treatment to be given *unless* there is a medical order to the contrary. This oddity in the law underlines the grave importance of communication about one's wishes, especially communication with the physician.

Nevertheless, the *moral standing* of advance directives, written or oral, is still key. That is, does the document represent the wishes of the person who executed it? It is the moral right of persons to chart their own course of action. The precise form, the wording, the signature of appropriate witnesses— none of these should directly affect the *content* of the directive or its moral force, which is the crucial element. It is always puzzling to me that medical and sometimes ethical professionals focus more on the legal standing of the document itself rather than its power and authenticity as a reflection of what a person wants and has said that they want. Is it not more important that there is clear evidence of preference than that the preference is expressed in precise and legal orthodoxy? Arguably one of the most important speeches in American history, memorized and quoted by generation after generation of citizens, the Gettysburg Address was written on an envelope scrap—hardly an "appropriate" form!

A further difficulty with honoring such documents is a more practical one. Where is the piece of paper when it is needed? A properly executed document tucked in antiseptic anonymity under the clean underwear in a dresser drawer cannot persuade medical staff to forgo medical intervention, in the event that persons cannot speak for themselves. Its legal stance is rendered moot, or perhaps "mute," if it is not available to speak for the patient. And the power of a legal document often holds more weight with the treatment team than moral suasion. A living will which does not accompany a nursing home resident or a car accident victim into the emergency room, while still legally valid, has little probability of influencing the person's care. Likely treatment choices in such a case would include what a friend of mine has called a "full court press," whatever the patient may have specified on a missing paper.

A final difficulty has to do with the interpretation of what is written. It is impossible to construct an effective document that covers all potential circumstances. A few things can be anticipated and addressed: "Don't feed me artificially, unless I can regain my former level of function." "Don't resuscitate me ever." Beyond these obvious prescriptions, perhaps the best that can be hoped for is that the document represents a cry by the person executing it to refrain from ineffective treatment. As David Kelly graphically puts it, such a document "gives the physician at least a rough sense of our wishes. It says, in effect, 'Don't do stupid stuff to me.'"[27]

Of course the best way to overcome this difficulty of imprecision is to appoint a surrogate who knows the patient well enough to make decisions which reflect her values. Such a person would be able to interpret possible treatments not specified in a living will. A surrogate with similar perspective and values is the best choice, but what is essential is someone who would decide based on the *patient's values*. Appointing a surrogate who is a strong enough personality to fight for one's preferences against that out-of-state nephew or an overzealous doctor is not a bad idea either.

Research supports[28] that even with advance directives, most people do not die in the manner they had envisioned. Regrettably, written advance directives do not appear to solve the problem. Then why should we have them?

The answer lies in a two-sided strategy. First, it is essential to have ongoing communication among the parties involved: doctor-patient, surrogate-patient-doctor, family-patient. Much of the research lays the failure of advance directives to ambiguity of what is wanted by the patient. Second, it is important to have a knowledgeable and assertive surrogate.

Morally, the responsibility of the surrogate is to do what the person who appoints her would have wanted. This is known in the bioethics literature as the "subjective standard." There is at least some indication or direction as to what this person would want if the "subject" could speak for himself. The only time the subjective standard cannot be used is when nothing is known about the patient's wishes. In that case, what is called the "best interest" standard is used. When nothing is known about patient preference the judgment of the care team and/or the legal next of kin is substituted for the patient's own wishes.

Contrary to what may happen in practice, unfortunately, the best interest standard must never be used to replace the subjective standard, unless there is no indication of the patient's wishes. This is a very important moral point. To override a patient's life values and choices is morally wrong. It is a frank interference with a personal life plan. It is a violation of a person's freedom of conscience. As the *Catholic Directives* assert, "While every person is obligated to use ordinary means to preserve his or her health, no person should be obligated to submit to a health care procedure that *the person has judged*, with a free and informed conscience, not to provide a reasonable hope of benefit without imposing excessive risks and burdens"[29] [emphasis mine]. Notice the reminder in the *Catholic Directives* that the judgment of proportion is subjective, an exercise of the most personal and sacrosanct core of human agency.

In deciding for others, a surrogate—family member, friend, medical professional—can be plagued with doubt. "What if I did it wrong? What if I had decided to keep Aunt Tillie alive on a machine, even against her wishes? Maybe a cure will be discovered?" Decisions, even good decisions, are always more richly informed and clear in hindsight. It is important that the decision-maker use whatever tools are available at the time of the event—asking questions, consultation with others, prayer—but not carry around a series of "what-ifs" there after. Decision-making is an imperfect pursuit. That is why there is forgiveness, especially forgiveness of self. The human person is in process, knowing only part of reality that may influence choices. Decisions can be based only on that information available at the time they must be made.

No matter whether we decide to make written plans for how we wish to die, at early leisure or when the cries of death are loud and looming, there are three elements that should always be a part of that planning: *comfort, connection,* and *conversation.*

Promoting Comfort

Comfort suggests that a level of ease with the topic must be established among the participants in the discussion. As noted above, death is not an easy subject to talk about. Death, the identified "dirty" word, is rarely expressed in the prime time of human conversation. We are not at ease using the "d" word. If advance directives are to be efficacious, it is imperative that we become comfortable.

The advice of a couple who used to give sex education lectures comes to mind. They suggested that if someone cannot say "sexual intercourse," "penis," or "vagina" out loud without discomfort—and "death" would be equivalent—he or she should run the vacuum cleaner and say the word over and over again in the noise until they are comfortable. I gave a lecture on advance directives to a group of nursing home residents several years ago. I was most uneasy with the topic, especially so in an audience where the median age put the group at risk for not lasting through the presentation. It soon became clear that none of them were burdened with the high level of discomfort that I was experiencing. They lived each day in death's familiar company.

Most had not only made peace with its closeness, but kept an open date for it in the daily planner of their lives. Time for me to get out the vacuum cleaner and become comfortable with those nasty "death" words.

Comfort with death begins with an honest statement of how we feel. This applies both to persons considering advance directives and those with whom they will discuss their plans. The "script" to begin discussion might look like this: "I find death really difficult to accept. I'm not really very old, at least that's what my mirror tells me. And I know how hard it is for you to think that I, your mom, might die someday. I really want to plan for that time, though, even if it's a long way away. Could we talk about this?" Or: "Mom, you keep giving me your crystal. You say that you want me to have it to enjoy before you die. I am really uncomfortable with the idea that you will die someday, but maybe we can talk about it and about what kinds of medical interventions you would want in case you became really ill."

"When my dad had his heart attack, no one knew what to tell the doctor about the kinds of medical care he would want. Every time Dad had tried to talk to us about death, we changed the subject. Then it happened. Everything Dad feared came true. All of us, the children, were fighting and yelling at each other. We loved Dad, and our anxiety came alive in our discussions. I don't want the same thing to happen if I should ever get really sick. Let's find a time when the whole family can get together to plan for my deathday party. I'll bring the cake and conversation topic; you get the ice cream." Admission of painful feelings, creation of a safe environment for discussion, and bringing together the people involved help construct an atmosphere of comfort.

Sometimes comfort is achieved not by a forced confrontation of the *content* of advance directives but by designating *who* will be responsible. Since the advent of the PSDA several authors have raised the question of whether advance directives are really what people want.[30] For some, comfort may be deciding *who* should make decisions, even if that surrogate would decide differently from what might have been specified. In placing trust in another to decide for us, there is a recognition of essential human dependency and connectedness to others. There is the affirmation that we have limits in our ability to envision and to shape future choices.

Making Connection

Connection likewise promotes the process of making plans. Within an environment of honesty, discussion about advance directives must be a dialogue rather than a monologue. Talking "at" someone, however carefully things are worded, does not make the necessary connections that result in understanding of the other's point of view. I cannot imagine ever having had a connected conversation about death with my father, the man who denied the reality of a cemetery in favor of the comfortable fiction of a golf course. His death, from a massive heart attack, was very quick; no decisions about life support or artificial feeding ever had to be made. There are no guarantees that death will come in so uncomplicated a manner to most of us.

Connection demands that one understand and attempt to address the issues of the other, often unspoken. These can be issues of denial, fear, or even control that inhibit connection. Naming these roadblocks, rather than allowing them to perpetuate beneath the surface, goes a long way toward removing them as impediments to connection.

Sometimes making connections with others is impeded by cultural, racial, and even age differences. The white doctor who attempts to execute advance directives with the family of a dying African American may find resistance. No connection will be made until an understanding of the underlying fear that white doctors do not really want to treat effectively persons of color because they expect that those patients cannot pay for the care they get or—even worse—because the white doctors wish to commit genocide.[31] No one is likely to say this out loud, nor am I affirming the universality of such statements, but the message is there and no connections are made.

Elderly persons may fear that they are considered extraneous by the young, even young members of their own family. "How could they possibly understand? There is no point in talking with them about these things." Young persons, even those with serious or terminal illness, may avoid connections when the subject threatens their halcyon illusion of immortality.

Perhaps the most difficult situations in which to make the necessary connections concern the cases of critically ill children. Parental guilt or the feeling of impotence at their inability to protect the child from illness cloud the ability to communicate. While advance directives are probably the farthest thing from mind, major decisions about treatment and cessation of treatment are imperative. Without addressing family dynamics, guilt, grief, and the real medical and developmental state of the child, connections are not present.[32]

Having the Conversation

Third, there must be *conversation* about the issues with open-ended questions. "Tell me about how you would like your death to be," rather than "Do you want to be fed artificially?" Open-ended questions allow people to paint a total picture rather than have them feel compelled to make decisions about particulars. Whether conversation results in written directives or not, it is a valuable tool toward understanding the other person. It is never to early to begin such conversations. The Cruzan and Quinlan families did not expect to face the dying of their young daughters.

Whatever the specifics of our advance directives, whether we feel we have completed our lives or have much left to do, even if all that is left to us is suffering, our paramount nature is that we deserve all that is related to human dignity as they near life's end. Pain and symptom control, attention to our life goals as we lie dying, and our social context need be remembered.

CATHOLIC PERSPECTIVE AND ADVANCE DIRECTIVES

"Are living wills appropriate for Catholics?"[33] I give talks at churches, teach bioethics classes, and have casual conversations with people about end-of-life issues, and I know this is one of the most frequently asked questions. Concerns about following Catholic teachings are very present as people wrestle with tough end-of-life decisions. "The Catholic church doesn't believe in pulling the plug. And certainly it wouldn't be moral to starve my mother to death."

Much of the confusion and inaccurate information about Catholic tradition illustrated in these assertions is caused by the identification of living wills with a proassisted suicide and euthanasia stance. Ordinarily directives specify the patient's wish either *not* to be treated or to have treatment removed in case it is ineffectual. Advance directives can be executed that specify that someone *wants* certain aggressive treatments in the event that they cannot speak for themselves. The secular media, and even bioethical literature, often draw no distinctions between discontinuation of life-sustaining treatment and direct intervention intended to end a person's life. A television drama portraying a Supreme Court case easily equates "killing" with "pulling the plug." Sincere and believing Catholics may derive their theological conclusions from the simplified dogma presented in the media rather than the same dictates of their tradition. Jack Kevorkian's actions become identical in the public mind—including the Catholic public mind—with those of the parents of Nancy Cruzan. Nuances are lost.

Contributing to the confusion is the reality that many, perhaps most, advance directives stipulate what is *not* wanted by the person. Do *not* resuscitate; do *not* initiate artificial feeding. Do *not* try to keep me alive if the technology is expensive and not very helpful. All such requests are clearly in keeping with Catholic teaching.[34] These interventions do not aim at the death of persons, but rather seek to permit the unavoidable process of dying to move forward. Often they are implemented in situations where the "person" is no longer available and will not return. Catholic congruence with the most common stipulations of advance directives, especially those which ask that someone not be treated aggressively when little hope exists for a good outcome, rests on Catholic principles and presuppositions: the qualities of the human person, the common good and attention to social justice—not to use up limited medical resources in futile situations—and the imperative against direct killing.[35]

Since documentation supports the reality that advance directives do not help patients get what they want, however, why should a Catholic—or anyone else—take the trouble to make them? Let us return to the characteristics of the human person outlined in chapter 1. First, the human person is both physical and spiritual. While certain forms of piety and thinking have emphasized the spiritual nature of human beings, Vatican II underlined the intrinsic unity of bodiliness and spirituality. What happens to my body happens to my person. What affects my body affects my person. As I near death, the paramount preoccupation of my person is often with my body. It is appropriate that I give attention to planning for it. I have a moral duty to care for my body in a responsible way to the end of my life. It is part of my moral duty to prepare thoughtfully for the spiritual aspects of my last moments.

Second, I am essentially related to those around me. With that in mind, is it caring on my part to leave to uninformed others the difficult task of having to make decisions for my body. Further, the difficulty of decision-making for others is increased by the dual suffering of loved ones around the deathbed. What of the daughter insisting on treatment for her mother that the daughter herself would not want? It certainly is not a process of calm decision-making for another's well-being. Rather, it is crisis decision-making, informed both by anxiety and the anticipation of a loss. In stressful situations, it is difficult to decide well. When care is planned, a great service is done for those we love, even when the document remains anonymous beneath the underwear.

The common good argues in favor of advance planning. As a member of a human community I have a moral responsibility to consider the implications and impact of decisions I make on others. To employ limited technology for little or no benefit is to act directly against the needs of others. Not only is every individual life a limited entity, the resources available to sustain that life are likewise limited. There are only so many kidney machines and so many nursing home beds to care for vegetative patients. Money, even with the illusion that this is "insurance" money, is limited as well. While it is never clear a priori whether I should have this particular medical intervention before the real choice arises, the idea that one is not morally obligated to "extraordinary means" is clear in the Catholic tradition. Any intervention that has less benefit than burden is not a good moral choice.

Resuscitation is rarely effective. In less than one-fourth of cases the person does not even reclaim life itself. In the rare cases where resuscitation works, that is the patient does not die, the quality of life is generally below what the person had before and is often only a vegetative existence. Often they never escape the hospital, dependent on repeated attempts to revive them.

If artificial feeding is introduced, the patient may continue to live; however, prolonged artificial feeding often leaves the person open to danger of infection, which in itself may hasten death. Burdens are great, in either case.

Catholic teaching never requires someone to choose a treatment option with little hope of a good result and much expectation of burden.

SOME FINAL THOUGHTS

The advantage of planning ahead is "to improve shared understanding of patient's values and preferences, improve patient-centered decisions, alleviate the burdens on surrogate decision makers, and avoid over- and under-treatment."[36] These words make sense from the point of view of the Catholic tradition. First, the human person is called by God to continue to create himself or herself until death. What is done to a person's body is really a part of this self-creation. From the moral point of view, the dying person's values and preferences should not be set aside simply because they are too sick to fight or to respond or in the face of the guilt or anxiety of those around them. To do so is to commit violence on the person's values. Whether or not this planning results in actual documents is left to the decision of the person.

Decision-making is best done when the decider can look at the issues and the possible choices without the limiting forces of impediments. If a person lacks sufficient knowledge or freedom because of time constraints, fear, or the shock of knowing that death is imminent, that person will not decide as well as a person without those constraints. Thinking about whether one wants aggressive treatment, palliation only, home or health care facility, or chocolate on the tongue is better done before those choices are urgent.

Arguably one of the most important decision-making processes involves the disposition and care of one's body when near death. "Death occurs only once for each person," says George Bernard Shaw, "but every person dies." We carry our Franklin planners; we make dates for casual dinners with friends; we put money in accounts for retirement. Does it not make sense to plan for this once-in-a-lifetime event?

QUESTIONS FOR DISCUSSION

1. Describe the various forms, both legal and moral, that advance directives may take.
2. Discuss the ways in which advance directives can be helpful and the ways in which they can be of little use.
3. Give an expanded definition of "do everything" as it is discussed in this chapter.
4. Discuss ways to promote good communication about someone's end-of-life care wishes.

NOTES

1. In 1976 only one state had a living will law. By the late 1980s forty-one states had such legislation. See Ezekiel J. Emanuel and Linda L. Emanuel, "Living Wills: Past, Present, and Future," *Journal of Clinical Ethics* 1, no. 1 (spring 1990): 10.

2. Ernest Becker, *Denial of Death* (New York: The Free Press, 1973), 27.

3. See Lawrence Schneiderman and Nancy Jecker, *Wrong Medicine,* (Baltimore: The Johns Hopkins University Press, 1995), 23.

4. Diane E. Meier, "Palliative Care: What Patients and Families Need to Know" (lecture presented in Cleveland, Ohio, April 14, 2001).

5. See a recent discussion of the Hugh Finn case in light of a Catholic perspective. Michael Panicola, "Catholic Teaching on Prolonging Life: Setting the Record Straight," *Hastings Center Report* 31, no. 6 (November/December 2001): 14–15.

6. Most state laws provide for written documentation of preferences. There are, however, some states where a person's preferences need not be in written form. It is wise to become familiar with the peculiar statutes of one's own geographic area.

7. What "terminal" means is often a sticking point for the implementation of the patient's wishes. In a sense we are all "terminal," that is to say that all are on a progressive course which will lead to death. Yet when should someone be pronounced "dying"? When should the medical approach shift from attempts to do what is medically possible to a mode in which the patient's choices for end of life are honored?

8. This power of attorney should not be confused with the legal jurisdiction of a person who might be designated to manage a person's estate, for example, or be placed in charge of other legal matters. The DPAHC has a specific task: to make decisions about medical care when a person cannot make those decisions. While the two may be the same person, the law provides for a separation of these tasks, since the best person to administer one's money may not always be the person best qualified to make decisions about health care preferences.

9. Ohio law does not allow the surrogate to remove life-sustaining technology unless the patient has specifically initialed that she would not want such technology used.

10. Ohio has expanded its living will laws to allow persons to specify that, while they don't want resuscitation, they do want other forms of aggressive treatment or "comfort" care.

11. See James H. Pietsch and Kathryn L. Braun, "Automony, Advance Directives, and the Patient Self-Determination Act," in *Cultural Issues in End of Life Decision Making*, ed. Kathryn L. Braun, James H. Pietsch, and Patricia L. Blanchette (Thousand Oaks, Calif.: Sage Publications, 2000), 47.

12. See Joan M. Teno, et. al., "Do Advance Directives Provide Instructions That Direct Care?" *Journal of the American Geriatric Society* 45, no. 4 (April 1997): 508.

13. See Linda Emanuel, "Advance Directives: What Have We Learned So Far?" *Journal of Clinical Ethics* 4, no. 1 (spring 1993): 11. Initial ambivalence or fear are often part of the conversation about advance directives, however. See discussion in the same journal, Edmund G. Howe, "The Vagaries of Patients' and Families' Discussing Advance Directives, especially 5–6.

14. The two appendixes at the end of the book may serve as a starting point for discussion. They suggest questions to help persons express either the cirucumstances under which they would prefer to die or compose a summary of their lives.

15. To advocate a position of "chart their own course of dying" is not an endorsement of suicide as an acceptable option. Suicide, assisted suicide, and euthanasia will be discussed in chapter 8.

16. The case actually was much more complicated. Because Cruzan was hospitalized in a so-called right-to-life state, the parents had to fight a long legal battle to remove Cruzan's feeding tube. The battle ended a number of years after it had begun, and after the Supreme Court decision to return the decision to the state.

17. David F. Kelly, *Critical Care Ethics* (Kansas City, Mo.: Sheed and Ward, 1991), 143.

18. The Wanglie case was one of an eighty-six-year-old woman in an irreversible vegetative state, whose family demanded that she be maintained on a respirator, considered futile treatment by the doctors attending her. For an extensive discussion of the case see Marcia Angell, "The Case of Helga Wanglie," *The New England Journal of Medicine* 325, no. 7 (April 15, 1991): 511–12.

19. Kelly, *Critical Care Ethics*, 170.

20. Do not resuscitate orders (DNRs) in a living will ordinarily are suspended for surgical procedures. A person should look into the specific rules of the facility in which a procedure such as surgery is scheduled.

21. *Directives*, 33.

22. There are two fallacies that can enter into this situation. The first is that pain cannot be relieved. This erroneous belief is often the basis for people wanting assistance in dying. Fear of pain can be a powerful motivator. Studies have indicated that most terminal pain can be managed and eliminated. See *When Death Is Sought: Assisted Suicide and Euthanasia in the Medical Context,* a study published by the New York State Task Force on Life and the Law, 1994. The study maintains that over 90 percent of pain in dying cancer patients can be alleviated by medication and that, in general, end-of-life discomfort can be treated effectively. Since the study was done, more concentrated effort has been made to address negative end-of-life symptoms. (see 40–41).

The second fallacy has to do with the idea that pain is in some way salvific: heroic Christian suffering. To romanticize pain and suffering is not good theology. As Kevin O'Rourke, former director of the Center for Health Care Ethics at Saint Louis University puts it, "Suffering in all its forms is an evil, and every reasonable effort should be made to relieve it." (*A Primer for Health Care Ethics*, 2nd ed. [Washington, D.C.: Georgetown University Press, 2000], 221.)

23. Dresser argues that respect for autonomy demands honoring the competent person's *actual* choice, not a choice for some future possibility in a situation of incompetence. See "An Alert and Incompetent Self: The Irrelevance of Advance Directives: Commentary," *Hastings Center Report* 28, no. 1 (January/February 1998): 28–29.

24. Competent persons' *current stated wishes* take precedence over any written or oral directives that they may have been set down in the past.

25. O'Rourke, "Suffering," 83.

26. The *Catholic Directives* are clear that a patient's request—written or otherwise—to do anything that would conflict with the conscience of medical personnel, to assist in abortion or euthanasia for example, should not be honored. (See *Directives*, 24.)

27. Kelly, *Critical Care Ethics*, 51.

28. The SUPPORT (Study to Understand Prognoses and Preferences for Outcomes and Risks of Treatment) research, published in 1995 (*Journal of the American Medical Association* 245 [1995]: 1591–98), attempted to improve the use and effectiveness of written advance directives, in particular the impact on preferences about resuscitation. As late as 1997 there was little evidence that having advance directives improved communication or changed resuscitation practice. See Joan Teno et al., "Advance Directives for Seriously Ill Hospitalized Patients: Effectiveness with the Patient Self-Determination Act and the SUPPORT Intervention, *Journal of the American Geriatrics Society* 45, no. 4 (1997): 500.

29. *Directives*, 32.

30. See, for example, Rebecca Dresser, "Advance Directives: Implications for Policy," *Hasting Center Report* 24, no. 6 (November/December 1994): S 3.

31. Trust issues that affect care of African Americans by white doctors are well documented. See Charles P. Mouton, "Cultural and Religious Issues for African Americans," in Braun et al., *Cutural Issues*, 75–76.

32. A good discussion of issues concerning dying children is to be found in Julie R. Van der Feen and Michael S. Jellinek, "Consultation to End-of-Life Treatment Decisions in Children," in *End-of-Life Decisions: A Psychosocial Perspective*, ed. Maurice D. Steinberg and Stuart J. Youngner (Washington, D.C.: American Psychiatric Press, 1998), 137–77.

33. John Dietzen, "Are Living Wills Appropriate for Catholics?" *Catholic Universe Bulletin,* February 7, 1997, 9.

34. A good deal of confusion still remains, especially with regard to the acceptability of artificial feeding and hydration. See chapter 7 for an extended discussion.

35. Even before the PSDA the American Church formally expressed concern for these issues. See Committee for Pro-Life Activities, "Guidelines for Legislation on Life-Sustaining Treatment" (Washington, D.C.: National Conference of Catholic Bishops: 1984), which noted that treatment "which only secures a precarious and burdensome prolongation of life for the terminally ill patient" could be appropriately discontinued. The committee reaffirmed the tradition of respect for human dignity, the condemnation of the direct taking of one's own or another's life, and the contextual and communal nature of end-of-life decisions.

36. News @vhaethics (a publication of the Veterans Health Administration National Center for Ethics), spring 2001, 1.

Chapter Five

When They Say Treatment Is Futile

"The functions of medicine are threefold: to relieve pain, to reduce the violence of disease and to refrain from trying to cure those whom disease has conquered, acknowledging that in such cases medicine is powerless." [Hippocrates]

What does it mean to speak of a treatment as futile? Who makes the decision and on what basis is that decision made? How can I be the one who authorizes the doctor to the plug: isn't there always hope? Doesn't the church teach that human beings should not be the deciders of life and death?

There are instances in medicine when the zealous and efficient work of the physician must yield to the dictates of reality, when what the healer does or proposes to do gives way to the inevitable, to the relentless progression of illness to death. Recognition dawns that further medical intervention has nothing of benefit to offer the patient, as Hippocrates observed centuries ago. One of the most difficult concepts in modern medicine—not so much to grasp, but to accept— is futility. With the advances in medicine and the consequent illusion of human invincibility, we are convinced that all human problems are conquerable through technology. Instant mashed potatoes, reaching out and touching people through e-mail, Dolly, the modern way to a new ewe—all sorts of technological advances support the convincing illusion that there are no barriers to advancement in all human endeavors, including medicine. There are in contemporary medical practice significant gaps between (1) what can be done, (2) what is being done, and (3) what should be done. The first is a question of fact, the second may indicate a lack of knowledge, the third is a moral judgment.

Futility is a slippery concept. What does it meant and whose task it is to make judgment? What are the consequences of futility for professionals and for the patients they serve? What are the implications for society and the common good that continuation of futile treatment has? What are the implications of religious belief, particularly a Christian perspective? What are the guidelines to help people make good moral decisions when faced with difficult dilemmas?

Modern American culture embraces the illusion of human invincibility, an illusion built on the promise of science and technology. With enough time and skill, even death can be conquered. It is perceived to be, as Callahan puts it, "a correctable biological deficiency."[1] Mrs. Sauell, an elderly woman whose life was slipping away, continued to exist in the intensive care unit. "The kidney specialist was satisfied that the schedule of renal dialysis was replacing her lost renal function; the pulmonary specialist was satisfied that the ventilator was maintaining her oxygen level sufficiently high to be compatible with life . . . the cardiologist concluded that Mrs. Sauell's heart was functioning at maximal capacity even though she was unable to leave the bed."[2] Technology, the god of modern life, was in charge.

The treatments rendered to Mrs. Sauell by well-meaning physicians "worked," if one looked only at the results on the individual systems of the body. Each physician, relying on the technology of the speciality, could point to positive results. Relying on the ethical principle of beneficence, and consistent with accepted standards of care, each continued to inflict good results on the patient. Yet overall, Mrs. Sauell did not improve. What was being done for her was futile, although the professionals were not able to articulate the reality.

If futility is a difficult concept for the profession itself, how much more so is it for patients and their families who are the ones faced with critical decisions about life and death and who grasp even the slightest scrap of hope? Eighty-six-year-old Helga Wanglie, dependent on a machine to breathe and permanently in a vegetative state,[3] was maintained alive at the request of her family. They insisted on the continuation of the ventilator support, against medical opinion that the treatment was of no benefit. In contrast to the Sauell case, it was the medical personnel who advised that treatment be discontinued. The family, understandably wanting Mrs. Wanglie to live and undoubtedly torn by the emotional impact of the situation, accused the doctors of "playing God" and insisted that the machines be continued.[4] Basing their claim on the ethical principle of autonomy, as interpreted in the American context, the family felt it appropriate to demand treatment for Mrs. Wanglie. No treatment seemed unreasonable to them in the face of option—her death—even treatment that professionals deemed "futile."

WHAT IS FUTILITY?

The term "futility" comes from the Latin, *futilis*, which means "easily poured out." There is an ancient Greek myth about the King of Argos, who ordered his daughters to murder their husbands. Although acting in obedience to their father's wishes, the women were still punished by the gods. They were sentenced for eternity to collect water, not in sturdy buckets, but in sieves. This action was doomed to failure; it was futile. In medicine the term futility is used in two ways. Futility can refer to a *quantitative* or *factual* assessment of what will not work. Futility can be *qualitative*, meaning that it has to do with the values and perceptions of the decision-maker and cannot be measured by scientific techniques.[5]

Quantitative Futility

Factual or quantitative futility can be either medical or physiological. It is *medically futile* to continue a person on kidney dialysis when cancer has invaded the entire body and is moving it toward death. The dialysis itself will be effective, but the underlying process of dying will not be put off. This is the situation in the case of Mrs. Sauell: her systems can be maintained, but the *medical reality* cannot be reversed. If Mrs. Sauell should go into cardiac arrest and the team attempted again and again to bring her back by resuscitation, their actions would likewise be *physiologically futile*, that is they would not even achieve the specific limited goals of the intervention. The bowel anomaly of an anencephalic infant can be surgically corrected (a specific treatment will have its own "good" effect), but the underlying condition cannot be changed.

The question of futility is whether the proposed or initiated treatment fulfills its proper goals in one or both of these areas (medical or physiological). Both types of quantitative futility demand assessments of fact, based on the medical realities of a particular situation. These facts—what is going on with this particular patient and what can be expected to result if certain treatments are started, stopped, or continued—must be considered along with general treatment guidelines for illness of this type. The result is an assessment of not only what *can* be done (chemotherapy is an appropriate proven medical intervention for cancer; antibiotics can be used to treat bacterial infection), but in finding an answer to the question, what *should* be done (will this patient respond to chemotherapy; is there an antibiotic that will have a curative effect for this patient's infection?). And the *should*, which is a moral evaluation, turns on the *can,* which is an evaluation of the medical facts and prognosis.

What distinguishes medical futility? First, treatments or interventions are *medically futile* when they cannot reverse or cure the underlying fatal condition. It is the task of costly machines to do their work, but their effectiveness is "easily poured out." Such actions may do what they are intended to do (keep the heart pumping or make the kidneys produce urine, for example), therefore they are not without efficacy. They are ineffective in reversing the underlying pathology of the disease. It is medically futile to provide medicine or breathing machines to keep the heart and lungs working for the person who can no longer breathe on her own because a lung cancer, spread now to other organs, has destroyed this ability. The physical body may continue its functioning—at least for a while—but the underlying cancerous condition will not be reversed. The case of Helga Wanglie, described previously, illustrates medical futility: the body was able to be maintained through artificial intervention, but the condition that brought her into the hospital in the first place was not reversed. It could be said with certainty that Mrs. Wanglie was never herself again.

It is medically futile to continue kidney dialysis for the patient whose body systems are beginning to shut down because they are dying, possibly of an unrelated cancer. The dialysis will do what it is intended to do, clean the blood of toxic materials, but the patient will not get better. In medical futility, a particular treatment may have the desired effect on a specific system or organ, but the underlying illness will continue to progress.

It is medically futile to repair the stomach or ill-formed heart of an infant who is born without a functioning brain (anencephaly). The child may be able to function vegetatively but will never be able to engage in truly human activity. The condition which impeded the proper development of the brain is not "cured" by successful repair of the other organs. Although such a poor prognosis evokes an emotional response of disbelief and denial, it is factual. Such a child will never be the hoped-for son or daughter of the distraught parents at the bedside. Often parents cling to desperate hope that impossible conditions will be changed. They not only allow but encourage multiple interventions without ever addressing the very real question of fact: with all this, what kind of life will my child have?

We can speak of a treatment or intervention as *physiologically futile*. What this means is that interventions will not even stem the problem that they are designed to fix. If I repeatedly stimulate the heart with medication and/or electrical shock, and immediately after each attempt the heart ceases to beat or returns to an arrhythmic beating, my actions not only do not reverse the underlying condition, they do not even produce the desired physiological result. Blood transfusions which do not stop the loss of blood from a bleeding internal organ will leave the patient with continuing blood loss and lowered blood pressure. To continue such activity is to persist in physiologically futile treatment. Such activity, although it is doing *something*, is not doing something which is of benefit.

Intervention that is designed to relieve pain but that will not cure the disease is not the same as futile treatment. Pain relief is an efficacious goal, even if it is clear that such an intervention will not cure the patient. In many cases it may cause harm to the patient and divert attention from helping the person to die with dignity.

A more mundane example is the prescription of antibiotics for a common viral infection. There is a certain comfort for both the patient and the physician in taking pills or other medicine. It satisfied the human need to *do* something, to exert some control in the face of illness. Antibiotics are known to be effective only against bacteria and do nothing to inhibit the growth of viruses. To prescribe antibiotics for a person suffering from a viral infection is physiologically futile: it will not produce the desired benefit; it will not destroy the virus. In a sense, one could say that the punishment does not fit the crime. The patient is subjected to an intervention that will not rehabilitate his or her condition, one that will not have an effect on the condition it proports to treat. It will neither prevent the progress of the disease nor reverse its course. Further, in light of what might be called a common good argument, continuing to administer antibiotics inappropriately and sometimes indiscriminately opens the possibility of developing mutated forms of organisms that have resistance to treatments that currently work against them.

Qualitative Futility

The second way to speak of futility is in terms of value or quality. A treatment or intervention is *qualitatively futile* if and when it no longer achieves the goals that the patient in question wishes to achieve. Its assessment does not depend completely on medical realities, but on the intersection of those realities with the values and priorities of the patient.

Mrs. L. missed her husband and had little zest for living in a chronically ill state. She perceived herself to be dependent on her family, an obvious disvalue to a woman who prided herself on being a self-sufficient individual. What she cherished in life died with her husband. Life, particularly life with a mobility-limiting hip fracture, held little meaning for her. Thinking clearly and resolutely, she made an autonomous choice to stop eating, to forgo a "treatment" that was keeping her alive. Forced artificial feeding would have sustained her life, but it would have violated her personal decision and undercut the specific goals she held for her life. Such treatment would not be futile in the quantitative sense of the word; it can be called futile in the qualitative sense: it will not produce an effect which, from the viewpoint and values of the patient, is an essential priority. "For those whose lives are always in a state of inner sickness . . . [one should] not attempt to prescribe a regime to make their life a prolonged misery."[6] Only the patient herself can be the appropriate judge of the proportion of misery present.

On the other hand it may be appropriate to continue, at least for a time, medically or physiologically futile treatment to achieve more important values. This, too, is an assessment of "quality." Perhaps Paul, a dying patient, wishes before he dies to make peace with that nephew in California, a distance away. Paul is resigned to die, since the progression of the disease cannot be reversed, but continued treatment will buy the short period of time it takes for the relative to make the trip to the bedside. The treatment will not stay or reverse the disease process. When word comes that the relative has decided not to make the trip, the sustaining but medically futile intervention will become qualitatively futile as well by definition: it no longer serves the desired goal—Paul's last reunion with the relative. Qualitative judgments of futility are proportional to the importance of the goals sought versus the severity of the costs—not only monetary—necessary to achieve those goals.

Suppose cancer-riddled Mary agrees to chemotherapy, knowing that it will give her a few extra months of life before she succumbs to her cancer. The therapy leaves her feeling ill and without energy—worse than she might feel without it. Yet she wishes to see the birth of her first grandchild. Once that grandchild is born, Mary may consider further therapy futile, since its burdens for her will outweigh the benefits of time that are achieved. Was this treatment medically futile from the onset? Yes, it could not reverse the course of the illness nor cure it. Was it futile in the sense of buying a portion of time for the patient, however? No. These distinctions can be subtle. They do not surface as the results of comprehensive laboratory testing, but they may require careful attention to all the factors present in a particular case. It is prudent to keep in mind the variety of good and humane solutions that may exist to these complex questions and not assume that there is only one morally right answer.

In addressing and evaluating qualitative or value-based futility, the essential dignity and integrity of the individual patient must be remembered and protected. We are self-directing subjects who must stand humbly before God with the choices we have made in our hands. We are not free to invoke others' choices as our own, but must own the unique moral path we have chosen. We are each summoned to conform our choices to "a law written by God" on the human heart. "To obey it is the very dignity of man; according to it he will be judged."[7] We are called to make decisions in the context of our relatedness to others, their needs and well-being.

Even God does not interfere with exercise of human freedom. This is true when human choices are directed toward the good (morally right actions), but it is true as well when choices are pointed toward evil (morally wrong actions). Human beings have an inherent freedom to create themselves as they choose. While this right is generally framed in American bioethics under the ethical principle of autonomy, the roots of it go beyond a liberal affirmation of individual freedom to what it means to be human,

a self-directing, self-creating subject. The freedom of the individual conscience is sacrosanct. The cautionary note, however, is that human freedom
seen within the anthropology of the Catholic tradition is designed to function most adequately in pursuit of the good.

Nevertheless, finer distinctions need to be made. It is not morally acceptable, from the Catholic perspective—even when one has chosen one's own
hierarchy of values—to act in such as way as to choose as an end that which
is not objectively good. The broader bioethics literature has featured articles
which endorse the taking of one's own life when and if that life becomes not
worth living—for whatever reason satisfies the individual. The argument is
based in the belief that human freedom to choose one's values and actions is
in itself absolute, without an objective referent. The argument asserts that
freedom itself is the overarching determinant of morality. As we have seen
above, Catholic tradition disagrees and deems suicide, evenly freely chosen,
an immoral action. It aims, with a clear intention but without proportionate
reason, at an objectively moral evil. To act directly against life is morally
wrong. We will discuss this more completely in chapter 8, when we take up
the question of suicide.

There are important differences among the following: (1) refusal of treatment, (2) expectation or demand of medically beneficial treatment, (3) pursu-
ing one's own goals, and (4) involvement of others in the pursuit of one's goals.

First, following the argumentation above, it is permissible for a patient to
refuse a proposed treatment, even beneficial or life-saving treatment, that is
offered. This right to refuse treatment is affirmed not only by the Christian vision of the human person which underlies it, but by law. To say so makes no
judgment about the moral character of such a refusal. Some refusals are
clearly moral (refusal of chemotherapy that is having no effect on a tumor);
others are less clear (refusal to eat, because life seems not worth living).[8] It
remains the *patient's* choice to make, however.

Second, it is appropriate that patients should expect their physicians and
hospitals to offer medical care and treatment that is designed to cure or palliate their illnesses. The expertise and commitment of physicians are committed "to providing competent medical service with compassion and respect for
human dignity."[9] To die in pain diminishes human dignity.

Third, the moral imperative on another to help me accomplish my goals is
a complex issue. While I have an inherent right to pursue my own goals, as
granted legally by the Constitution as well as inherent in human personhood
and moral subjectivity, I have no claim on your conscience to agree with my
proposed actions nor to help me achieve them. This stance, profoundly
Catholic in that it affirms the uniqueness of every conscience, is diametrically
different from that of Jack Kevorkian. He believed another's wish was his

compelling command. Perhaps I wish to die. I may even believe that this is a good action. However strong my wish or compelling my argument, it cannot bind me to do something that my conscience asserts is morally wrong. I have a right and, indeed, a moral obligation to follow my own conscience, whatever yours demands of you. It cannot demand the same of me. Pursuit of my own goals is what defines who I am. This tenet holds even when my moral trajectory of choice is hell. Otherwise moral freedom is a travesty.

Futility, especially qualitative futility, should not be interpreted as a generic category that can be defined precisely and applied evenly. There is no standardized test for it.[10] This is part of the difficulty in making application of church documents which affirm the goodness of life and importance of certain methods of preserving it. This is part of the problem with hospital policies which attempt to set guidelines for all care within their institutions.

Documents dealing with broad issues can only state the general principles involved. They cannot be expected to make application to every individual situation and case. Although definitions of futility can be framed in a general manner—we can speak of certain categories of treatment as futile; such definitions, like those defining what is generally ordinary and extraordinary, must be applied in a *case-specific* manner.

Judgments about futility are calculated judgments about the efficacy of this particular intervention on this particular patient. We know, for example, that cardiac resuscitation can be effective in restarting a heart.[11] We see machines in airports and other public places and we champion the movement to train service personnel to use them. Whether the procedure is likely to be effective here and now for this fallen patient is a judgment call, based on the expertise of the medical personnel and a factual assessment of the condition of the patient before them.

There are documented instances in a hospital, on whose ethics committee I sit, where an elderly patient was resuscitated over a dozen times in a period of two days. She died anyway. We know from sociology and psychology that human beings seek to avoid death and will do almost anything to preserve their bodies against the threat of harm. Our hands immediately pull away from a hot stove, even before our brains know that we are touching it. Adrenalin begins to pump when we sense that we are in danger and life is at risk. Yet in the end we must resist deflective actions that cannot stop the process that ends in death.

Judgments about the likelihood of a particular intervention to do work must be concrete, involving the assessment of the evidence in this case rather than plugging into general guidelines. Whereas we can speak of certain therapies as always futile—drinking pink grapefruit juice while reciting the Gettysburg Address will not change the course of my heart disease—here we use the term futility only and specifically with regard to specific treatment in a specific case. Judgments about whether certain therapies will work medically or phys-iologically, or are in keeping with the goals and values of the patient, are not to be made in a general way.

Resuscitation is a therapy that in theory works; it may not be helpful in this particular case. Vasopressor medicines that help the heart continue to work are valuable tools for the physician; they may not provide more than a moment's respite here and now for this particular individual; they may only prolong the dying process and increase the pain and discomfort not only for the patient, but for the family keeping vigil at the bedside. Chemotherapy seems to cure some cancers, buys time for others, is a futile treatment in many. Sometimes the dis-tinctions among these possibilities are not known until the therapy is tried and the results are evaluated. It is up to the patient, the patient's surrogate, or the patient advocate—perhaps the hospital chaplain or another family member—to ask the important questions that help the decision-maker to evaluate whether such interventions are indeed futile.

WHO NAMES FUTILITY?

The answer to this question can be reached by examination not only of the ethical principles of beneficence and autonomy, but by looking at the various moral decision-makers in a concrete case and defining their moral goals. Since medical and physiological futility are judged by the standards of med-ical efficacy, the duty to suggest and implement appropriate treatment, the proper decision-maker is the physician. It is the physician whose primary moral goal as a professional is the health and well-being of the patient. It is the physician who is morally bound to act with beneficence toward those en-trusted to his or her care.

Judgments about instances of medical or physiological futility are essen-tially judgments of fact or assessments about reality: will a particular medi-cine stop this disease process? Will shocking the heart bring that organ to the point of where it can again function effectively? Sometimes getting to the "facts" is not easy. Nevertheless the physician is the person who best under-stands what might work or not work in a particular case. It is a question of medical expertise to determine whether the expected *effect* of a particular treatment will indeed provide a *benefit* to this patient.[12] It is the moral re-sponsibility of the physician to use medical expertise to determine what will be of benefit. When that benefit is established, it is the moral responsibility of the physician to articulate that benefit (and perhaps its negative implica-tions and risks) to the patient and/or the patient's surrogate. At that point it be-comes the patient's or the surrogate's time to decide.

Ultimately it is the moral responsibility of the patient to make decisions about his or her own care. In the realm of qualitative futility, a shift in thinking from the professional assessment to the personal choice must be made. It is the patient or the patient's surrogate who best understands the values regarding life and its living that the patient holds. It is the patient and the patient's values that reign over other considerations when making decisions in this arena. This principle is consistent with personal responsibility of conscience as well as American culture. The physician's area of competence is medical fact and the art of applying the medical arsenal to this specific case. Only the patient can assess what is of value to him or to her. There is no medical test which demonstrates the titer of an individual's tenacity toward life or the desire to continue it.

A good example is the case of Nancy Cruzan, the young Missouri woman whose family and friends testified that she would never want to live in a persistent vegetative state or be kept alive by artificial feeding. It was important that her family knew and articulated her preferences for treatment, even though their battle to have them honored was a long and frustrating one. While the "treatment" was working in the physiological sense—patients can be fed and/or ventilated for years—the values of the patient, as articulated by her family, were not being served. The treatment therefore was rendered "futile" by reason of the patient's values. One could make a strong case for quantitative futility as well, since Nancy's condition was not going to be cured by artificial feeding. In this case, the decision to remove artificial treatment became a decision of quality, not quantity of life. Life had lost meaning for Nancy as a particular individual with a particular set of values. Nancy lay in a hospital bed, unable to communicate or interact in any human manner. As the prolonged court battle demonstrated, however, not every person involved in the case agreed as to what should be done. It was her decision, or that of her surrogates to make, since it was her values that were being weighed.

In Catholic tradition, moral teaching has emphasized not only the *objective* components of the decision—what I do—but has taken into consideration the *subjective* components, why I act and my concrete ability to act freely and to understand the implications of what I do. Decision-makers are not merely the agents of particular actions, the actions themselves linger on as a part of them, actualizing their values, religious and otherwise, and making them the kinds of persons they have chosen to be. There is no definitive "test" for this aspect of decision-making; there is no way of ascertaining without a doubt if the decision is a good one or a bad one. All persons must stand before God with their decisions. And all difficult medical decisions carry with them elements of both good and evil.

Richard McCormick, an outspoken defender of the Catholic tradition in bioethical matters, makes a clear distinction between *causality*, to make something happen, and *culpability*, a moral responsibility for making something happen.[13] When a surgeon cuts into someone's belly to remove a tumor, the patient will wake up with a great deal of pain. Although the surgeon's action *causes* the pain, it is a secondary result of the surgery which the doctor does not directly intend. The doctor is not morally responsible or blameworthy, *culpable*, for bringing pain to the patient.

A determination of futility may require that a respirator be removed from a dying patient. Someone has to do this. Someone has to remove the equipment or turn off the machine. Does that person's action allow (cause?) the dying to proceed? Does the nurse or physician who "pulls the plug" or the family member who consents to the removal of life-sustaining technology participate knowingly in such an action? The answer to both questions is "yes." Would the patient have remained alive for a time if the respirator had not been removed? Likely, yes. Therefore we must conclude that there is at least some causal element in the consent of the family and the action of the health care professional to stop or remove life-sustaining treatment. The *moral* question has to do with blame, however. Catholic tradition has used the term "culpable" for morally blameworthy actions. Catholics of a less tender age may remember the catechetical analysis of serious moral fault: it is a big sin; I know it is a big sin; I want to do it anyway. To stop futile treatment is not blameworthy. While the death of the patient, *which I recognize* cannot be avoided, there is no intention to kill. The distinction turns on the inevitability of death in this particular case, in the face of any action or lack of action persons might take and in the weighing benefits and negative consequences to the patient on a respirator. While the current American debate and its response in the legal system document a variety of strong and divergent opinions,[14] the position is consistent with Catholic tradition.

Does life as it is being lived have continued meaning to the patient? The patient's values weight the decision, even in the face of other medical considerations. It is not immoral for a patient to refuse a life-saving transplant, if that person believes that the personal benefits do not outweigh what are perceived as serious burdens.

The bottom line is that patients have the right to *pursue* but not to *impose* their own agenda. Personal integrity, religious perspectives, difference in values from those of the professionals—all are sufficient reason for patients to depart from the offered care plans of their professional consultants. This is true even if the choices they make are eccentric or even bad choices. Patients have a right both to refuse treatment based on their values and to receive good treatment within the judgment of the medical community.[15]

Professionals have not only the right but the responsibility to refuse treatments that are futile in the sense of medical or physiological goals. No doctor is required to provide steroids to athletes, Laetrile to desperate cancer patients, or abortions to women who wish them. Helga Wanglie's doctors had a moral responsibility not only to the truth of the medical condition but to the common good to refuse continued futile treatment to Mrs. Wanglie. This odious responsibility would hold, *even in the face of advance directives demanding that "everything" be done.* A "full court press" advance directive holds no moral power to trump the honest medical assessment that a possible treatment will not benefit the patient. "Everything" must be efficacious or it should not be done. Beneficence, not maleficence, is the goal of medical treatment. Individual conscience, professional values, and the mission of the institution in which care is sought stand as testimony to this principle.

CONSEQUENCES FOR PROFESSIONALS AND PATIENTS

As we examine the theoretical underpinnings of futility it is necessary to keep in mind that these issues have ramifications in the real lives of real people: patients, families, professionals alike. Each player is this drama comes to the stage with a particular set of values and goals, a unique set of underlying presuppositions—a unique "role" to play. Everyone brings what can be called "hidden agenda," those goals and presuppositions which may not even be recognized by the people themselves, but which help shape their actions and decisions. Hidden agenda refers to the motivations, fears, feelings, and so on that underlie how we think about things and often what we do. It does not refer only to things which people intentionally keep hidden, but to those things they do not even see themselves.

In his classic article[16] discussing active and passive euthanasia (discussed in some detail in chapter 2) Rachels outlines a case that illustrates what can be meant here. He draws the scenario of Jones, who watches a small child drown and does nothing, because Jones wishes to gain an inheritance upon the death of the child. His "hidden agenda" is the motivation that is not readily seen by describing the facts of what happened: child slips in tub and drowns. While Jones seems not to be responsible for the drowning, Jones's motive to endorse the death of the child and his lack of action to prevent the drowning constitute moral culpability, *even without direct causality.*

Hidden agenda are not limited to nefarious motives, as they are in this case. Sometimes the issues and feelings below the surface include power tugs of war among the participants. James Nelson speaks of situations in which there is use of "a crowbar for wrenching decision-making from families"[17] Sometimes such a situation emerges when families' agenda may be lack of trust in the medical judgment. At other times it may be the physician's need to exert his authority, based on the "doctor knows best" model of medicine prevalent in earlier times. Since, as Lantos has observed, "[t]he doctor-patient relationship (DPR) is not a relationship between equals"[18] there is the potential for doctors to leverage their position unequally over patients and patient's families. Such power plays are not announced, but can exist underneath the surface of decision-making events. Lantos enumerates other issues that may color decisions about treating or not treating in discussions about futility. Concerns about money, trust among the parties, and the need to cling to hope in the face of no hope may enter tacitly into decision-making.

The announcement of futility carries with it the connotation of failure for the professional and the ominous sentence of death for the patient and for the family. No one wants to fail; few face death without a spectrum of feelings from fear to anger, from sadness to regret. All these things lurk beneath the surface of discussions about futility; all make such a naming very difficult. The effects of this naming go well beyond the medical implications. They are not to be taken lightly, as they have major impact on the various players in the serious drama of death.

SOCIAL IMPLICATIONS OF FUTILITY

Pronouncing that treatment is futile or continuing to treat in the face of futility have consequences for society. Implicit in either are questions of justice and implications for social policies regarding assisted suicide and euthanasia. Particularly in the United States, we tend to speak of rights and what is owed the individual without a nuanced understanding of either where such "rights" originate or of their implications. American rights appear to exist independently of considerations of the influence of our exercise of "rights" on others. It is rare for those who invoke the notion of right to explicate what justifies or underlies such rights.

First, let us consider justice. Demand for continued futile treatment by patients is not simply a matter of individual free choice and a right to autonomy, it is also an issue of justice and the common good. All medical resources are limited goods. There are fewer organs available for transplant than there are persons who will die without them; there are fewer dollars available for health care expenses than there are patients with medical bills. It is a matter of responsible and just allotment of such treatment in the face of limited resources. Is this rationing of treatment? Of course it is, but it is also an act of justice.

Justice is the distribution of goods in an equitable manner. Since medical goods are limited, it is just to supply them to those who need; it is unjust to provide them for those who will not be helped by them. Utilization of futile treatment, like providing a drink from a leaking sieve, satisfies the need of no one and pours out the precious good without efficacy. While the notion of rationing health care gets consistent bad reviews in the media, there is no other way to distribute a commodity that is limited. The important thing, however, is that rationing be done with justice and that limited medical resources not be poured into the sieve of futility.

The judgment of whether or not to continue medically futile intervention turns not only on the free choice of her family but on responsible and just management of health care. Such management dictates that she not be entitled to that treatment. It is not a question of "playing God," as Wanglie's family accused the hospital of doing, it is a question of acting as responsible stewards of health care resources both real and financial that are available. For every Wanglie kept alive, several Smiths and Joneses will not get the nonfutile medical care they need and could have if Wanglie were not consuming the resource. And Wanglie is not alone. For many, an overwhelming portion of the health care dollar is spent funding the last year of life. Do not make the mistake that this is a question of money alone; it is often a question of proper and effective management of money. Remember the sieve. If fresh water is poured into a flawed container which allows the water to seep out, no one's thirst will be sated.

The second case at the beginning of the chapter illustrates the issue of justice from the opposite point of view. Rather than the demands of the patient or patient's family to continue to pour water into the sieve, the plight of Mrs. Sauell is the result of the zeal and denial of the medical care personnel who will not cease treatment. It is not only dollars and intensive care resources that are spent, it is the human resources of care personnel. To think about these issues without a consideration of the social implications is to think about them inadequately. If all moral agents should not act without consideration of the social implications of their behavior, this is true of medical persons as well.

Intersecting with justice issues in futility are public policy and law, illustrated by the currently "hot" topic of legalization of assisted suicide. Sometimes the throw away phrase, "right to die," is not really a cry for assistance in dying, but an assertion by patients that they not be forced to endure treatments that have little or no benefit to them: *futile* treatment. Without the connection of these issues, clearly the assisted suicide debate in this country is not airing all the issues.

FUTILITY AND CHRISTIAN FAITH

An anthropology derived from Christianity—we are not without limits in either our choices nor our potential—puts a distinct filter on issues of futility. First, if we are intrinsically connected to other human beings in the relationship of community, the choices that we make must take these others into consideration. Helga Wanglie's family cannot make a choice isolated from other potential users of her life-sustaining technology; they must take them into account.

Decisions to forgo treatment are ultimately *social* decisions, dictated by the notion that we are social beings, connected to one another in reality and in faith. We are stewards of the goods and resources given in this life and must use them carefully and justly. We must take into consideration not only the cost to ourselves and our families but the burden decisions we make place on the greater society. One has only to listen to the testimony of nurses in a neonatal intensive care unit about how hard it is to continue to treat aggressively an infant that had no hope of recovery but whose family continues to demand that the child be kept alive. The emotional cost to others may be more horrific than the financial cost.

Second, Christians and their approach to human existence in this world have a different perspective toward medical intervention because of their belief that existence in this world is not the totality of human life. Ignatius of Loyola's dictum to work as if everything depends on God and pray as if everything depends on us, should not be lost in this discussion. The viewpoint of the Christian includes not only the notion of life after life—a fuller continuum along which death and futility fit—but the specific teachings from Catholicism that may apply. There is a perspective of equanimity that a Christian has toward death that may not be shared with those who have not this faith.

SOME DECISION-MAKING GUIDELINES

Persons who are nearing death and their families need to learn what questions must be asked as they enter into decision-making. They must ask specific questions about proposed treatment in the particular situation in which they find themselves. Good decision-making requires sufficient factual information to understand the implications of the various choices available. Daniel Callahan, an ardent champion of facing human mortality, has discussed the difficulty we have with end-of-life decisions. Increasingly, he points out, modern dying brings with it anxiety, "based upon the growing difficulty of making a clear determination that a patient is dying, and that nothing more of life-extending benefit can de done."[19] Add to this reality the emotional overlay of grief, guilt, and general disease that accompany the event.

It is imperative that decision-makers arm themselves ahead of time with a set of questions which need answers. No prognosis of an illness is absolutely certain, but physicians and nurses have a pretty good instinct based on experience and medical knowledge as to when enough is enough and life is slipping away. Further, it may be helpful to call upon an advocate for the patient and for the family who can help frame questions soberly and without the emotional strain that families feel. Resources such as the pastoral care department and the ethics committee may be tapped.

Pastoral care personnel are trained to be comfortable at the bedside of the dying and are viewed as patient advocates. In a community hospital in the Midwest a dying man in his fifties, who had been hospitalized and in great pain for over a week, had refused to sign a do-not-resuscitate order. Wrongly, the care personnel had connected this resistance to an assumption that he didn't want pain medication.[20] It was the pastoral care team that finally intervened. They uncovered an unresolved issue causing him guilt and an inability to die in peace. By asking the right questions, in this case not specifically about a medically factual issue but a psychological one, futile attempts to hold the dying process at bay were stopped, the man was given medication to ease his severe pain, and he died peacefully a short time later.

A hospital ethics committee can be called in to help the proper questions be asked to determine if further treatment is futile. Contrary to the belief of many, ethics committees best function not as decision-makers but as bodies to help good decisions be made. Members, often trained in ethics, can help patients, families, and medical personnel arrive at the facts needed to come to decision: Who is the proper decision-maker? What are the morally relevant facts? Are there emotional or other factors, either with the patient, the patient's family, or even with the medical personnel, that need to be addressed? What are the values that the patient seeks here? What is the best solution? I have seen ethics committees relieve conflict between families and the doctors, ease guilt long after cases have been decided, and help really good decisions be made. Anyone who wishes may ask for a consultation from the committee. Family members, the patient herself, or any member of the care team may and should request help in difficult moral dilemmas. And there are rarely more difficult events than those where futility is involved.

Let us return to the quotation at the head of this chapter about the goals of medicine. To recognize what futile treatment is and to accept its implications is to open the door to a much better level of care for those who are on the brink of eternity. When we try to do the impossible, seriously to think that we can "play God" in the face of reality, we sap energy from the real task that faces each of us at the end of life: care. To relieve pain, to alleviate the results of a ravaging disease, to stand by in hope for the resurrection and in preparation for new life is a better task.

The "good death" of the Middle Ages, with no technology and only human touch and tears to connect the worlds of now and then, wasn't such a bad thing after all. When medicine has little to offer there is still much to be done to make death a good transition for the dying person and for all those who gather at the bedside. To understand and to address the issue of futility brings clarity and peace. Futility does not have to be a bad word. Nevertheless, it needs to be put in place relative to the larger arena of life's end.

QUESTIONS FOR DISCUSSION

1. Why is it necessary in medical situations to differentiate between what *can* be done and what *should* be done?
2. What is futility? What are the various kinds of futility? Who makes the judgment as to when futility exists?
3. Is not initiating or stopping treatment judged to be futile the same as killing a person? Explain your answer?

NOTES

1. Callahan, *Troubled Dream*, 58.

2. Schneiderman and Jecker, *Wrong Medicine*, 134.

3. Medically there are certain conditions of unconsciousness that contain some hope that the patient will recover. In the case of Mrs. Wanglie, however, it was determined that she would never recover her human capacity to think, to communicate, or to reason.

4. See S. H. Miles, "Informed Demand for 'Nonbeneficial' Medical Treatment," *New England Journal of Medicine*, 325, no. 7 (August 15, 1991): 512–15.

5. Many authors have made this distinction. See, for example, Lawrence J. Schneiderman, "The Futility Debate: Effective Versus Beneficial Intervention," *Journal of the American Geriatric Society* 42, no. 8 (August 1994): 884–85.

6. The words are those of Asclepius, an ancient Greek physician. Quoted in Schneiderman and Jecker, *Wrong Medicine*.

7. *Gaudium et Spes*, 12.

8. Instances of such refusal are not so uncommon, even beyond the private world of Bertha. It is said that Joseph P. Kennedy, faced with the loss of his third son (Bobby, assassinated as he was running for president) also stopped eating and waited to die. The compounded pain of several tragedies in his life finally became too much to bear.

9. This is taken from the ethical code of the American Medical Association. "Principles of Medical Ethics (1980)," reprinted in *Biomedical Ethics*, ed. Thomas A. Mappes and Jane S. Zembaty, 3rd ed., (New York: McGraw-Hill, 1991), 54.

10. See Howard Brody, "The Physician's Role in Determining Futility," *Journal of the American Geriatric Society* 42, no. 8 (August 1994): 875–78.

11. The statistics for such treatment indicate a very poor survival rate. Therefore, while resuscitation can be an effective tool in some cases, it is not the panacea that it is often thought to be.

12. Laurence Schneiderman, et al. "Medical Futility: Its Meaning and Ethical Implications," *Annals of Internal Medicine* 112, no. 12 (1990): 949–54.

13. See Richard A. McCormick, "Vive la Difference! Killing and Allowing to Die," *America* 177, no. 18 (December 6, 1997): 9.

14 See McCormick's discussion, "Vive le Difference," 7–8, and the earlier article, James F. Bresnahan, "Killing and Letting Die: A Moral Distinction Before the Courts, *America* 17, no. 3 (February 1, 1997): 8–16.

15. This right has been supported by law, however, as illustrated in the case of Nancy Cruzan and others.

16. James Rachels, "Active and Passive Euthanasia," in *Biomedical Ethics*, 369.

17. James Lindemann Nelson, "Families and Futility," *Journal of the American Geriatric Society* 42, no. 8 (August 1994): 879.

18. John D. Lantos, "Futility Assessments and the Doctor-Patient Relationship," *Journal of the American Geriatric Society* 42, no. 8 (August 1994): 868.

19. Daniel Callahan, *Troubled Dream*, 23.

20. There still exists the mythology of associating pain-relieving drugs, especially morphine, with the hastening of death by slowing respiration in the dying person. Recent studies have debunked the myth, but hospitals and even families still buy into it and pain relief is withheld.

Chapter Six

When the Patient Cannot Respond: Coma or Persistent Vegetative State

They draw the curtain while the technician removes the ventilator, bowing to the patient's advance directives. The gathered, weeping, lay down their good-byes at the bedside. Breathing comes as labored punctuation to the prayers for the dying. Modern science, repentant, waits outside the *shekinah* of the divine will. Three weeks pass. Breathing is less labored, as the steady procession of nearly mourners continues. Conversation is future-driven, speculating how long it will take for the pneumonia to do its work; or it is retrospective, paging through the leaves of his life from the chapters before technology inflicted both hope and desperation.[1]

This was the scene several years ago at the bedside of a dying priest. He had collapsed while exercising. Following bystanders' efforts to resuscitate him the emergency squad took him, convulsing and clearly wrestling with death, to the hospital. Although medical personnel worked over him for a long time, applying the latest in life-saving technology, the sad conclusion after a week of hope was that his cognitive functions would never return and the person who had been well known and loved was not coming back. The decision was made to remove life support and allow death to enter the hospital room and claim its prize.

The scene is not uncommon in the context of modern end of life care. More than 50 percent of people die, against their expressed wishes, in hospitals. There the constant and devoted support system is a gaggle of machines rather than a gathering of family and friends. Modern medicine has the ability to do wonders to bring people back from the brink of death—or does it?

The patient in the final episode of life whose human functions are limited to the biological presents a special emotional and moral conundrum. A person, because of the abilities of modern technology, can hover in a noncommunicative state between life and death. We shall look at the nature of coma and persistent vegetative states from the medical point of view and from the moral perspective. We will examine the moral questions in light of Catholic teaching and draw some conclusions.

THE MEDICAL CONDITION

There is a great deal of confusion not only among the public but also among those of the medical community as to the status of persons whose cognitive functions seem irreparably lost. From the point of view of the nonmedical person, much of this perplexity has been fueled by the miracle cures portrayed on television[2] as well as by apocryphal stories told and perhaps embellished to comfort families in pain. There is the young mother who wakes from a several-year-long coma to embrace her babies now grown and—in full makeup and vigor—leaves before the last commercial to go dancing with her husband. There may be stories of brain-damaged young men who graduate with honors from Yale. Even the marvelous biography told in the movie *A Beautiful Mind,* while not an end-of-life story, was garnished with Hollywood touches for the hope-hungry audience.

Headlines scream from the pages of local newspapers accusing ghoulish transplant surgeons of preparing not-yet-dead bodies for the taking of organs. Ugly questions are raised. If life support is terminated, aren't we killing a person? How can one take organs from someone who isn't yet dead? Isn't it God's place to decide when someone should die? How can human beings play God?

Adding to the confusion is the ongoing debate about when death actually occurs. The term "death" may be attached to the irreversible stoppage of the heart (cardiac arrest), irreparable damage to the entire brain (whole brain death), or even the situation in which the upper brain loses function permanently but the brain stem and therefore the biological systems continue to function (persistent vegetative state). Any of these definitions can be troublesome, as death is a slippery physiological concept, not so much a point in time as it is a gradual movement from a fully functional person to a biological system that no longer performs the minimal operations of life and becomes a "corpse," ready for burial.[3] A neurologist quipped that no definition is totally helpful in capturing the concept of death but "you know it when you see it."

What are the medical facts which apply to the patient who cannot interact because of an assault to the brain? The brain is a marvelous and mysterious organ, the site of human function. It allows us to remember past events, weave experience into the airy stuff of dreams, and to feel pain and sorrow.

Its corollaries in the peripheral nervous system protect us from the hot stove before we are conscious of its heat, send messages of pleasure and pain, and "oversee" the processing of food and fluids. It is rare that these movements come into the spotlight of human attention. It is rarer still that we nuance our understanding of which parts of this exquisite system comprise the uniquely human. And when that is gone, even rarer still that we embrace the task of letting go.

As suggested by these various definitions of death, the human brain functions at two levels. The lower brain controls what are sometimes called the involuntary or "animal" aspects of the human person. This means that, often below the level of human consciousness and immediate control, many functions that sustain the processes of life persist without attentive effort. Human beings breathe, they swallow; blood and antibodies flow efficiently through the human system to maintain and enhance its function. Above all this bustle is the command system, the activity of the higher brain: the process of thinking, of remembering, of dreaming, and of communicating knowingly both with self and with others.

Regrettably, sometimes the functions of the upper brain, that through which the human person is expressed and completed, are impaired without sustained damage to the lower brain and its functions. Sometimes the impairment to the upper brain is irreversible and permanent. If such a condition exists, identity-making ceases to be. The human person, distinctive in hopes and in the haphazard exigencies of daily personal choices, no longer functions. While some have called this condition "upper brain death" or "neocortical death,"[4] the patient is "not dead yet"—to parrot Monty Python—and can continue to appear as integrated as before.

I offer examples of three conditions which can gravely compromise upper brain function. The first is present when the *brain fails to develop fully*, the condition found in anencephalic infants. Although their bodies may perform many of the autonomous activities shared by parents, family members, and caregivers, such children do not and will not possess the material and physical ground from which persons and personal identity can develop. The sometimes observable actions of grasping, sucking, or even response to what might be considered "painful" stimuli are simply reflexes or nonintentional activities. The underdeveloped brains of anencephalic infants do not support the capacity to "translate neural activity into an experience."[5] However regrettable it may be, they cannot and will not ever function as complete human beings.

The second condition is *coma*, which is defined as "a state of pathologic unconsciousness,"[6] in which a person is unaware of the environment and unarousable by external stimulation. Coma patients appear to be asleep. Although they may exhibit movements and symptoms associated with normal sleeping and/or discomfort—grimaces, perhaps even crying—it is a medical conclusion that they experience no pain.[7] Something happens which causes an assault leading to dysfunction in the upper area of the brain, the place where blind sensation is translated into human awareness. Some coma patients may recover their previous level of function and some may deteriorate to a permanent vegetative state. The possible outcomes in a comatose patient should reveal themselves within two weeks: partial recovery, persistent vegetative state, or death.

The third condition where the upper brain is not functioning normally is called *persistent vegetative state* (PVS).[8] This designation is given to either a transient condition (toward recovery) or to an enduring condition in which a patient has sustained sufficient damage to the brain that human functioning and response are absent and do not return (Karen Quinlan is an example). Causes of PVS include trauma, anoxia (deprivation of oxygen to the brain), stroke, and degenerative or metabolic disease.[9] Persons in PVS go through sleep/wake cycles and may appear, because their eyes can be open, to be awakened and oriented to their surroundings. Family members and caregivers may interpret movement as responsiveness, perhaps clinging to the hope that the devoted care given is not in vain. PVS patients are not aware of their environment, although normal bodily functions—so-called vegetative activity—continue. PVS is considered "permanent" after three months if the cause was nontraumatic. After this time "recovery is rare and is associated with moderate to severe disability at best. . . . [L]ife expectancy is approximately 2 to 5 years,"[10] although some people have been known to live much longer. Any slim favorable prognosis is often further compromised by the physical and life context of the episode that caused the condition (age, how long the brain was without oxygen, a history of drug and medication use, the nature of the precipitating cause).

Patients' families should be made aware that there are certain medical indicators that can be observed or tested early on to determine the likelihood of recovery. While no diagnosis is ever foolproof, the likelihood of accurate prediction that a person in PVS will not return to a former state of health approaches 100 percent. Doctors who respond to family queries with a blanket "we don't know and can't tell what will happen" are not giving the decision-makers the whole picture, the data needed for good decisions to be made. Professionals may share the denial that is a common companion to the dying process. While no prediction is "for sure," methods to obtain the data relevant to offer an informed and highly accurate prognosis are generally available in such situations.

In summary, it can be said that expectation of recovery from incidents that gravely compromise the upper brain function of the human person is bleak at best. And even with recovery, studies show that often the person is left with serious and permanent consequences and with limited function. And the sicker and older the persons are at the time of the incident that puts them in PVS, the worse the prognosis is. This reality is demonstrated time and time again by such cases as Quinlan and Cruzan, who were young and healthy; and by Wanglie, who was at the upper scale of the age spectrum. The former two survived for years without regaining function; the latter survived as well, but with the need for continued crisis intervention during the remaining years of her existence. Bottom line: no case of long-term coma or of PVS holds hope for recovery to a previous state of wellness after a few months have passed. Many can be accurately predicted to hold little hope after a few days. It is important to examine the concrete situation of the specific case before informed decisions can be made by those tasked with making them. It is important that families ask and receive truthful answers to the real condition that exists and its prognosis. If Grandma is never coming back, the decision-makers must move to the difficult job of deciding between continuation of aggressive medical intervention and the election of possible "comfort."[11]

THE MORAL QUESTION

A patient comes into the emergency room—descriptions always have the person "rushed" to this beehive of professional competence and personal trauma. He is nonresponsive; his body is convulsing uncontrollably; the family members stand by in the shock of this unforeseen event. Various chemical and/or electrical interventions are initiated. It is a scene from any prime-time medical drama. Things calm down and the patient is stabilized. What is not clear at this juncture is whether the patient will recover. Certainly initial treatment is the moral thing to do, in most cases, with the hope that the person will return. It is never definite at the onset of such an event as to whether function will return, since assault to the brain may or may not be reversible. Aggressive treatment in this setting is unquestioningly "ordinary," or what is called "standard of care." Intervention for patients whose prognosis is unsure is indicated to stabilize their condition so further decisions can be made.

Let us add a bit to the scenario: the patient is an elderly frail woman and this is her fifth trip to the emergency room in recent weeks. Each time she is treated and sent back, unresponsive, to the nursing home where she has lived for seven years. During that time she has not known her family members and has developed an increasingly aggressive and painful cancer. She has been on dialysis in the nursing home, she has severe infections from time to time requiring antibiotics and other interventions. Is this repeated invasion really "ordinary" for her? Should even the initial emergency treatment be given?

Now to the moral calculation, particularly in light of the Catholic tradition. Morally relevant are the facts of the case: what is the likely prognosis and how likely is it? In the case at the beginning of the chapter, the man was clearly healthy and functioning before the episode. Yet previous function does not necessarily predict the extent of damage to the brain or the possibility of recovery; this may take some time to answer. Treatment until such time as it is clear whether he will regain function is a good moral position.

In the second case the situation is different. Quality of life is poor. She is clearly grasping life by an increasingly slender thread, or perhaps even entering into the process of dying from the cancer eating at her body. Because she is frail, the interventive techniques—especially any that would require chest compressions or use of paddles as resuscitation does—likely would cause more harm than good. It could be argued that her life has become a burden, even to her. Perhaps the best moral position is to allow the process of dying to move forward, even without a clear picture of whether resuscitation would return her to her previous baseline of function. Such a decision would be an appropriate application of the principle of double effect. It recognizes any effort to revive her as extraordinary, presenting a disproportion of burden over benefit.

The first moral response to any medical situation is to follow any expressed wishes of the patient. It is the patient who has jurisdiction over her life. If the patient has stated, either in the form of a living will (the legal standard) or clearly to family or surrogate in some other form (the moral standard) what she wishes, those wishes should be honored *unless* there is a medical reason to consider the treatment futile. In such cases medical judgment should trump patient directives that insist on continued ineffective intervention. The directives of a patient may save the family or the medical personnel from having to make difficult and disconcerting decisions. Having such discussions among family members long before such events saves a lot of grief at the actual time of an event.

But the PVS patient is *not* dying, the condition which activates the living will or the durable power of attorney. Therefore there may be objections— possibly from the medical personnel—to honoring the wishes of the patient as set out in such documents. It is accurate to insist that under the law the living will or DPAHC (Durable Power of Attorney for Health Care) do not become operative until and unless the patient is "terminal." Morally, any directives stand as an indication of what the person would have wanted in such a case. The moral considerations should override any concerns about legality. As ethicists Thomas Shannon and James Walter note, "Statements that individuals make about their death or the circumstances of their dying are extremely important."[12] Following both the principle of autonomy and the

Catholic tradition of respect for individual decisions of conscience, the stated wishes, even of a patient who is not dying, should be honored.

What should be done when it becomes clear that a condition will not reverse itself and the wishes of the patient are not present to guide the decision? What kind of treatments, if any, should be maintained or initiated? Possible interventions might include cardiopulmonary resuscitation, support for breathing by means of a ventilator or may expand to the consideration of artificial nutrition and hydration.

What can, and more importantly, what should be done about the comatose or PVS patient is dependent on two things: the reality of the patient's condition and the possibility for regaining function. Therefore it is imperative to get the facts about the patient's condition and prognosis. It is not possible nor is it morally necessary to ascertain *beyond any doubt* that a person in either state will not regain some function. It is highly improbable that very many will do so. Once the degree of probability of the degree of human function that is possible is established, the moral questions about what should be done can be considered.

What principles go into the decision? First, the respect and awe for the person and for her life-project must be addressed. In the context of the Catholic perspective on the human person, what someone chooses to do or directs to have done from the reflective depths of one's own conscience must be respected. This is particularly true when that person can no longer speak for herself. In modern bioethical terms, the principle of autonomy must be honored. Short of expressed directives from the patient that either go contrary to the consciences of those tasked with carrying out those wishes ("Please, if I am irreversibly comatose, put a pillow over my face and hold for several minutes") or fall under the umbrella of futile treatment ("Please, keep shocking my heart again and again if I go into arrhythmia, even if the regular heart beat cannot be restored"), the patient's plan should be followed.[13]

There are a number of ways this "plan" can be expressed by the patient. If his wishes are known—and each person has a moral responsibility to let others know what is wanted in such cases—these wishes should be honored. Again, every personal life project is sacrosanct: each shapes the kind of moral person he wishes to become in his relationship with God and others. "The free and informed judgment made by a competent adult patient concerning the use or withdrawal of life-sustaining procedures should always be respected and normally complied with, unless it is contrary to Catholic moral teaching."[14] The Catholic anthropological perspective affirms this position. Human persons are moral entities charged with creating themselves as they interpret God's unique call to them. To interfere with such trajectory is to certainly "play God," in a role that even God does not accept.

Second, the principle of totality affirms that the whole of the person takes precedence over any part. To continue to maintain biological systems—"parts"—is to undermine the importance of the whole person. When the "person" has departed even in the face of continued biological life, the obligation to maintain that "life" is subverted to a consideration of the good of the whole. As Jesuit John Kavanaugh states, "To be a human person is to be inseparable from the facticity of body. To be a human person is to abide in time and history. A human person is unthinkable, unimaginable, without the endowment of reflexive consciousness that makes possible not just bodies but personal embodiment."[15] The still precious human being who exists in PVS no longer has this ability.

Third, and particularly in cases where someone's wishes are unclear, the moral task is to weigh the specific benefits and burdens that come from different options. What is in the best interest of this particular person? If a person has no reasonable likelihood of recovery from the event, the "burdens" of continued treatment in the face of very little benefit suggest that treatment should be forgone or withdrawn. In becomes, as the Catholic tradition states, "extraordinary."

The extreme burden to the patient is dramatized in physician Lawrence Schneiderman's characterization of the PVS patient. He sees such existence as similar to the ancient practice of exile, which condemned someone to a fate "worse than death." He argues that, even though the victim is not aware of the "punishment," it is still harmful. The ongoing maintenance of such a patient, "enslaved to perpetual inertness, emotionless, helpless, unlike any other form of human existence, isolated from every human connection and communication," he suggests, is wrong. It is not only ethically permissible to remove interventive life-sustaining technology, says Schneiderman, but it is "an obligatory act of beneficence."[16] The burdens to the exiled patient are certainly more onerous than the benefits.

Schneiderman's perspective is similar to that of the Catholic tradition. The *Catholic Directives* note that "the duty to preserve life is not absolute, for we may reject life-prolonging procedures that are *insufficiently beneficial or excessively burdensome*"[17] [italics mine]. Is this equivalent to an intent to *kill*, to commit murder, as some have affirmed? Is it motivated by a hatred of the patient or malice toward him? No. The intent rather is to avoid prolonging a human life that no longer functions as such.

Benedict Ashley notes, "Human bodily life by its intrinsic teleology has its value from its service to activities of the whole human person, and activities of knowledge and free choice. When these activities become permanently more and more difficult or impossible, the corresponding obligation to preserve bodily life diminishes."[18] Ashley's opinion is that such an admonition applies to the individual in PVS. While such a patient is not dying and *can* be maintained by medical interventions and constant care, such a patient cannot exercise uniquely human abilities, cannot consent to actions, cannot laugh or cry, cannot in short function humanly.

The intent, the strong moral obligation, is to preserve the dignity of the person as he lived and to affirm the Christian belief that life is not totally described by existence in this world. The motivation is to preserve the patient's dignity in the face of an unavoidable, if not imminent, death or no chance of return to human function. It may be helpful to stand back from the crisis situation and assess what scenario truly protects and enhances the dignity of the dying: a sterile room with tubes and technology, medicine and machinations; or the human drama of good-byes and grieving, tenderness and touch. This is often an easier task in the calm of reading a book about decision-making than in the quotidien vigil at the bedside of the stricken loved one.

Fourth, a social standard is applied. This standard evokes the principle of the common good. The human person is essentially related to others; the social implications or the impact upon others of human decisions are part of the process. The *Catholic Directives* are clear that among the considerations for treatment is weighing of the burden to "family and community," including the burden of expense.[19] Notice that there are two groups that may be considered in this area: the family and the broader community. Among the "greater community" are those who are tasked with ongoing care for such patients. With regard to the former, the burden to the family not only in terms of emotional stress but also in terms of financial implications can be part of the moral calculus. Keeping in mind the dignity of the person as the first and foremost consideration, it is still appropriate—especially when overarching burden to the individual in PVS is already there—to look at how continuing treatment impacts on the family.

Further, although the financial implications to the health care system tend to be lost in the emotional and urgent fog of questions about letting go, these costs are an important aspect of the moral question. Likely family or caregivers do not even know what the cost is. Third-party payers take the impact, as do the hospitals themselves. These considerations cannot take a backseat in the process of decision-making. If persons and their choices have essential impact on society, their deliberations must consider that impact.

It may be possible to keep alive on a respirator and/or with artificial feeding[20] a comatose spouse or a child who, in the realm of miracles, may one day open her eyes to see the strained smile of her parents gazing at her. It may be that a person will live for a long time in PVS without support to breathing, if that person is artificially fed. It may be possible, in the world of miracles, for such a person to "come back." The negligible *possibility* does not balance the lack of any reasonable *probability* that this might happen, nor the excessive cost of maintaining that anemic hope. It is estimated that a large and disproportionate portion of every health care dollar is spent on treatments clustered near life's end. Inflating these statistics, of course, are the numerous futile interventions that are used without probability of success. Grandma *may* wake up someday or a cure may be found to counteract the brain damage she has sustained. The burden of treating her while we wait, however, is significantly greater than the rumor of benefit that is present in the real situation. If Grandma is to dance again, let it be in the ballrooms of heaven.

Fifth, those who are adamant about a right to life and its sanctity sometimes espouse a kind of vitalism: as long as the *body* continues to function, it must be maintained. The principle here would be that the biological life of a human being has in itself an intrinsic and hegemonous worth, in a sense acting as a trump to other competing values. While this is the position of certain individuals, a few holding it on individual religious grounds, and some religious groups (Orthodox Jews, for example), it is not the position of Catholic faith. Some confusion is present here if the two strong pillars of Catholic thinking (respect for the value of life and the distinction between proportional and nonproportional interventions) do not stand together. To emphasize exclusively the first is to fall into the trap of vitalism, that the body has some absolute value that cannot be set aside. To look only at the second is to risk a crass utility which stresses the bottom line and forgets to honor the human value. Some have indeed tied withdrawal of treatment from such patients to a spectrum of a future world of mass mercy-killing, a "soylent greening"[21] of America.

In a very sensitive and insightful article, Paul Schotsmans, a Belgian bioethicist, notes that "This mentality [keeping a patient alive even when it is clear that death is inevitable] is often inspired by alsolutizing the norm of 'respect for life' (the sanctity of life principle) and subsequently leaves very little room for accepting the process of dying in a manner that is humanly worthy."[22] Respect for the sanctity of the body rather demands that it not be battered and betrayed with interventions that have little hope of success. Treatment of this kind, notes Schotsmans, "leads to a profound impoverishment of the mystery that humans represent in all their relations and dimensions."[23] Belief in the ultimate disposition of the person in the afterlife promised in Christian faith likewise argues for "letting go" when it becomes clear that hope for recovery of the person is slim to none.

Sixth, there is the issue of the slippery slope. This catchword is often invoked as a cautionary barrier to stopping treatment in patients such as we have been discussing. It is used as the moral justification for continuing intervention for PVS patients. What is the slippery slope? Picture a person facing a steep hill, the grass slick with moisture from a recent rain. Clearly to negotiate the slope without falling and tumbling down in the manner of Jack and Jill—which resulted in a "broken crown" for unlucky Jack—is difficult. Better never to set foot on the hill, so as to avoid the probable difficulties connected with doing so.

In ethics the idea functions as an admonition: don't do something that might weaken or compromise the value not chosen in the particular action. Such a compromise would make it easier to set aside the value in the future. Don't make exceptions to rules so as not to erode the power of a good rule. Certainly don't cease treatment of the PVS patient, or inevitably you will begin to be at home with all forms of euthanasia.[24] Keep your foot off that problematic incline. That way you won't get into trouble. In fact it is this reasoning and, in some instances, the juxtaposition of end of life issues with abortion that has caused political pressure to ban anything that even hints at "killing," including the removal of life support after it has been determined that such intervention is futile.

It is important to consider the slippage of respect for life that a particular act might effect, especially in a culture that seems to eschew its value. The slippery slope is always ahead of the person or persons who must make hard decisions. Yet the very danger of the slippery slope might serve as a warning to decision-makers to be sober and to be careful as they move ahead in their actions. It is a reminder that, even though every moral decision must be judged on the circumstances that are peculiar to the specific case, the negative consequences must be acknowledged and regretted. Nonetheless, to neglect actions that are morally right simply because they carry with them some evil is to avoid moral responsibility.

Facing the death of a loved one or certainly one's own death is never easy. But, as Schotsmans states, "A humane accompaniment of the dying is not possible unless the relationship between the dying person and his bystanders is taken with utmost seriousness. The work required will take a great deal of effort on the part of all involved." It is not easy to make the decision to cease aggressive intervention, to stop ventilator support, to make the choice not to feed artificially. One regrets that something better cannot be done for the patient, something that would bring him back. Yet to make this decision is the humane method of "treatment," it is the human worthy method of care.

THE THEOLOGICAL OPINIONS

The Catholic tradition has become translated into two theological positions on this issue: on the one hand it has emphasized the value of life as a basic good; on the other hand it has concluded that this value, although very important, is not in fact absolute. There is a the distinction between what is "official"

Catholic tradition and what may be only theological opinion. In the minds of the average person in the pew or in the Lazyboy in front of the evening news, these distinctions are often blurred. This blurring becomes a stumbling block to good decision-making in the crisis situation of having to decide about the life and death of a loved one.

How one uses the conclusions from doctrine and from theology in making decisions should vary. Doctrine is the official position of the church on a particular issue. Theology is the ongoing discussion which attempts to understand more deeply the central tenets of faith and to integrate them into new contexts. The more central and enduring a teaching, the more important it is as part of the decision-making process. If a teaching or a conclusion about how one should live appears clearly and consistently in scripture, for example, it is the bedrock from which Catholics build their moral edifice. If the church makes a statement as doctrine or dogma in a particular area, certainly that statement holds grave weight for Catholics in their processes of making decisions. Scripture and tradition have long been the twin peaks of Catholic thought, casting a clear and definitive shadow of influence over moral questions. That being said, there are few areas where there is clear and consistent tradition; and concerning many contemporary end-of-life questions there is rarely anything specific either in scripture or tradition. Further, many of the conundra raised in the application of modern technologies—life support machines, feeding tubes, electrical shock to regulate heartbeat—could not even have been conceived a generation ago.

In Catholic tradition, theological opinion covers a wide range of views. It is an essential component of Catholic life, particularly in the development of doctrine and in working out of moral solutions to new problems. Theologians, those for whom the term is a professional designation and those who are simply reflective believers, wrestle with what the tradition presents and attempt to apply that tradition to the business of living.

There are two threads of contemporary theological opinion[25] that have tried to offer help in drawing conclusions about patients whose level of brain damage is severe enough that they cannot return to a former level of human function. The first is represented in the work of William E. May and others, who stress the basic goodness of human life and the subsequent moral obligation to preserve it. "Human bodily life is a great good. Such life is personal, not subpersonal. . . . It is possible to kill innocent human beings by acts of omission as well as by acts of commission."[26] May argues that life as a "basic good" has a strong claim on continued existence. While refusal of treatment as "useless or excessively burdensome" may be morally appropriate in some instances, there is the temptation in such refusal to "devalue the lives of the noncompetent or to regard such persons chiefly in terms of the utilitarian values they may represent."[27] May sees such terms as "vegetable," "terminal," and "brain death" as pejorative dehumanizing terms which reinforce a proeuthanasia stance.[28] These arguments represent what might be called an unnuanced "prolife" stance. The major value emphasized is life, the basis for other human activities. Other values recede in the discussion to a place of lesser importance. May and those in agreement with him continue to refer to the "personhood" of patients whose cerebral cortex is irreparably damaged.

This theological position warns of the slippery slope to euthanasia and a diminution of life as a value. It champions the value of care for all human beings, especially the vulnerable, and emphasizes the importance of self-sacrifice in attending to them. While it recognizes in principle the notion of excessive burden (action is extraordinary and therefore not morally obligatory), it cautions against concluding too quickly that such a burden exists. The stance, following the reasoning that in Rachels's argument (discussed in an earlier chapter) that doing or not doing are morally equivalent, points out that evil can be done as easily by omission as by commission.

While the point of view, rightly, holds up the value of life and the need to move slowly, it seems to downplay the concrete decision-making process and the facts that may accompany the actual dilemma and influence its moral outcome. Unnuanced, it may translate into condemnation of morally appropriate termination of futile intervention. It avoids a serious recognition that some interventions are extraordinary and need not be initiated or continued. It is possible that May's position also feeds into the wrong-headed notion that suffering has an intrinsic value (good in itself) rather than that suffering is appropriately accepted as a means (evil but proportionate) to a good end.

In opposition to May and others are those who recognize the significance of the inability of the person in PVS to carry on any kind of personal life. While affirming life's value and respecting the intrinsic and enduring dignity of *persons*, they make a distinction between life in general and human life in particular. "Human biological life is a necessary condition for the achievement of the basic human goods."[29] As a "condition" it is to be respected as the substrate for humanness but does not in itself hold the same value as personhood.

Such a stance does not commit the decision-maker to an unnuanced obligation to sustain the life of a PVS patient, who will never return to the activities associated with persons, any more than it commits someone to retain a diseased arm because it was once biologically alive. Neither does it result in a disrespect for the biological entity that previously supported human activity, anymore than it would suggest disposing of a human corpse in a dumpster. "When it is medically clear that such matter [the brain, the integrating organ of humanity] has been destroyed, then it seems impossible to argue that a substantial union of body and soul remains or that an obligation to sustain life remains."[30]

While respecting human life, those who espouse this position argue that irreversible loss of the "human" part of human life moves the discussion to one of proportion: is there a greater good to be accomplished by sustaining biological life in the face of the clear loss of the potential to sustain the human project? Rather than seeing terms such as "vegetative," "terminal," and "brain death" as pejorative terms calculated to weaken respect for persons and for life, this position would view those terms as the neutral assessment of a medical reality—important information to assist in rather than to define the decision-making process. It is the medical facts of a particular case that influence the calculation of proportion in the difficult choices that face people like the families of Karen Quinlan, Nancy Cruzan, and Helga Wanglie. As technologies advance and the ability to sustain bodies becomes better and better, the temptation to do so—whether on principle or from emotional bias or denial—becomes increasingly alluring. The moral determination remains clear: those interventions which pose a greater burden than benefit are extraordinary. Extraordinary interventions are never morally obligatory.

SOME FINAL WORDS

To emphasize only one aspect of decision-making is to become backed into a decision-making corner. It is rarely a position from which good choices result. One of the rich and helpful traits of Catholic tradition is its ability to look at a number of criteria before making a final moral judgment: the value or values involved, the real context of the decision, and the methodology to weight values that has been worked out over centuries. As to the question of value, it is clear that both theological positions honor and cherish life. The theological position of May and others honors it almost ahistorically, that is to say, the value of life is considered so fundamental as to exclude considerations based on the real circumstance of the case. The second position, illustrated here by the comments of Wildes, Ashley, and others, honors human life in the context of real situations. This may be a more difficult place from which to decide. To stand in it is to assent to regret both the complexity of the situation and the urgent responsibility to *be* responsible for what is done and what is not done.

Richard Gula, in his book on euthanasia, gives four guidelines that might be helpful to summarize what has been said here. While he is addressing specifically the issue of euthanasia, what he says represents the best of Catholic tradition and holds together the elements emphasized by both positions. It could be helpful for those who must decide what to do when PVS is the diagnosis:

1. Life is not an absolute good nor is death the absolute evil.
2. The patient's "free and informed choice" is the guide for applying or avoiding life-sustaining intervention.
3. Treatments are not required that do not reverse the terminal illness.
4. Withholding treatments should "intensify efforts to comfort."[31]

Standing at the bedside of a person still vital and interactive in the memories of those in attendance is a terrible place to be. The decisions to withhold or to withdraw treatment are terrible decisions. They require careful deliberation and exquisite courage. The dying priest in the scenario given at the beginning of the chapter lingered for almost a month after life support was removed before his last labored breath came. Each day his friends saw their tear-moist hopes for his recovery evaporate. However morally right the action was, it took courage to turn off the machines. It took courage to wait with hope not for recovery, but for resurrection!

QUESTIONS FOR DISCUSSION

1. What are the medical conditions that may compromise the function of the upper brain?
2. What questions should be included in the moral considerations concerning treatment or removal of treatment of a person whose brain lacks function?
3. Is Catholic theological opinion of one mind on this issue? Elaborate your answer.

NOTES

1. Dolores Christie, "This Is My Body: A Good Friday Reflection," *Emmanuel* 102, no. 3 (April 1996): 153.

2. A study of several popular television series demonstrated that 92 percent of persons over sixty-two years of age obtained their knowledge of the efficacy of cardiopulmonary resuscitation from watching television. On television, this intervention resulted in an over 60 percent survival rate, in contrast to the minimal survival rates reported in real-life studies. In actuality these figures decrease with the age and medical condition of the patient. A rumor of miracles abounds on the small screen and in the minds of a large number of the public. See Susan J. Diem, et al., "Cardiopulmonary Resuscitation on Television: Miracles and Misinformation," *The New England Journal of Medicine* 334, no. 24 (June 13, 1996): 1578–82.

3. This idea is not universally conceded. By contrast others have proposed the idea of death not as a process but as "the event which separates the process of dying from the process of disintegration." See Charles M. Culver and Bernard Gert, "The Definition and

Criterion of Death," *Biomedical Ethics*, ed. Thomas A. Mappes and David DeGrazia, 4th ed. (New York: McGraw-Hill, 1996), 313.

4. See Ronald E. Cranford, "The Persistent Vegetative State: The Medical Reality (Getting the Facts Straight), *Hastings Center Report* 18, no. 1 (February/March 1988): 30. Cranford does a good job of discussing the medical condition associated with PVS.

5. Chris Borthwick, "The Proof of the Vegetable: a Commentary on Medical Futility," *Journal of Medical Ethics* 21, no. 4 (August 1995): 206.

6. Andrew Garrow et al., "Anoxic Brain Injury: Assessment and Prognosis," *UpToDate* 2002 <http://www.utdol.com/application/topic/topicText.asp?file=cc medi/22605> (September 22, 2002).

7. The perception of pain is a *conscious* experience associated with the cerebral cortex, which does not function in such cases. What is observed are responses to stimuli at lower noncognitive levels of the nervous system: we pull away a hand from a hot surface well before the brain registers the heat and pain, for example.

8. Some have eschewed this term, believing that it presages the perception of the patient as "a vegetable," with "demeaning and grave consequences to the patient in question," that is a loss of rights due a functioning human being. See Raphael Cohen-Almagor, "A Concise Rebuttal," *Journal of Law, Medicine, and Ethics* 28, no. 3 (fall 2000): 285. The author prefers the term "post-coma unawareness."

9. Charles Weijer, "Cardiopulmonary Resuscitation for Patients in a Persistent Vegetative State: Futile or Acceptable?" *Canadian Medical Journal* 158, no. 4 (February 24, 1998): 491.

10. Garrow, "Anoxic Brain Injury: Assessment and Prognosis." It is reported that in the United States today there are an estimated 10,000 to 25,000 adult PVS patients. The annual cost of caring for them is nearly $7 billion.

11. The "comfort" here is mostly for the caregivers, since the patient in PVS is unable to process sensations and therefore does not experience pain or pleasure or any normal human feeling.

12. Thomas A. Shannon and James J. Walter, "The PVS Patient and the Forgoing/Withdrawing of Medical Nutrition and Hydration," *Theological Studies* 49, no. 4 (1988): 644.

13. The consciences of others may never be held bound to one's wishes. If there is a disagreement between the designated decision-maker and the physician that cannot be otherwise resolved, particularly one in which the physician believes his or her conscience would be compromised, the decision-maker should move the care of the patient to another physician.

14. *Directives*, 59.

15. John F. Kavanaugh, *Who Count As Persons? Human Identity and the Ethics of Killing* (Washington, D.C.: Georgetown University Press, 2001), 47.

16. See "Exile and PVS," *Hastings Center Report* 20, no. 3 (May/June 1990): 5.

17. *Directives*, V: Introduction.

18. Benedict Ashley, "Dominion or Stewardship: Theological Reflections," *Birth, Suffering, and Death*, ed. Kevin M. Wildes et al. (Boston: Kluwer Academic Publishers, 1992), 97.

19. *Directives*, 32.

20. The discussion of providing artificial feeding and hydration to patients who will die without them will be taken up in chapter 7.

21. *Solyent Green* is a futuristic movie in which citizens must submit to active euthanasia when what is deemed their useful span of years is complete. Each individual may personalize his death experience with special music, choosing a color for the room in which death comes, and so forth.

22. Paul Schotsmans, "When the Dying Person Looks Me in the Face: An Ethics of Responsibility for Dealing with the Problem of the Patient in a Persistent Vegetative State," in *Birth, Suffering, and Death: Catholic Perspectives at the Edges of Life,* ed. Kevin Wildes et al. (Boston: Kluwer Academic Publishers, 1992), 136.

23. Schotsmans, "When the Dying Person," 136.

24. In some states the strictness of advance directive statutes, favoring continued treatment even in the face of futility unless the patient has stated otherwise, is a result of legislators' and lobbyists' fears that a weaker law would promote widespread euthanasia and even encourage abortion.

25. This section relies heavily on the work of Kevin Wildes, "Life as a Good and Our Obligation to Persistently Vegetative Patients," in *Birth, Suffering, and Death*, 145–54. In this article Wildes summarizes and analyzes the theological literature about such patients, in particular the differing positions of contemporary theologians.

26. William E. May, et al. "Feeding and Hydrating the Permanently Unconscious and Other Vulnerable Persons,*" Issues in Law and Medicine* 3, no. 3 (1987): 204.

27. May, "Feeding," 205.

28. May, "Feeding," 206.

29. Wildes, "Life as a Good," 153.

30. Wildes, "Life as a Good," 152–53. Wildes finds himself in agreement here with Benedict Ashley, "Domination or Stewardship," 97, who argues that for PVS patients, among others, it is "proportionately burdensome" to prolong life. Ashley's point is that as the ability to perform human activities—those mediated by the higher brain—becomes more and more diminished, the obligation to preserve bodily life likewise diminishes.

31. Richard M. Gula, *What Are They Saying About Euthanasia?* (New York: Paulist Press, 1986), 137–46. Gula's development of each of these points may be helpful to the reader.

Chapter Seven

When the Patient Cannot Eat:
Artificial Nutrition and Hydration

His disciples were hungry and began to pick the heads of grain and eat them. "I do not want to send them [the crowd] away hungry, for fear they may collapse on the way" (Matt. 12:1). I was hungry and you gave me food, I was thirsty and you gave me drink (Matt. 25:35).

Italian mothers never let a visitor leave their homes without a full stomach and a little something "for later." *Mange!* A groaning board of food and drink is the rule for the celebration of birthdays, holidays, weddings, even funerals. Coffee clatches, cocktail parties, cotton candy at the circus—all are stable elements of human comfort and communication. Even the religious dimension of human existence is built around food. There are the sacred meals of Passover and the Last Supper; there are the milk and honey of Mithraism and the harvest festivals of ancient nomadic peoples. The Bible, in a cursory estimate, contains several hundred references to food and drink and over 500 to water. Food and drink not only nourish, they give comfort, they symbolize the bonds of community and personal relationship in every era, every culture, and indeed in every religious tradition.

It is little wonder that the feeding and hydration of persons near death, as well as those in PVS, is such a controversial and emotionally charged question. Much of the literature that surrounds this issue was generated in the late 1980s. This flurry was largely in response to several cases that hit the front pages and the courts at that time about the morality and legality of withdrawing or withholding nutrition and hydration from patients, some of whom were not actively dying. While the controversy may have subsided in terms of both its notoriety and the proliferation of scholarly articles, many people are unclear about not only their own thinking on this issue but on the position of the Catholic tradition. How do we face the personal and painful decision about whether to begin or to continue artificial nutrition and hydration either for ourselves or for someone about whom we care. It is important to look at the methods currently used to feed and to hydrate patients, the emotional elements that cloud the decision-making process, the various opinions as to whether such therapy should be given—particularly within the Catholic tradition. What can help those faced with these decisions?

HOW DO I FEED YOU? LET ME COUNT THE WAYS

What is the function of eating and drinking, the "nutrition and hydration" of medical lingo? From the physiological point of view, of course, both food and water are necessary to maintain life, to bring about growth, and to produce the energy needed to perform both the tasks of daily living and the project of self-creating. Human beings, like all animate creatures, need both commodities to exist, to move, to thrive. This is the first and most basic service provided after birth and throughout life.

But for human beings food and drink have other functions and deeper meanings. Is there anyone who cannot identify with the urge to reach for a bag of potato chips or a chocolate chip cookie to ease the pain of an argument with a friend? Some "drown" their sorrows in a lingering series of martinis or a parade of vintage chardonnay. Most find the latest hamburger combo too much to resist, especially when they feel depressed or stressed. Human beings seek comfort in food and drink, easing their pain, and feeling good as a tasty morsel or swallow slips from mouth to memory. Is it not the pleasure aspect of eating and drinking that prompted the ancient Romans to emit what they had consumed so they could begin to gorge themselves again? Food and drink not only nourish, they provide both pleasure and comfort.

They are likewise powerful symbols of human connectedness. Beer commercials do not picture the lonely drinker but the person contentedly sipping in the midst of friends. The beer becomes the link to friendship, the glue that keeps the party going. A football game or a high school formal is not complete with, respectively, the communal suds and hot dog—don't they come in links?—or the predance dinner and the trip to the car for a shot of whiskey. Television entices viewers by depicting a not-so-elderly and clearly healthy woman sharing an Ensure moment with her grown daughter. From the first oozing of mother's milk until the last drops of water on drying lips before death, food and drink are symbols of caring, compassion, and connection between and among people. From Halloween trick-or-treaters to the friends who drop in unannounced; from convention banquets to hamburgers on the grill, human beings come together around food and celebrate their community with drink. It is no wonder that these items have such power to insert themselves into both the *kronos* of everyday life and the *kairos* of life's end.

The question here, however, is not a grocery list of ordinary food sundries; it is rather the difficult decision as to whether to feed and hydrate *artificially* a person approaching death. When someone can no longer take a morsel of food or a sip of water by mouth, it is the question of whether a person or her surrogate should refuse artificial feeding and nutrition. As with any moral decision, it is important to get at the facts.

The prescription for artificial nutrition offers three basic options. For patients who cannot feed themselves, either temporarily or permanently, technology gives solutions. The first method is through insertion of an IV (*intra-venous*— into the vein) needle through which dissolved nutrients can be administered in a sterile fluid. These lines generally are placed either in an arm or under the collar bone through what are called central venous lines or simply, central lines. Both methods allow the administration of nutrients in a manner that is, for the most part, minimally invasive and not extremely uncomfortable; although neither are risk or aggravation free.[1] The second method commonly used for giving nourishment and hydration is by the NG (naso-gastric) tube, a slightly fatter plastic tube inserted through the nose and into the stomach so that nutrients may be administered. Third, a method considered by some to be more humane and certainly more convenient for caregivers, a PEG (percutaneous endoscopic gastrostomy—inserted into the person through a hole from the outside abdominal surface into the stomach) tube can be placed. This device can be positioned for long-term or even for permanent use. It is seen by many as an important medical advance, "an unobtrusive, safe, and effective medical intervention for patients unable to eat by mouth."[2] It removes the anxiety that persons are not receiving sufficient nutrition and eases the burden imposed on caregivers to spend long periods of time feedings patients who can still potentially take nourishment by mouth but are unable to feed themselves. In some cases it has become the gold standard for long-term feeding and hydration, the "value-added" for many nursing home residents, especially those with conditions such as dementia or PVS. Many have championed this advancement; scientific studies have been done to demonstrate its efficacy. In some cases PEG feeding is not only recommended but presented to families as necessary treatment for loved ones.[3]

If it is decided that fluid only (not food) should be given; a patient can be hydrated periodically for a limited time (five to seven days) through what is called a "butterfly needle," placed under the skin. Proponents see this method as avoiding the more interventive, expensive, and cumbersome techniques detailed above and may have medical benefits to the dying cancer patient who needs hydration to eliminate the toxins from pain medication.[4] It is a method that does not require hospitalization or professional expertise, but can usually be managed by the home caregivers.

WHAT TO DO?

In what circumstances might artificial feeding or hydration be offered as an efficacious intervention? The less permanent and less invasive methods are often used in conjunction with other hospital procedures in acute situations. Medical personnel may insert an IV for a short time in the patient who has surgery or one who comes into the hospital emergency room dehydrated. IVs are effective ways to administer medication. A three-year-old who had surgery to remove ten inches of bowel was successfully fed first through a nasogastric tube and then through a central line until his own system could take over the process. A patient admitted to the emergency room with a severe dehydration and disorientation due to electrolyte loss was given an IV which was able to restore the necessary chemicals to his body and to bring him back to normalcy.

There are two situations in which the benefits of artificial feeding and hydration are not so clear. First, there is the instance of a patient who is actively dying. Often the case is one of terminal disease, perhaps cancer. Second, there is the situation of a person in PVS. That patient is not actively dying, but there is no serious hope that such a patient will return to her former state of human activity.

What can be said about the person near death, where there is a predictable and likely short course before the last breath will be taken and grieving can begin? Before good decisions can be made, it is essential to understand the facts of the particular case. The first thing is to consider the medical state of the patient: what are the chances that the patient will return to his former state? In the case of certain terminal illness, the chances of such recovery approach zero. A cancer that has invaded most major organs and that has provoked the gradual shutdown of physiological systems will not go away. The patient with such a disease will undoubtedly die, and probably sooner than later. A massive heart attack will likely end in the death of the patient, even in the face of early intervention and excellent technology.

Studies demonstrate the negative effects of feeding and hydrating patients who clearly have only a short time to live. It is part of the normal dying process for physiological systems to shut down. Circulation slows, the desire for water lessens, fluids that are a part of healthy bodies are diminished as the biological organism moves toward death. For patients with symptoms of congestion, vomiting, edema, and other conditions enhanced by sufficient levels of bodily fluids, shut down of bodily systems may actually bring relief. Reduced levels of fluid in the system can increase the level of electrolytes and actually effect a kind of natural anesthesia, relieving pain and perhaps reducing the need for high doses of pain medication, which have their own problematic side effects. To hydrate dying patients may not create the good effect it is meant to do. Particularly in elderly patients the mortality rate after placement of feeding tubes seems to be very high, indicating that the intervention does little to stop the progress of the mortal illness.[5]

Physician Joanne Lynn and bioethicist James Childress have noted specific problems associated with artificial feeding and hydration. For example, the pain related to gaining access in burn patients, or the difficulties with the body's ability to process nutrients and fluid as in the case of cancer patients or babies with short bowel syndrome, suggest that such interventions be classified as futile.[6] Dying patients may experience discomfort when food and fluids are maintained artificially. "Terminal pulmonary edema [swelling caused by fluid in the lungs], nausea, and mental confusion are more likely when patients have been treated to maintain fluid and nutrition until close to the time of death."[7] Rather than providing a peaceful and dignified death, then, such interventions actually enhance the discomfort of the dying person. In demented patients it is often necessary to add restraints and sedation to the "treatment" that accompanies end-of-life nutrition and hydration, in order to stop them from removing the uncomfortable tubing.

But what of the use of semipermanent or permanent feeding procedures for those who will not die soon but who will not return to their previous level of intellectual function? What about patients who are not actively dying, such as those in PVS? As discussed in the previous chapter, it is possible to predict with fairly good accuracy the survival and/or recovery potential of persons with conditions such as PVS. If a patient has made it clear beforehand that she does not wish artificial nutrition and hydration, the question becomes an easy one: follow the advance directive of the person involved. Below we shall discuss whether such a decision is in keeping with Catholic tradition.

The medical reality of such patients is clear: there will be no return to a former state of health. Such patients may linger for months, perhaps years, in a state of dependence and noncommunication. Unlike a Helen Keller,[8] who was able to break through to others after much time and effort, people in PVS neither remember their history nor wish for the future. They do not connect in the present. Often these patients are young, exemplified by Karen Quinlan and Nancy Cruzan. The horror of the events that put them in such a state is exacerbated by their youth and the destruction of the promise of their lives. They are sentenced to lie in bed, curled into a fetal position, for an undetermined period of time, not able to communicate or realize their hopes and wishes. Should what Thomas Shannon and James Walter call "halfway tech-nologies,"[9] in this case feeding tubes, be introduced?

While it does provide life-sustaining nutrition, the introduction of a device for artificial alimentation is certainly an affront to the dignity of the person. The body is invaded, the foreign device is attached to the person. No wonder so many patients try to remove them. No wonder it is sometimes necessary to restrain them so they will not remove the offending device. And is it possible that such attempts at removal are not caused by a demented state but rather by the person's desperate attempt to regain dignity?

In addition to the burden imposed on the patient, there is the persistent bur-den to caregivers and to family. Rightly, those who endorse artificial feeding have insisted that burdens to others are not the central moral consideration. Nevertheless, to consider how the specter of this burden to others might play out *from the perspective of the patient* is an imporant aspect of the decision-making process. If asked, most people would not want their loved ones or even paid caregivers to have to care for them in this manner. For some it may be the fear of such a future existence that drives them to contemplate suicide. Human beings are often called upon to be heroic in their efforts of care to-ward others. Yet, if little or no benefit is happening for the sick person, such a burden merely becomes an evil chosen for itself: perhaps the caregiver feels good in doing it. But evil, however good it feels and however heroically it may be portrayed, is still evil.

THE EMOTIONAL COMPONENT

There are many emotional factors which influence decision-makers in their ability to think clearly on this issue. These factors can act as impediments to moral decision-making at both the freedom and knowledge level. At the very least they expand the dimensions of the process. First, there is the matter of maintaining control. Most human beings like to have command over things that affect their lives or those of people about whom they care. Disease and death and other medical exigencies erode not only the feeling of control but its reality as well. "Why did I get cancer? Why wasn't my little brother some-where else besides in the path of that drunk driver? What did my wife ever do to deserve being in a persistent vegetative state?"

These questions have no satisfactory answers, nor do the questioners ex-pect any; they merely express the utter helplessness that people feel when faced with tragedy. There is often little the questioner can do to reverse the events or to stop the spread of a death-dealing illness. Yet there are some places where the illusion of control can be restored. One of the most obvious places where influence can be exercised is in choosing to *do* something to reverse the situation or to remedy it, even something that reason labels futile. The author is reminded of a two-year-old, standing helplessly beside the scattered pieces of a dish he had accidentally broken. "Fix it!" he demanded "It can't be fixed, but it's OK" older wiser adults assured him. "Try! Please!" the child's plea was urgent and desperate. At the dark-night vigil before the dawn of death adults are like that child: "Fix it. Try!" Artificial feeding and hydration are actions that cry out the imperative, "Fix it. Try!" often in the face of futility. In some cases this may be the only intervention left. Maybe the disease or the accident cannot be addressed, but at least the patient can be fed. "Do it. Try!" As Stuart Youngner, physician and bioethicist, observes, "Few interventions highlight this illusion of control and the simultaneous sense of responsibility than the artificial provision of fluids and nutrition to a patient at the end of a chronic illness."[10]

The second issue has to do with the profound symbolic meaning of food and drink. We all identify with the examples given above. How important food and drink are to human interaction! How important they are as a statement of care and of love! Studies have shown that over 40 percent of health professionals believed "that 'even if life supports such as mechanical ventilation and dialysis are stopped, food and water should always be continued.'"[11] "You expect me to let my mother, my little brother, my wife, my patient, starve to death?" Of course no reasonable person—none of us—could comfortably say "yes" to such a question. Even those who do not see artificial feeding and nutrition as a favorable treatment option for dying patients believe "the symbolic connection between care and nutrition adds useful caution to decision making."[12] While they do not totally endorse this position Shannon and Walter suggest that, for some, the removal of nutrition signifies "that the individual has been marked and put outside the community, outside society."[13] It seems to indicate that the person lacks value in himself or has no usefulness in the community. Food, even artificially administered food, then becomes a "symbol of inclusion." The emotionally charged and symbolic meaning of food and drink moves decision-makers beyond what they would reasonably choose, and often beyond what they would want for themselves. It is a much dearer choice than other forms of intervention.

The third difficulty is the notion that to say "no" to artificial nutrition is often viewed as a voluntary saying "yes" to death. It seems to lay on the decision-maker moral responsibility for someone's death. Gilbert Meilaender, a proponent of artificial feeding, notes, "When we stop feeding [he is talking here about the patient in PVS], we are not withdrawing from the battle against any illness or disease; we are withholding the nourishment that sustains all life."[14] Such impassioned words provoke guilt and responsibility in the most level-headed.

A good example of such an attitude is seen in a patient, a medical doctor himself, who lay unconscious with little hope of regaining his former state of health or cognition. His son, the DPAHC, communicated to the medical personnel that the father's wish was not to be fed artificially. A member of the hospital staff stopped the patient's wife in the hall and said, "Do you know that your son is trying to kill your husband?" Such inflammatory language, such framing of the issue in accusing and negative moral language, simply clouds the moral issue of what can and should be done with emotional material that is not easily set aside. In the case described, a feeding tube was eventually placed. There was pressure from hospital personnel to have it inserted. The son finally agreed, against not only his father's expressed wishes but his own. The patient was subsequently transferred to a nursing home where he endured for several months, never regaining his former self. This was not what he had hoped for nor what he had asked for.

It is very difficult to be the person responsible, morally responsible, for making the decision to forgo or to withdraw food and fluid, even when it is the right decision. Logic may reassure that the decision-maker neither causes nor assents to the death; emotion bears the burden and the guilt. In the case of dying children the situation is exacerbated. How can a young child, not yet having an opportunity to live, be condemned to death? How can anyone take on the formidable moral responsibility of making that decision? Some might add: "How can anyone play God?"[15]

The fourth emotionally charged area is that which Elisabeth Kubler-Ross describes as associated with the grieving process. Patients and their loved ones, as well as other decision-makers, are likely to experience anger, denial, and guilt when facing the end of life. If one is feeling these emotions, especially that of denial or guilt, it is very difficult to stop treatments, especially those such as feeding. "My child isn't dying. Why should I even have to think about whether to stop feeding her?" "It's my fault my husband is in this condition. If only we had not argued yesterday, he would be OK." How can a person who hasn't yet faced that death *is* real assent to discontinuation of the very stuff that makes life continue? And facing the reality of death is a process that cannot be forced along in time.

Finally, persons may have trouble making the decision to withdraw or withhold nutrition and hydration because of religious beliefs. One may perceive, consciously or unconsciously, that the tie between religious ritual and food is very strong. It is. And people may see the awesome decision they are asked to make as taking the place of God's decision. Often the discussion is formulated in such terms. That only makes the decision more difficult.

The religious aspect may take the form of vitalism—the maintenance of biological life becomes the critical value. Although Catholic tradition does not enshrine vitalism, a misunderstanding of it may cause decision-makers to insist on artificial nutrition and hydration on religious grounds as necessary to honor the "sacredness of life."[16] Distinctions between living and human living, between morally appropriate (proportionate or ordinary) means to preserve life and those which are inappropriate (disproportionate or extraordinary) are often blurred in the misted vision of those who face the death of loved ones. In general there is what Callahan calls a "stubborn emotional repugnance against a discontinuance of nutrition,"[17] even when it is the right thing to do.

THE CATHOLIC PERSPECTIVE

Similarly to the question discussed in the previous chapter—that of discontinuation of other treatments for patients in PVS—the issue of feeding and hydrating has generated two different poles of theological opinion. On the one hand there are those who insist that, because such technologies are readily available and not particularly costly and because nourishment is such a normal and basic human activity, it is almost always morally appropriate to use artificial means when natural eating and drinking can no longer be performed. Some theologians would go so far as to see this intervention as morally mandatory "as it is neither useless nor burdensome."[18] These individuals place an uncompromising emphasis on the value of life against other considerations.

In the late 1980s there was a flurry of articles about this issue, including statements by bishops conferences and other groups. May and his associates, who represent one aspect of Catholic theology but not necessarily its mainstream, hinted that to neglect to feed people who could not feed themselves was not far from euthanasia and was the first step on the slippery slope to deliberate killing. They describe death from dehydration and malnutrition as "slow, very painful, and disfiguring,"[19] and invoke the admonition from *Gaudium et Spes* to feed the man dying of hunger so as not to be responsible for killing him. The statement "dying of hunger" is powerful emotional leverage to maintain artificial feeding. But patients in PVS are neither dying nor able to experience symptoms of hunger, since the portion of the brain that registers a feeling of hunger is not operative. In 1987 the New Jersey State Catholic Conference invoked the state Supreme Court to continue feeding Nancy Jobes, a severely brain-damaged young woman. The Conference document stated, "that nutrition and hydration are basic to human life and consequently must always be provided to a patient."[20]

With regard to the perceived burden of such ongoing intervention, May has suggested more recently that preserving the lives of such person is worth the expense, and that families alternately "can remove them from these costly institutions, take them home and do the best they can with the help of such services as hospice care, volunteers from the parish or neighborhood, etc."[21] One wonders about the burden to the caregivers in modern America as well as to the patient, cared for by nonprofessionals who may not be able to keep the body of the victim free from bed sores or from infection (a common complication with long-term artificial feeding). Is this not part of the heavy burden that not only the family but the patient will bear? Hospice, which will be discussed in chapter 9, is a paid service only in the anticipated last six months of life. It is not a viable reimbursable option for care of a person who will never recover but whose life expectancy may be many years. Patients in PVS have the potential to survive for a much longer period of time.

On the other side of the argument are those who have insisted that it is not morally necessary to provide food and fluid to those in PVS. Other Catholic theologians responded to the question. Perhaps the best work at the time was that done by Jesuits John J. Paris and Richard A. McCormick. Their joint article reprised the traditional church teaching regarding "extraordinary" intervention, noting that until such signature cases as Quinlan "there was little ambiguity or hesitancy about ending artificial feeding for dying patients." They quote conservative Protestant ethicist Paul Ramsey, who counsels those who care for the dying not to have recourse to "pretended remedies" but rather to maintain comfort and company. Although the argument certainly can be made that patients in PVS are not dying, the moral principles—as will be demonstrated below—remain the same.

In what might be called the alternate chorus in the dueling voices of the episcopacy, then-bishop of Providence Louis Gelineau supported the opinion of moral theologian and local priest Robert McManus. McManus concluded that the proposed removal of "artificially invasive medical treatments" providing food and hydration for PVS patient Marcia Gray was morally appropriate. Such treatments were "futile and thus extraordinary, disproportionate and unduly burdensome."[22] Acknowledging the contrasting theological opinions, the bishop deemed that McManus's conclusion "does not contradict Catholic moral theology and in no way supports or condones the practice of euthanasia."

That is likewise the opinion of Shannon and Walter, who expand some of the points made by Paris and McCormick in their work. (The reader may wish to read the entire article, perhaps one of the most thorough on the subject.) Shannon and Walter agree with the position that human life has value. They affirm, however, that this value is never the final word. "[I]n the Christian framework, life—even human life—is not of ultimate value."[23] It is transcended by justice, freedom, charity, the good of the neighbor, and other values. That prioritization in illustrated in the endorsement of such magnanimous actions as martyrdom and self-sacrifice.

What are the distinctions concerning the value of human life and its relationship to other values? Richard McCormick, rightly, has emphasized that "Every human life, regardless of age or condition, is of incalculable worth."[24] In fact, says McCormick, "not only do human beings *have* value, they *are* value." The point, however, is whether continued physical life for a given individual contains the potential to share or to obtain those values or goals for which the physical is the fundamental substrate. Although McCormick in this article is discussing treatment for severely impaired newborns, such as anencephalic infants, the principles are the same in PVS. These precious human beings will never be able to function as human persons, to pursue and to fulfill life goals. Like McCormick and many Catholic moralists, Shannon and Walter resist the trap that looks at the utility of persons, that is, the benefit or burden their existence provides for society. Certainly the "bottom line" is a standard moral calculus for American ethics. Rather the authors insist on the moral significance of the potential to fulfill what they call a "teleological" obligation of the person,[25] that is the duty to work toward human goals and ultimate ends. The morality turns not on the good for society but rather the good for the patient and the patient's human functioning.

Christian anthropology affirms the dignity of the human being, the image of God in fleshy form. It underlines as well the essential connectedness of humanity one to another and the limitedness of every human biologically bound individual. Decisions about artificial feeding and hydration must take into account what values are being preserved and which must necessarily be set aside, albeit regrettably. Is the dignity of a person preserved by the invasion of the body by medical means to insert a feeding tube, particularly in a case where the burdens seem to outweigh any benefits? Is that dignity promoted by a terminal sentence to a bed-bound noninteractive existence for an extended period of time? Is communication and human community promoted by artificial feeding; or perhaps more to the point: does keeping a person alive with no hope of ever carrying on the ordinary activities of human living serve that person's ability to function as a person as well, including their responsibility to the well-being of those others?[26] Is the solitary digestion of the evening meal of concentrated nutrients comparable to the communal chewing on the Thanksgiving turkey?

The *Catholic Directives* affirm a presumption in favor of feeding and hydration, even artificial feeding and hydration, of all patients.[27] They go on to say to qualify the statement, however: patients should be fed "as long as this is of sufficient benefit to outweigh the burdens involved to the patient." As demonstrated above, the benefit of artificial nutrition and hydration to the patient in PVS seems to be nonexistent and the burden excessive. Shannon and Walter offer some insight here: "Burden can accrue to the patient precisely though the administration of modern technology and can be a consequence of a life lived merely at the biological level with no hope of restoration or further pursuit of temporal or even eternal goals."[28]

Medical intervention to one's body, however painless, is arguably an affront to dignity. This is especially true if the intervention is done without permission of the patient or in defiance of expressed instructions in a written or oral living will. Feeding tubes are open to infection, dependent on the attention of others, and require good nursing care to protect the immobile body from bed sores and other complications. For the patient there is no psychological or spiritual benefit. This is especially true in patients who can still be fed by mouth and in whom tubes have been inserted. Even the physical contact of another human being is denied them in favor of the efficiency of the tube. Is this "ordinary" or "proportional"? As philosopher and bioethicist James Drane states, "Even when the administration [of artificial feeding] is not burdensome (i.e., because the patient is unconscious), the overall effect of this technology may be overwhelmingly burdensome in the sense of keeping a person from a humane death by dragging out the dying process for years or sometimes for decades."[29] Drane compares this idea with the American "right to die" notion. Where is resurrection destiny in all of this? Perhaps there is a limbo after all, but it is created by human beings not by the divine.

A second qualifier found in the Catholic Directives is that concerned with motive. Therapy can be initiated (and one presumes withheld, since there is no moral difference between the two if the motivation is held constant), "even if this therapy may indirectly shorten the person's life so long as the intent is not to hasten death."[30] Catholic tradition has uniformly condemned any action that *intends* the death of another. Again, the insights of Walter and Shannon about the PVS patient are helpful: "The patient's death, while foreseen, results from the justified discontinuance of a technology that itself can neither correct the underlying fatal pathology, that is, the permanent inability to ingest food and fluids orally, nor offer the patient any reasonable hope for what we have defined as quality of life."[31]

Which of us would want to be fed and hydrated artificially if it became clear that there was no chance of reversing a PVS? Most would not. Yet every day precious persons are cursed with such care; doomed to live out a vegetative existence and postpone their final "resurrection destiny" because life transcended other goals. The bottom line for Catholics is that even though the specter of benefit is raised in the feeling-laden situation of artificial feeding (although not all would agree that keeping the body alive is per se beneficial) if the burdens are excessive, one has no moral imperative to endure them.

The general rule should be the more functional the person is and/or the higher is the probability that the person will return to former function, the greater is the responsibility to consider artificially administered food and fluids. The closer to death or the less functional the person is, and the longer a noncognitive state persists (permanently in the cases of persons in PVS); the greater the burden to the patient. As the burden increases, the moral proportion decreases and the moral compass moves in the direction of no artificial intervention.

WHAT ARTIFICIAL HYDRATION AND NUTRITION CANNOT DO

There is one thing that artificial feeding and nutrition can do: preserve the body of the person for hours, days, perhaps years. Unfortunately there is much that such intervention cannot do. It cannot reverse the underlying pathology that has brought the person to this isolated place. It cannot restore the person to the earthy road to eternal life. And, while the emotional bellies of those who decide against artificial nutrition and hydration for someone they love may continue to growl in disapproval, such intervention will not nourish the decision-makers' hearts or their hopes.

As the Jesus of history gave way to the Christ of faith, he did so without accepting the final offer of drink (Matt. 27:34). His next food and drink would be on "the day when I drink it with you in the kingdom of my Father"(Matt. 26:29). The Johannine Jesus took the proffered wine from those standing near the cross (John 19:30), but found his "food" in doing the Father's work (John 4:34). There were more important values to be served in the dying and the rising of a savior. Centuries later the Catholic tradition counseled patients that it was morally permissible to refuse foods too expensive and/or repulsive to their palates. Can we today force the acceptance on the vulnerable dying of nutrition that we would not ourselves choose? Answers to questions of food and drink for the dying are never easy nor without pain. But they are decisions that require thought and patience.

QUESTIONS FOR DISCUSSION

1. What are the reasons that underlay conclusions that the dying must be fed and hydrated? Which of these are relevant moral considerations and why?
2. What are reasons or situations in which the dying should not be artificially fed and hydrated? Why?
3. What emotional factors influence the wish to nourish and to hydrate those near death?
4. Is there an official Catholic position on artificial nutrition and hydration? Explain your answer and apply to a particular situation.

NOTES

1. Greater detail can be found in Storey (1992), "Artificial," 69–70.

2. Terence F. Ackerman, "The Moral Implication of Medical Uncertainty: Tube Feeding Demented Patients," *Journal of the American Geriatric Society* 44, no. 10 (1996): 1265.

3. Decision-makers may appropriately explore further whether and why such an intervention is "necessary." Sometimes the necessity speaks more to the ease of care. While he does not necessarily agree, Ackerman mentions this as a possible scenario, especially in nursing homes: the accusation is that greater priority is thought to be placed on "the convenience of staff members than on the interests of patients." See "The Moral Implication," 1266. Alan Meisel notes his own impression of the discomfort felt in nursing homes when the removal of feeding tubes is proposed. It appears, from his discussions with a variety of professionals that it is "devilishly difficult, if not impossible, to have tubefeeding withheld or withdrawn from a nursing home resident who is not longer able to be fed by mouth." (See Alan Meisel, "Barrier to Forgoing Nutrition and Hydration in Nursing Homes, "*American Journal of Law and Medicine* 21, no. 4 [1995]: 339.) In some cases, where the decision made is to continue supplying nutrition and hydration to a given patient, there are other methods that can be used.

4. Dying patients who are still somewhat active and not hospitalized may be taking medicines for pain. Often these need to be excreted from their systems, although lowering of the medicine's dosage with no artificial hydration will often achieve the same result. Fluid is an essential component of this excretion process. Other symptoms associated with progressive dying may be relieved as well by artificial hydration. For further discussion see Eduardo Bruera and Neil MacDonald, "To Hydrate or Not to Hydrate: How Should It Be?" *Journal of Clinical Oncology* 18, no. 5 (March 2000): 1156–58.

5. See Mark D. Grant et al. "Gastrostomy Placement and Mortality Among Hospitalized Medicare Beneficiaries," *Journal of the American Medical Association* 279, no. 24 (January 24, 1988): 1973. This study, done in 1991, included 81,105 patients sixty-five and over. Of the patients studied, 15 percent died in the hospital; 23 percent died with thirty days. The patients who fared best were those whose condition was food-related, malnutrition for example. Older patients and African Americans did less well than their counterparts. Most patients were nursing home patients rather than being cared for at home.

6. See Joanne Lynn and James. F. Childress, "Must Patients Always Be Given Food and Water?" *Hastings Center Report* 13, no. 5 (October 1983): 18.

7. Lynn and Childress, "Must Patients," 19.

8. I am grateful for this reference to John F. Kavanaugh, *Who Count*s? 69.

9. Thomas A. Shannon and James J. Walter (1988), "The PVS Patient," 623. The idea of "halfway" is that the condition or pathology that the patient suffers is not reversed by the intervention, it merely substitutes for a function that the person is unable to perform due to the condition. It is a similar concept to medical futility: a bodily function can be maintained but the underlying disease or pathology is not changed.

10. Stuart J. Youngner, "Two Times What?" Quantity and Quality of Life in Tube Feeding Decisions, "*Journal of General Internal Medicine* 12, no. 2 (February 1997): 134.

11. Study quoted in Youngner, "Two Times What?" 134. Over 12 percent thought that discontinuing artificial feeding was the same as killing the patient. The ideas of proportion and intention are still not patent to the general public, even the professional sector.

12. Lynn and Childress, "Must Patients," 21.

13. Shannon and Walter, "The PVS Patient," 642.

14. Gilbert Meilaender, "On Removing Food and Water: Against the Stream," *Hastings Center Report* 14, no. 6 (December 1984): 11.

15. Earlier in the book the idea of "playing God" was addressed. Here the issue is one of emotional reaction to a difficult situation.

16. I am grateful for the insight to Door Goold et al. "Conflicts Regarding Decisions to Limit Treament: A Differential Diagnosis," *Journal of the American Medical Association* 283, no. 7 (February 16, 2000): 912.

17. Daniel Callahan, "On Feeding the Dying," *Hastings Center Report* 13 (October 1983): 22.

18. William E. May, *Catholic Bioethics and the Gift of Human Life* (Huntington, Ill.: Our Sunday Visitor, 2000), 268.

19. May et al., "Feeding and Hydrating," 207.

20. New Jersey State Catholic Conference, "Providing Food and Fluids to Severely Brain Damaged Patients," *Origins* 16 no. 32 (January 22, 1987): 584.

21. May, *Catholic Bioethics*, 269–70.

22. Louis Gelineau, "On Removing Nutrition and Water from a Comatose Woman," *Origins* 17, no. 32 (January 21, 1988): 547.

23. Shannon and Walter, "The PVS Patient," 633.

24. Richard A. McCormick, "To Save or Let Die: The Dilemma of Modern Medicine," reprinted in *How Brave a New World? Dilemmas in Bioethics* (Garden City, N.J.: Doubleday and Company, 1981), 350.

25. Shannon and Walter, "The PVS Patient," 636.

26. Shannon and Walter caution against a utilitarian approach to quality of life. They argue that the argument for quality of life can be made from the connection between the medical condition of the patient (PVS) and the patient's ability to pursue life's goals and purposes. See "The PVS Patient," 635–36.

27. *Directives*, 58.

28. Shannon and Walter, "The PVS Patient," 639.

29. James F. Drane, *Clinical Bioethics: Theory and Practice in Medical-Ethical Decision Making* (Kansas City, Mo.: Sheed and Ward: 1994), 87.

30. *Directives*, 61.

31. Shannon and Walter, "The PVS Patient," 641.

Chapter Eight

When the Patient Is Ready to Die: Suicide and Its Companions

Isn't it better to help someone die than to have them die a long, painful death? Is it wrong to pull the plug? Doesn't someone have the right to die by choice and have help doing it?

A week-old infant born without an anus and with little hope for survival is allowed to die without surgery to the digestive tract, ultimately from starvation. The question is raised whether it is less cruel simply to end the child's life now.[1] A thirty-something AIDS victim asks a doctor to prescribe medicine to help him die, since the pain and embarrassment of his condition has become unbearable. An elderly Florida man puts a pillow firmly over the face of his demented wife. He holds it there until she ceases to breathe. Stories of suicide, assisted suicide, euthanasia, and allowing to die surface in the news and in the medical and ethical literature. They have been the threads of the fabric of assisted suicide laws enacted within the last ten to fifteen years in the United States and abroad.[2]

It is estimated that half of dying patients at least consider the possibility of assisted suicide as an option for their future. Ten percent of these actually consider suicide for themselves. This is particularly true of persons with progressive deteriorating diseases such as Lou Gehrig's disease (amyotrophic lateral sclerosis) and AIDS.[3] While not all patients who consider suicide go on to request help killing themselves, it is significant that such thoughts are a part of the dying process of many.

What is clear on the American landscape is that there is no agreement about the morality of such actions and whether there are morally differences among the various narratives. Those who follow the news and those who sit in the pews of Catholic churches are confused as to how to describe and define actions that lead to death and how to determine their moral value. It is important to tackle these issues. We will address definitions and distinctions, look at the reasons people consider suicide and follow through on their thoughts, discuss the distinctions between the Catholic approach and that which represents the diversity of American culture.

DEFINITIONS

There are many names given to the purposeful and sometimes precipitous ending of life: suicide, assisted suicide, active euthanasia. *Suicide* is the direct taking of one's own life. In the Catholic tradition it refers to actions *intended* to kill oneself. A person deliberately takes a large overdose of medicine; someone jumps from the top of a tall building. For those interested in techniques Derek Humphrey, founder of the Hemlock Society, has written a how-to book detailing methods for ending one's life. His book, *Final Exit*, serves as a macabre and graphic "textbook" for those who seek to commit suicide and for those who would assist them.

In the Catholic tradition and for purposes of defining the moral content of certain actions, the term "suicide" is *not* applied to actions that may result in death but are not directly intended to do so. Examples of such actions would be throwing oneself in front of a car to save the life of a child; going into a burning building to save another's life; or, for Christians, the sacrifice of Jesus on the cross. The tragic destruction of the New York World Trade Center in September 2001 provided many examples of heroic sacrifice of life. Courageous persons, in some cases knowingly, forfeit their lives for what they see as more important values. Often such people are fully aware that their own lives will be lost. These are *foreseen consequences which they knowingly and freely choose. They do not directly intend* their own demise; they accept it as a proportionate evil in the service of a greater good. Suicide, on the other hand, is the intentional taking of one's own life without a proportionate reason. And for many, that proportionate reason is likely the competing value of saving another's life.

Whether suicide is to be assessed as morally wrong for a particular person is further determined by the amount of *freedom* the person has at the time of making such a decision and following through on it. A person who is severely depressed, for example, may not be truly free to see options to suicide for the seemingly unbearable hurt he feels. It is possible that a person experiencing severe anxiety or pain as he nears death may not be morally responsible for taking his own life. Such persons often cannot see beyond their pain to alternate solutions to suicide.

The Catholic tradition is clear about the objective gravity and wrongness of suicide, but also emphasizes the need to be cautious in assigning moral blame to a person who has taken her own life. Friends and relatives of a suicide victim may be consoled that not all actions that might be labeled morally wrong in an objective sense are indeed blameworthy at the subjective level. In a pastoral context, every effort should be made to emphasize that ultimately only God can assign moral blame for any action, and that suicide must be clearly free and knowing before it can be given this label.

Assisted suicide is the consentual forfeiture of one's life with the help of another. It is currently legal in some places such as Oregon, the Netherlands, and Belgium.[4] In the United States, the most notorious instances of assisted suicide featured the involvement of Jack Kevorkian in the deaths of many people. Persons judged to be competent solicited the trained pathologist to help them die. Many of the cases that make the news in the national debate over legalization of assisted suicide in the United States portray suffering, desperate people who were unable to end their own lives and therefore enlisted the help of others—often medical professionals—to their final exit.[5] Assisted suicide implicates another person in the project of self-destruction.

Euthanasia, the term means "good death," is the taking of another's life for benevolent reasons. Traditionally a distinction has been drawn between the terms "active" and "passive" euthanasia. *Active euthanasia*, like suicide and assisted suicide, refers to actions directly *intended* to end a life. A lethal dose of medication to "put someone to sleep" as we do pets; a pillow or plastic bag over the face to cause suffocation; a resolute push of the wheelchair over the scenic cliff—all are *active* euthanasia. It is an activity which has its principal intended result the death of the subject.

As defined in the Catholic tradition, *passive* euthanasia[6] is more complex. The term can refer to inaction: the elderly cancer patient whose heart has stopped beating is not resuscitated; no kidney dialysis is ordered on a patient whose cancer is metastatic; the pneumonia in the PVS patient is not treated; the anencephalic newborn is not given surgery for a bowel anomaly. *Passive euthanasia* may refer also to action which hastens the trajectory of death: the respirator is stopped, the medicine to stimulate the heart is removed, artificial feedings are discontinued, all treatments that do not bring the person back to where they were medically and personally are suspended. While it is often confusing to call such actions "passive," since clearly some involve *doing* something; that is the distinction that the tradition has made. The distinction turns on the intention and on the assessment of whether what I do, or do not do, promotes a proportionate good effect,[7] that is the return to health and function of the patient. Although the distinction has a long tradition in Catholic thinking, it is found in the secular bioethics discussions as well.[8] It is not always clearly defined or clearly understood, however.[9]

Active euthanasia involves doing something that directly results in death as its *primary* consequence. Passive euthanasia is generally defined as any action or omission which, while *not directly intending the death*, has the death among its (foreseen) results. It is often this distinction—the difference between killing and allowing to die—on which the morality of a particular choice turns.[10] For Catholic moral theology, *what the agent directly intends* is a key element in the moral equation. In the American public debate about assisted suicide and about the starting and discontinuation of treatment, the distinction between active and passive euthanasia has often been lost. In the Catholic tradition passive euthanasia refers to actions or omissions which may have more than one result, but the result intended is *not* the death of the subject.

Often a differentiation is made between *voluntary* and *involuntary* euthanasia. Clearly the first refers to the act of ending the life of another *with* her consent. It is related to assisted suicide, except that the hand that brings death is not that of the patient.[11] The second refers to actions that end someone's life *against his wishes*. Sometimes there is confusion about the subject's wishes, perhaps because he has not or cannot express a preference (a comatose patient, for example). Euthanasia is often situated as an act of kindness (she never would have wanted to live like this, implying consent) or as an act of utility (he is no longer a useful member of society and has become a burden). Involuntary euthanasia is the intentional taking of another's life without that person's expressed consent and with the direct intent to do so.

It is important to remember that *passive euthanasia*, or allowing someone to continue the process of dying without ineffective medical interference is *not* the same—at least as viewed in the Catholic tradition—as active involuntary euthanasia. The specification of one's wishes regarding cessation of futile treatment at life's end in a living will, durable power of attorney for health care, or in some other form are intended to clear up any ambiguity about the person's wishes. Such directives allow caregivers to forgo treatments or discontinue interventions that patients would not have wanted. They do not allow action directly aimed at ending a life. Caregivers and family members should be comfortable that such cooperation with the wishes of a loved one is an appropriate endorsement of their love and respect for the dying person's wishes.

REASONS TO CHOOSE DEATH

Why do people wish to die? Pain, suffering, depression, and fear of abandonment or of the process of death itself all contribute to desperation. There is some evidence that people may wish to die for none of these reasons, but only because life for them has ceased to have meaning.[12] The American system champions both autonomy and the right to privacy. It is the unexamined embrace of these values that led to the legalization of abortion and supports efforts at the legalization of physician-assisted suicide.[13]

Most persons do not like pain. We call those who do "masochists," and believe them to be abnormal. From infants in utero to single-celled creatures, animals instinctively move away in reaction to painful stimuli. The synaptic nerve response to the hot stove or sharp needle, even before the mind engages the assault, demonstrates the basic level at which all resist pain. Pain is a symptom of something gone wrong in the biological system, an attack to its integrity and its well-being. It is a warning signal that the body sends to alert the person to something wrong. An instinct at the very basic level of biology resists pain or tries to find its origin and eliminate it. Nevertheless data indicate that many people actually die in pain, spending their last few days in what physician and author Sherwin Nuland has called "a plethora of purgatory."[14] This is true for a number of reasons.

First, only recently have doctors and other health professionals listed pain as "the fifth vital sign," something to be consciously monitored in patients along with temperature, respiratory rate, blood pressure, and pulse. Since pain is a largely subjective phenomenon, however, it is not as readily calculated as the other vital signs; nor has it been addressed adequately in past medical practice.[15] Evidence suggests that this is true even in the enlightened twenty-first century.

Second, there is still a reluctance to give strong pain medicine such as morphine, due to its addictive properties. Standing at the bed of a man dying of lung cancer, I heard a nurse respond to his anguished request for medication by telling him, "It's not time yet for your pain medication." And if that is not enough, patients and professionals alike fear the unpleasant side effects of strong pain-controlling drugs.

Third, the prevalent misconception that use of heavy pain relievers suppresses respiration and may cause death to come more quickly gives caregivers pause that they may in fact be "killing" the patient, or at best, hastening the death. As one reads the abundant literature on end-of-life issues, this message comes up again and again *even though recent studies have demonstrated that it is not true.* Yet the myth prevails and with it the experience of pain.

Because pain has been so poorly addressed in the medical arena, many patients pose the question, "Isn't it better to take one's life *before* unbearable pain intervenes and there is no longer the opportunity to do something about it? Isn't it better to help one to die rather than to watch them slowly and painfully get there without help?" In 1994 a task force was set up in New York to look at the issues connected with assisted suicide and euthanasia. The members "were particularly struck by the degree to which requests for suicide assistance by terminally ill patients are correlated with clinical depression and unmanaged pain."[16] One can assume that such correlation is peculiar neither to the 1990s nor to the state of New York.

Severe or intolerable discomfort need not exist for the vast majority of dying patients. Recent advances in pain control and alleviation of unpleasant side effects have resulted in a great deal of attention to this problem and even the inception of a medical specialty in palliative care.[17] Many concerned with good pain control near life's end as well as heading off requests for suicide are making great strides. The possibility of addiction for a person who is going to die anyway is a ludicrous consideration, and studies have shown that most people who take addictive medication and recover from the illness that required it do not become addicted but rather stop taking medicine when they no longer feel pain. Today almost no person needs to die in discomfort. Efforts at palliative care can and should be as aggressive as any curative interventions. Families and patients should explore these issues before death and severe pain are knocking loudly at the sickroom door. They should be reassured that the dying person will be supported to any extent necessary on their journey. Physical pain is not a mandated federal marshal needed to accompany the dying on the last flight home.

Pain may exist in other than the physical body. Sometimes the greatest suffering that a person experiences is psychic or spiritual, rather than physical. A middle-aged former priest hospitalized and dying of a physically painful cancer was suffering from a sense of unresolved guilt consequent to what he perceived as his failure at priesthood. Not until the pastoral care department helped him articulate his anxiety and deal with it was he able to die at peace with himself and with God.

Diane, the patient featured in a controversial 1991 article in the *New England Journal of Medicine*, was described by her compassionate doctor as experiencing "[b]one pain, weakness, fatigue, and fevers."[18] Diane was frightened of what she envisioned would happen as her disease progressed, and if she did not end her life: increasing discomfort, dependence on others and loss of control, and the ultimate choice between mind-numbing sedation and great pain. Not only was there an anticipation of bodily pain, Diane did not want to suffer the loss of independence and control. As she saw the scenario, the only solution was to take her own life.[19] Sadly, that is exactly what she did.

Much has been written in the Catholic tradition about the efficacy of pain. "Offer it up," was a common cliché in the everyday Catholic piety of the past. The idea was that a sufferer should turn over the distress to God, achieving some religious good by the pain endured. The greater the pain, the greater the (spiritual) gain. Even Nike has borrowed the idea to sell sports equipment! The passion of Jesus was, and often still is, held up as an example of the good to be found in suffering. The *Catholic Directives* join other official Catholic documents when they reinforce this image of the good of pain which can "take on a positive and distinctive meaning through the redemptive power of Jesus' suffering and death."[20]

What is often overlooked in this enduring counsel to the would-be pious is that pain is not an end in itself but a *means* to an end. To undergo "redemptive suffering"—proportionate and necessary pain as a means toward a good end—is morally appropriate. The biblical reference to a woman about to give birth in pain as a prodrome to the joy of having a child, the "tough love" recommended to parents of teenagers (as painful to the parents as to the children!), the hard work of a scholar in the throes of birthing an article—all are "pain" as a means to a proportionate end.

To seek pain for its own sake is nothing less than sadistic and morally evil. To endorse the spiritual benefit of such activity is bad theology and bad piety. This fact cannot be stressed too strongly. Pain in itself is a physical or ontic evil. Since evil can never be chosen as a morally acceptable end *in itself*, the only reason for its endurance must be a proportionate one, that is one accepts pain for a greater (proportionate) good. When one looks more closely at the examples that are often given, including that of Jesus on the cross, it becomes clear that the *pain* is not to be chosen as an end, but may be used as a means to something richer and more to be valued.

There is the fear of the process of dying itself. Several years ago, *The New York Times* carried a personal article about the lingering death of the author's mother. "It was bad enough in past days when death came quietly, inevitably, typically in a bedroom of the family home. But it is much worse now when death nears, or seems to near, in a sterilized hospital room full of equipment that can do so much."[21] Many people both welcome and fear the technology that may keep their bodies alive, but may also sentence the dying to prolonged futile treatment in the impersonal and sterile setting of the hospital intensive care unit. Tubes, needles, machines, the foreign and often noisy environment: not the idealized setting one's pictures for one's own death. We fear not only the loss of control but the intervention to our person and peace that accompanies such treatment.

The dialogue between dying cancer patient and nurse in the play, "W;t," captures the idea:

> VIVIAN: I know. I can't figure things out. I'm in a . . . *quandary*, having these . . . doubts.
> SUSIE: What you're doing is very hard.
> VIVIAN: Hard things are what I like best.
> SUSIE: It's not the same. It's like it's out of control, isn't it?
> VIVIAN: (*Crying in spite of herself*) I'm scared.

SUSIE: (*Stroking her*) Oh, honey, of course you are.
VIVIAN: I want . . .
SUSIE: I know. It's hard.
VIVIAN: I don't feel sure of myself anymore.
SUSIE: And you used to feel sure.
VIVIAN: (*Crying*) Oh, yes. I used to feel sure.[22]

Depression can contribute to a desire to die. While depression can exist without terminal illness or impending death, it is often a concomitant symptom. It is a strong predictor of suicidal thoughts. A therapist has observed, "There is no suicide without depression and only 30 percent of depression is treated."[23] Among the questions that professionals and family should ask the person who talks about suicide or who asks about help in dying is whether the presence of a depressed attitude contributes to or motivates such wishes. Depression can and should be treated, apart from the symptoms of the terminal disease itself. It should not be used as a reason to hasten death. Nuland notes, "[A] very large proportion of the elderly men and women who kill themselves do it because they suffer from quite remediable depression. With proper medication and therapy, most of them would be relieved of the cloud of oppressive despair that colors all reason gray."[24]

Jon Fuller, Jesuit and medical doctor, has suggested that patients' requests for assistance in dying are a function of the erosion of trust in the medical profession to accompany the dying with support in pain and anxiety management. If a person believes she will die alone, in pain, abandoned—whether this is the true appraisal of the situation or not—she will be more likely to want to be preemptive in avoiding such a scenario. Fuller believes that "If patients trusted that their physicians would appropriately treat pain and anxiety as they approached death, there would be no need to look to suicide as a means of escape, and the angry and anxious backlash [the current physician-assisted suicide movement] would not have developed."[25]

Perhaps the greatest aspect of fear that accompanies the dying process is that it will take a long time. Patients envision a siege filled with pain, uncertainty, increasing medical interventions. They worry that the frame of their dying will be a collage of incontinence, needles, bed sores, and other unpleasant experiences for themselves and their caregivers. Bodies that are dying are "marginalized, problematic bodies."[26] The young wife whose mother died a lingering death from primary breast cancer views the lump in her breast as a dire sentence with a protracted and painful dying. The man recently diagnosed with AIDS anticipates a dehumanizing and prolonged death. We are all fearful of a lengthy journey toward the doors of death. The process brings "a potent reminder of frailty, vulnerability and mortality."[27] Such a spector is an ideal breeding ground for thoughts of suicide, where control is ours and the avoidance of disagreeable processes is possible.

In contrast, studies show that most deaths occur very quickly after the person begins to go downhill, generally in less than six months but sometimes in a matter of hours or days.[28] The time frame of dying is not as long as one imagines, and one's quality of life before that downward turn can usually be pretty good. Further, the dying process need not be artificially extended by futile medical intervention that only increases the isolation and suffering for both dying persons and those they love. Perhaps the perceptions of its length can be foreshortened by a dying process controlled by dignity and pain management, as well as the tender companionship of friends and family rather than tubes and treatments.

For families and caregivers the most important thing to realize is that requests for assistance in ending the life of the patient near death are frequently motivated by concerns other than a true wish for death. Once concerns are addressed, studies show that patients no longer ask for help to die.[29] It is imperative that those who respect the dignity of the dying listen carefully not only to the words of request patients speak but to the underlying fears and concerns that may precipitate asking for death. To cut off conversation when persons raise the issue of suicide ("You don't really mean that. Let's talk about something else") is to reinforce the idea that the dying person no longer has a place in the community of family and friends, and that suicide may be the best solution. Their serious concerns about pain or fear of what is to come are marginalized, and so are they.

From the moral perspective it is essential to realize that thoughts about ending life—thoughts of death and of suicide—are not only normal but driven by the feelings associated with the process. And these feelings mitigate or attenuate the moral responsibility not only for wishes and thoughts about and for death but also the severity of the moral responsibility for them, especially if the thoughts become reality. Because Diane fears the process of death, she is driven to an action that is not in itself objectively moral. Even an animal caught in a trap will chew off its own leg to escape its projected fate. A recent news story recounted the story of a young man who did much the same to free himself when his arm was caught.

Fear and anxiety are impediments to moral freedom. "Survival" may be pictured by the desperate as an end to the present suffering, and "suicide" may be the means they believe are necessary to get there. Impediments to one's clear thinking and to one's freedom can mitigate and sometimes totally overpower the freedom necessary for moral responsibility. Hopefully those who care for the dying can help eliminate the impediments, and thereby eliminate the urgency for taking one's life.

OPTIONS FOR DYING

Within the American debate on the issue, there are often cries of a "right to die."[30] A right to die is an assertion that autonomy trumps other values. It is fueled by the anxieties and issues of loss of control. In a recent survey nearly 50 percent of doctors and 65 percent of the general public indicated that assisted suicide should be permissible in some circumstances.[31] As the answers were probed more carefully, it became clear that even doctors that opposed assisting their patients to die would be comfortable giving sufficient pain medicine "even at the risk of hastening death."[32] Only 6 percent of those who claimed to believe in physician-assisted suicide reported that they had actually helped a patient to die. The author of the article wonders if this is a distinction without a difference. The blurring of the distinction so clear in Catholic tradition is part of what has spurred this onerous debate, particularly in the United States. This lack of a clear distinction in people's minds has resulted in such judicial responses as the Oregon law making assisted suicide legal. Even without a law permitting physician-assisted suicide, patients already have a *legal* and often a *moral* right to refuse treatment (passive approach) and even to stop eating and drinking to hasten death.[33]

As death approaches, three options are available to the person dying and to the caregivers. The first option is to strive aggressively to maintain life. It involves a predominantly medical model: aggressive intervention aimed at curing the underlying disease or the use of various medications or techniques aimed at maintaining the physiological well-being of the body. It is the type of intervention that was discussed in chapter 5. Such intervention might be a surgery to remove a cancerous organ or X-ray or chemotherapy to kill the fast-growing cells that characterize cancer. Physiological interventions might include such minimal treatment as the administration of medicine or such maximal interventions as cardiopulmonary resuscitation. It is such interventions, often futile, that prolong and complicate the process of dying. When the interpretation of the patient's condition is limited to this model, it is very logical to focus only on what can be done medically and not see the complete person. It is a model of comforting control for the caregivers, and it is of little value to the dying human being.

It is easy to understand how aggressive intervention can happen. A loved one collapses; 911 is dialed and the person is taken to the emergency room. The patient may even have clear advance directives, but in the panic of the moment no one thinks about them or pauses to find these important papers. The documents may be set aside by hospital personnel for a number of reasons. The drama, anxiety, and even the hope of the ER plays large in real life just as it does on prime-time television. There is the feeling of shock and of desperation—wanting all the bad things to go away, wanting it to be different, wanting the problem to be "fixed." It is the everyday stuff of the ER to use dramatic intervention aimed at reversing or stemming the progress of an event that no one wants. The more high-tech equipment is available, the more the promise of miracles persists.

Narrow focus on the medical can easily lead to the application of futile treatment. What must be asked is: "Is this intervention helping?" Is the person gaining anything? What criteria should be applied? In fairness to this model of medical intervention, it is not always clear what the outcome will be in an individual case. When Karen Quinlan was brought into the ER no one, including the professionals, knew that to save the life of a previously vital young woman on that fateful day would be to condemn her to years of vegetative existence in a nursing home. Intervention was appropriate. Human hindsight is always richer in understanding than is foresight. Yet the implementation of advance directives and family discussion about what a person—even a young and healthy person—wants will be helpful in enriching foresight. Thinking beyond the tense and chaotic moment of the emergency is needed if families are to make good decisions. We must be clear that *not* treating or stopping treatment are both substantially and morally different from killing.

A second model focuses on the natural process of death, letting the dying die. It allows the participants to assess realistically what is going on: is there really any potential for this human person to live a human life again? This model could be described as more passive. It recognizes and respects the entrance of death into the life of both the dying person and those experiencing the event with them. Perhaps the practices surrounding death from former times are still valid: chicken soup, warm blankets, and the touch of a loving hand may still have their place in the setting of death. Perhaps the preferred setting for death is a domicile of familiarity and hospitality instead of the citadel of hospital sterility.

Christians believe that the sting of death has no power, that death is only a passage to the arms of God. Or do we? From the Catholic tradition, it is a valid position regarding death. What do we intend versus what do we foresee? What are we able to do, and when should we stand attentively at the bedside and surrender to the mystery and reality before us? These questions are important ingredients in the decision-making process.

THE CATHOLIC SLANT

In the first chapters in this book I outlined the perspective of the Christian tradition about the human person. The reader may recall the discussion about the qualities of the human person, many of which are important in the consideration of the morality of suicide. Human persons have an intrinsic dignity, based in the image of God. They are characterized by an intrinsic relationship to the material self and to other people. Finally, human life is a limited reality, pointed ultimately toward its ultimate end in God.

Life is a precious good, which every person possesses in trust. If God is the author of human life, it is incumbent on human beings to treat this divine creation with awe, respect, and care. Catholic belief holds that to act directly against this good is a grave evil. The *Catholic Directives* summarize what has been the consistent position of the church: "Catholic health care institutions may never condone or participate in euthanasia or assisted suicide in any way."[34] There exists a long-standing Catholic tradition against the direct annihilation of one's own life or assisting in the destruction of the life of another. As a base-line principle this is essential.

Returning to the theme of autonomy: every person is called to make choices of self-determination, choices that define and shape who he or she will become. Autonomy is always conceived and circumscribed within the circle of human responsibility to the self, to God, and to others. This is clearly stated in the encyclical, *Veritatis Splendor*, "Human freedom belongs to us as creatures; it is freedom which is given as a gift, one to be received like a seed and cultivated responsibly. It is an essential part of that creaturely image which is the basis of the dignity of the person."[35] John Paul cautions repeatedly that freedom is not license but seeks its true fulfillment in the truth and in consideration of humanity's essential relationships.

A traditional argument against suicide articulates the ultimate irony that to take one's life is to destroy the very freedom that one uses to do so. If I kill myself, or have another help me to die when there are still choices that I can make in life, I eliminate that very freedom that I say I exercise in the act of taking my life. People who commit suicide, Nuland graphically observes, "have committed a felony against themselves."[36] The well-known philosopher Immanuel Kant viewed suicide as self-contradictory, since it invokes free will to justify its own destruction.[37] Karl Barth, the prominent Protestant theologian, calls suicide, "a frivolous, arbitrary and criminal violation of the commandment [Thou shalt not kill], and therefore self-murder."[38]

Suicide may feel like the ultimate act of self-assertion. For the frail and the dying, whose bodies no longer respond to their direction, who lie at the mercy of medical technology; it may appear to be the *only available* act of self-assertion. This perception is a contradiction and belies the underlying self-interest for human beings to continue to live.

Ultimately, to take one's own life or to assist in the taking of another's life is to deny the very reality of what humanity is. It exercises an illusionary freedom while it negates the dignity of the person, the person's relationship to others, and the ultimate sovereignty of the divine. A human life is an awesome reality which cannot be dismissed in the name of autonomy. Autonomy, certainly the nonnegotiable prerequisite to truly human action, remains an insufficient justification for the purposeful attack on human life.

The illustration given at the beginning of the chapter deserves to be revisited. The young man with AIDS who asks for physician-assisted suicide is not a fiction. His true story is told by physician, Richard Selzer, in his own autobiography.[39] The physician was asked to help Ramon die. After a period of questioning and satisfying himself that the patient was not depressed and really wanted to die, he provided Ramon with the lethal dose of medicine, promising to finish the job himself if the pills did not work. The date for the suicide was determined, everyone was in agreement that no one but the patient would be present. This was to avoid legal implications for both the physician and for the man's partner. All seemed in order, until the partner decided to return home earlier than was agreed. The dying man was taken to the hospital, where his stomach was pumped and he was returned to his former state of chronic illness. The words of his partner: "I had to call the ambulance, didn't I? What else could I do? He was alive."[40]

The ironic and surprising twist to the story, a testimony to an intrinsic will to live, was that Ramon, now having traveled to the brink of the death he sought with resolve and freedom, discovered that death was not what he really wished. He was glad to have been saved before the medicine took its deadly toll. "'Do you want to be treated for the pneumonia?'" asks Sulzer as the salvaged but still ravaged patient lay in his hospital bed. "Ramon nods. 'Do you want to live?' Ramon nods. 'Do you want to die?' Ramon shakes his head."[41] Even a brief span of life circumscribed by a terrible disease seems worth living. Ramon died only twelve days later.

The Catholic view of human persons sees persons as images of God, formed to create themselves and eventually to find their way to God again. The personal and autonomous task between birth and death is one of stewardship. Courtney Campbell captures this idea when he observes, "[H]uman beings are entrusted with caring for and respecting the divine gifts that may come in the form of one's own life and body, or in the presence of others with whom we create relationships and covenants out of the equality of mutual dependence."[42] That stewardship does not include the direct destruction of the life it bears. To take one's life is to cast aside the hope that God cares more for us than we ourselves do. It is the ultimate act of illusion, that somehow we belong exclusively to ourselves. It affirms that human beings, rather than God, are ultimate.

The Catholic vision of humanity that Campbell's statement underlines is that persons are essentially related to one another. This relationship demands both receptivity and responsibility from both sides of the partnership. In considering suicide, this may be the most pertinent element to examine in contrast to a contemporary American ethos of individuality. Embodied in the national embrace of autonomy is the notion that it is a disvalue to be unproductive or dependent. Not just the image of self as good only if successful, useful, accomplished, independent; but the concern that others, too, value us only in these terms can be the platform from which thoughts of suicide are launched. The opposing qualities of dependency, neediness, and incompleteness are not honored nor embraced. They are seen to diminish the dignity of persons. As people lose utility or other valued qualities, their lives become less and less important to maintain. They exist as a drag on the prosperity and progress of the culture. Bottom line thinking, while generally applied to business, taints our vision of ourselves and our relationship to others. The movie *Solyent Green* demonstrated this vision: people who reach a certain age are euthanized. When their personhood is no longer valued, their bodies are still useful as a commodity, a source of food: the ultimate utility!

That is not the vision of humanity seen through the lens of Catholicism. As Kavanaugh points out, "Usefulness, meaningfulness, even pain or suffering do not give us value. Our value is a function of our being."[43] It is not a function of our accomplishments nor of our potential. Catholic vision sees humanity unadorned as the only thing necessary to dignity. Arguments of utility to justify suicide, assisted suicide, or euthanasia have no basis in Catholic tradition.

While not diminishing the intrinsic worth of persons, we may wish to examine qualities that may enhance the personality and the passing of the dying. Christopher Vogt suggests a look to the gospel picture of Jesus given in Luke. Vogt offers paradigmatic "virtues of dying persons," which are embodied in the Jesus of the passion. These are patience, compassion, and hope.[44] The Jesus of Luke's gospel exhibits not an absolute autonomy, but a willingness to share that freedom with those who controlled the drama of his death. Reluctant to suffer, Jesus chooses passion and death as what he perceives to be "a necessary part of his faithfulness to God."[45] In healing the ear of the servant (Luke 22:51) and reaching out to the crucified thief (Luke 23:43). Jesus demonstrates compassion even as he suffers without it. As he moves through the dreadful hours of pain; he trusts that God's strength, symbolized by a comforting angel (Luke 22:43), will carry him through. Vogt's point is that it is not only caregivers that can be actively relational in the dying process, the dying can assume an active role as well. To enter into the passion of Jesus is not an exercise in masochism but the final self-creating activity of the ebbing life.

Turning the view outward, people may see not only their diminished utility but may focus on the burden they have created for others as they die. For the retired father of a family who has spent decades earning the bread and board of a comfortable life, the idea of years of dependence as his body gives in to Lou Gehrig's disease may seen too much to bear. The ads for retirement communities and for extended living facilities emphasize the virtue of independence and decry the awfulness of dependence on others, particularly family members. It is easy to buy their message.

Sometimes the belief that dependence is a bad thing is reinforced by family members and other caregivers. A newspaper story recounts the situation of an eighty-four-year-old woman who had lived with her daughter for twenty years. As the older woman began to show signs of diminished physical abilities—her hearing became impaired—the daughter told her that it was OK for older people to commit suicide when they cannot any longer care for themselves.[46]

The anguished looks of those at the bedside of the dying conveys a clear message: "Hurry up. We can't handle this for very much longer." Such negative feelings coexist in cozy ambivalence with feelings of regret that death is imminent. Often the elderly and the infirm of any age are marginalized by society and told in one way or another, "You are not useful. You are causing us pain." They read the reflection of their own hopelessness in the eyes of those they love. The young cancer victim who sees the anguish in the expressions of his parents may wish to spare them further grief. While the parents, if questioned, would insist that they do not want the son to die, the message they send may say otherwise. The Eskimo grandmother who walks out onto the frozen wasteland at night to avoid slowing down the tribe in their migration may be responding to the cultural message that she is a burden rather than freely choosing this end for herself.

If and when physician-assisted suicide becomes legal in more than Oregon, the potential for pressure to precipitate death against the psychological, physical, and financial burdens it brings will likely increase. While I vehemently disagree and have never found it to be true in my experience with hospital patients, Gregory Pence argues that the desire to avoid futile treatment is prompted by medical staff, "confused, frustrated, and angry about its mistakes, disagreements, and the inability to provide either a cure or a good death,"[47] Even if his conclusions are not accurate, such *perceptions* of how caregivers feel about lingering death can influence the freedom of the dying and pressure them to acts of self-destruction. Daniel Callahan, a longtime proponent of allowing people to die without aggressive intervention, details a possible scenario in which assisted suicide has become the norm.

People with a terminal diagnosis will find themselves facing a doctor who may not only pose it as an option, but even the first option, the most sensible, the most humane. "I can help you to die—or you can take these treatments, which are expensive and may be painful, and then apply for hospice care that may or may not be available. Which do you choose?[48] While in theory suicide may be a free act, there are many things that can impact on that freedom. Those factors lobby strongly against its legalization, whatever the morality is.

In sharp contrast to the American perspective the Judeo-Christian tradition emphasizes not only the interdependence of persons but the special respect due those who are vulnerable. From the admonition of the eighth-century prophets to be mindful of God's presence in the cry of the poor to the care of Jesus for the frankly vulnerable embodied in children, widows, and the sick, care of the needy and dependent has been held up as a cardinal virtue. In recent years the so-called principle of vulnerability has been added to the bioethical lexicon.[49] Standing beside the twinned principles of autonomy and beneficence must be the conviction that those who are sick and dying—the vulnerable—must be treated with the most exquisite care. And those who are vulnerable bear a "familial" relationship to all of us. Catholic anthropology asserts this essential connection of all persons to one another.

TERMINAL SEDATION

Earlier in the chapter the window that some deaths may be painful deaths was left open, if only a crack. Most deaths, if properly handled, can be pain-free and dignified. There are some situations in which pain is so great that it cannot be relieved by ordinary methods. The medical response to these cases is *terminal sedation*, the deliberate induction and maintenance of a final deep sleep intended to spare the patient intractable pain or suffering as she slips into death.[50] Some have called this practice "sedation of the imminently dying."[51] The assumptions for its use are that the patient is very near death, her pain or anguish cannot be relieved in any other fashion, and that she consents to this intervention. This might be the scenario of a late-stage cancer patient, whose body systems have even lost their ability to process food and water.[52] The humane medical response of terminal sedation would allow her to "go gently into that good night," as Dylan Thomas suggests. The underlying case of death is the disease, while the purpose of the sedation is to relieve pain.

The moral response from Catholic tradition is summed up in the *Catholic Directives*, "Patients should be kept as free of pain as possible so that they may die comfortably and with dignity. . . . Medicine capable of alleviating or suppressing pain may be given to a dying person, *even if this therapy may indirectly shorten the person's life so long as the intent is not to hasten death* [emphasis mine]."[53] While terminal sedation may or may not shorten the patient's life; it most certainly precludes any further conscious human activity. The same *Directive* reminds us that "a person has the right to prepare for his or her death while fully conscious [and] should not be deprived of consciousness without a compelling reason." Assuming that an opportunity is provided for the dying person to conclude whatever she perceives to be unfinished business, within the parameters of the existing medical situation, terminal sedation is an appropriate and moral response. The action fulfills the criteria set down by the principle of double effect and allows a peaceful leave taking.

Terminal sedation has been used also to describe the practice of periodic (24 to 48 hours) medicating to allow a patient in severe pain respite from the uncomfortable symptoms of disease or the dying process. After the designated period of sedation, the dose of the sedative is gradually decreased until the patient is again conscious.[54] "Palliative sedation" and "respite sedation" are sometimes used to describe this practice. From the perspective of Catholic teaching, there seems to be no moral difficulty with such intervention: it relieves pain, at least for a time (a good thing), and does not raise the question in any way of an intent to kill. Caregivers of those whose pain seems enduring and intractable may wish to explore this option with medical personnel.

The concept and use of terminal sedation has been expanded to include another application. It is the use of "terminal" sedation for persons not terminal, what has been called "sedation towards death."[55] A case will illustrate the scenario.[56] A nonterminal patient with spinal cord paralysis with no physical discomfort claims to be "in agony" and requests terminal sedation. The physician thinks about issues of autonomy, relief of suffering—of both patient and physician, whose compassion shares the patient's pain—and the inability of the patient to do anything for himself. Since terminal sedation seems to be an acceptable treatment legally,[57] why not use it in cases such as this? Is not the purpose of the action relief of suffering and not the death of the patient? Is it not the duty of the physician to act compassionately, to "midwife"[58] the patient through the dying process? The fallacy in this argument is to assume that a narrow legal umbrella intended to allow assisted suicide to patients very near death can and should be applied to other situations. *Legal* is not the same thing as *moral*, a further difficulty is to confuse the wishes of the patient (which may lead to immoral actions) and the duty of someone other than the patient to go along with those wishes. Even in Oregon physicians have no legal obligation to assist in suicides.

Margaret Farley, a Catholic moral theologian, has suggested that there may exceptions to the no-kill rule, believing that circumstances do make a difference in the moral quality of an act. "Is it possible," she asks, "that when death becomes inevitable and surrender to God is made in the face of it, then communal bonds can be preserved and not violated in an active as well as a passive dying-into-life?"[59] She suggests that death itself can be an "active" process, a consentual decision to die. "[A]ction and passion, giving and receiving, embracing and letting go, become two sides of the same reality."[60]

The case for compassion, for aid to the dying seems strong. How can this scenario be judged from a moral perspective? An analysis from a Catholic perspective sees "terminal" sedation for a patient who is not indeed "terminal" as essentially the same as voluntary active euthanasia, and therefore as morally wrong. Its purpose is death, rather than the relief of pain or suffering.

The image of "midwifing" is an interesting one, but one that needs further explanation. The function of the midwife is to be present in support to the woman in labor. The midwife has neither jurisdiction nor ability to make the birth happen, but rather only stands by. Perhaps this is the proper image for the physician. She does not precipitate the death anymore than the midwife precipitates the birth, but she does companion the person on the journey to new life. Terminal sedation in the person who is not near natural death is not distinctly different from putting a pillow to the face of the sufferer: its primary aim is the death of the patient. When the primary aim is a disvalue, in this case death, the action is morally wrong. The closer the action which results in death gets to the aim of the agent (the person with the pillow or the pill) the more the moral integrity of the act is compromised. While a case could be made for compassionate ending of the life of another, the case cannot be made to deny what such an action does to the person performing it. The residual in the *agent* is a residual of directly intending and causing the death of another human being. It is difficult to find a proportionate reason for such an action.[61]

Ron Hamel has offered some helpful guidelines for use of terminal sedation:

- the patient is irreversibly terminally ill; usually in a state of advanced deterioration
- all well-established therapeutic strategies have been attempted and have proven inadequate
- the only realistic means available to palliate may hasten death
- the intention is not to hasten death but to relieve pain
- the patient has had the opportunity (if possible) to prepare for death
- informed consent has been obtained
- life-sustaining treatment should be withdrawn
- the dosage of medication is proportionate to relief of symptoms and is not increased as long as symptoms are alleviated[62]

Hamel agrees that use for "existential suffering," which can be sedation toward death may be much more problematic.

THE "GOOD" DEATH

What, then, does "euthanasia," or a "good death" look like to Catholics? It is certainly one in which the person dies with dignity intact, with the support of medical attention to pain and suffering and the human attention to friends for the journey. It is one that holds as many elements of human personhood as can be held. The "good death" is one in which forgiveness and reconciliation are central.

One of the most difficult parts of suicide and its companions are the feelings of guilt and alienation that are part of it. For the person who suffers and lingers, thoughts of suicide may bring guilt. If suicide is actually carried out, guilt is the predictable legacy of those who remain. "What should I have done to prevent it?" "It must be my fault. I should have given better care."

What of someone who has committed suicide? Does this last act, so definite, finally consign the deceased to death-after-life in the eternity of isolation that we call "hell"? Certainly the Catholic practice of former times which forbid the burial of suicides in blessed ground suggests this. How are we to resolve such a horrendous action and make peace with it? Karl Barth says it well: "God sees and weighs the whole of human life. He judges it according to His own righteousness which is that of mercy."[63] We cannot know even our own hearts. How can we know the heart of another or the mind and mercy of God? If a patient does succeed in committing suicide, those who are left to grieve should do several things. (1) Leave the judgment about the state of the deceased to God. We cannot know the heart of another, particularly what impediments may have driven someone to suicide. (2) Forgive ourselves. Let go of guilt for the event. People who wish to kill themselves are resolute. There is little that can be done to prevent self-destruction. The cause is not something that we have done or neglected to do. (3) Talk about feelings. Feelings about a suicide, like all feelings about significant events, are mixed. It is important to acknowledge grief, sadness, shock, sorrow. It is equally important to recognize relief, anger, and any other emotions that may not seem to us "appropriate." Feelings are what they are. They must not be judged through a filter of moral rightness.

Human life is an awesome value. Dignity demands that we care for life as long as we can and cede that life into the arms of God when we can no longer do so. The direct taking of life through suicide, assisted suicide, or any type of "mercy killing" has no place in the sacred space where God comes to meet the dying. While we have a right to die with dignity and without the prolongation of the process, we do not have to corresponding right to take life directly. To do so, even once, is to erode the very value inherent in our humanity.

QUESTIONS FOR DISCUSSION

1. Differentiate among the terms suicide, assisted suicide, active euthanasia, passive euthanasia, and murder. What does Catholic teaching say about each of these?
2. List some reasons why people entertain thoughts of suicide or assisted suicide. Which of these, if any, do you consider morally valid reasons and why?
3. Differentiate between the terms "legal" and "moral" as they are applied to assisted suicide.
4. What is "terminal sedation" and what moral guidelines for its use can be applied from a Catholic perspective?

NOTES

1. See "Not Compassion Alone: On Euthanasia and Ethics," *Hastings Center Report* 25, no. 7 (Special Issue 1995): 48.

2. The urgency to make assisted suicide legal in the United States has yielded a statute in only one state, Oregon.

3. A summary of studies in this regard is given in Paul B. Bascom and Susan W. Tolle, "Responding to Requests for Physician-Assisted Suicide," *Journal of the American Medical Association* 288, no. 1 (July 3, 2002): 92–93.

4. The Dutch and Belgian laws permit physician-assisted death only under certain stringent conditions. In the Netherlands the term is not "assisted suicide," as it is in the United States, but rather "euthanasia."

5. The headlines of a local newspaper on January 13, 2003, report the lastest doctor-designed suicide machine, seized by customs as he tried to leave his native Australia. (Cleveland Plain Dealer, 8 A.)

6. Because the meaning of the term *passive* is confusing, it is common today among moral theologians to speak rather about *intended* and *foreseen* consequences. Many Catholics still use the term *passive euthansia*, which is why we use it here.

7. It is essential to emphasize the idea of some *proportionate* good, since both passive and active euthanasia include among their consequences the death of the subject.

8. See, for example, Candace Cummins Gauthier, "Active Voluntary Euthanasia, Terminal Sedation, and Assisted Suicide," *Journal of Clinical Ethics* 12, no. 1 (spring 2001): 43–46. Gauthier discusses active voluntary euthanasia and gives a good explanation of the principle of double effect.

9. Rachels, "Active and Passive Euthanasia," discussed in detail in chapter 3.

10. As was discussed earlier in the book, morality is not judged *solely* on the basis of the agent's intention. It is necessary that there exist an objective proportionate good toward which the agent aims. This is a most important qualifier in the assessment of moral rightness or wrongness. On the other hand, a "bad" intention, such as

wanting the death of another, can render a non-act (I don't do something to prevent a death which I want) is a sufficient criterion to render an act morally wrong. James F. Bresnahan has raised the issue of intentional ambiguity, "A doctor can really intend to kill but disguises this by pretending to do what can be, in moral intention, an honest acceptance of unwanted side effect, namely death." See "Palliative Care or Assisted Suicide?" *America* 178, no. 8 (March 14, 1998): 17. While it is theoretically possible for a physician to wish a patient dead, this seems a highly unlikely situation. Few doctors would entertain such a perfidious intention. In fact, the situation is often just the reverse: doctors fighting to continue treatment in the face of patient and family objection. Bresnahan's comments serve only to muddy the clear distinction in Catholic teaching between active and passive and to encourage a climate of mistrust between patients and caregivers.

11. Even though the act is similar, voluntary euthanasia may have legal implications that are greater than those of assisted suicide. Nicholas Dixon has argued that they are morally similar, however, particularly as they involve physicians. See "On the Difference between Physician-Assisted Suicide and Active Euthanasia," *Hastings Center Report* 28, no. 5 (September/October 1998): 25–29.

12. Lawyer and ethicist, Dena Davis, has argued that opting for suicide is an appropriate response to a diagnosis of impending debilitating illness such as dementia or other progressive conditions. While suicide would "deprive me of some good years," says Davis, "the risk of waiting too long is even worse: one might fail to achieve one's goals or endanger others by being careless with lethal pills or weapons." Davis believes that the exercise of autonomy is so important that charting one's own death course overrides other factors. (See, "Rational Suicide and Predictive Genetic Testing," unpublished draft [January 15, 1997], 6.) Davis's position reflects at least one place on the continuum of the importance of autonomy that characterizes the American moral landscape.

13. Implicates another in the act of killing. The argument urging such complicity goes something like this: if persons are unable or unwilling to end their lives shouldn't it be the caring physician's duty to help achieve their goal? Certainly this is the argument of Timothy Quill and others. It side-steps the issue, raised elsewhere in this book, that one's demand on another's complicity ends where the other's conscience judges the action demanded as wrong: I should not help you commit an action that I believe to be immoral, even though you cannot accomplish it without my help. Even the Oregon law permitting physician-assisted suicide allows physicians to withdraw from caring for a patient requesting it, if the doctor believes assisted-suicide to be wrong.

14. Sherwin B. Nuland, *How We Die: Reflections on Life's Final Chapter* (New York: Vintage Books, 1995), 140.

15. There is at least anecdotal evidence to suggest that part of the reason the Dutch endorsed active euthanasia was because severe pain in the dying was not being addressed adequately. [Theo A. Boer, "After the Slippery Slope: An Evaluation of the Dutch Experiences on Regulating Active Euthanasia" (paper presented at the annual meeting of the Society of Christian Ethics, Pittsburgh, Pennsylvania, January 10, 2003).]

16. The New York State Task Force on Life and the Law, *When Death Is Sought: Assisted Suicide and Euthanasia in a Medical Context* (May 1994), ix. This book offers some good tools for anyone dealing with end-of-life issues. It includes appendixes with resources for hospice, assessment of pain and depression in a patient, and some principles for handling requests for euthanasia and assisted suicide by suffering patients.

17. Stanford University, for example, offers an intensive course to train physicians in the management of pain and related symptoms. It is interesting that palliative care has become a topic of some concern in the Netherlands, perhaps in the face of some dissatisfaction with the experience with the sanctioning of assisted suicide.

18. Timothy E. Quill, "Death and Dignity: A Case of Individualized Decision Making," *The New England Journal of Medicine* 324, no. 10 (March 7, 1991): 693. Dr. Quill has been a vocal proponent of physician-assisted suicide. The cases he uses to illustrate the need in his book, *Midwifing Through the Dying Process* (Baltimore: The Johns Hopkins University Press, 1996), are a mixture of passive euthanasia and frank assisted suicide. Such confusion is unfortunate.

19. Diane was given pain medication sufficient to cause death. Initially simply having the option for suicide gave her some degree of comfort.

20. *Directives,* General Introduction.

21. Andrew H. Malcolm, "The Ultimate Decision," *The New York Times*, December 3, 1989, 38.

22. Edson, "W;t," 64–65.

23. Kathleen Whalen FitzGerald, personal communication.

24. Nuland, *How We Die*, 152.

25. Jon Fuller, "Physician-Assisted Suicide: An Unnecessary Crisis," *America* 177, no. 2 (July 19, 1997): 9.

26. Elizabeth Hallam, Jenny Hockey, and Glennys Howarth, *Beyond the Body: Death and Social Identity* (New York: Routledge, 1999), 1.

27. Hallam, *Beyond the Body*, 21.

28. The time course of the final states of death can be less than a day or up to two weeks. (David E. Weissman, "The Syndrome of Imminent Death," *Fast Facts and Concepts # 3,* <http://www.eperc.mew.edu>)

29. Michael W. Rabow and Amy J. Markowitz, "Responding to Requests for Physician-Assisted Suicide: These Are Uncharted Waters for Both of Us," *Journal of the American Medical Association* 288, no. 18 (November 13, 2002): 2332.

30. Yale law professor and ethicist Stephen L. Carter has called it a "wrongheaded 'right.'" See "Rush to a Lethal Judgment," *New York Times Magazine,* July 21, 1996, 28.

31. Wayne J. Guglielmo, "Assisted Suicide? Pain Control? Where's the Line?" *Medical Economics* (October 11, 2002): 49. The survey included the opinions of 5,000 physicians. The distinctions between what we have called passive and active intervention were not made by all those surveyed, however.

32. Guglielmo, "Assisted Suicide?" 49.

33. This reality is pointed out by David J. Mayo and Martin Gunderson, "Vitalism Revitalized," *Hastings Center Report* 32, no. 4 (July/August 2002): 18. They note that the Oregon law is actually more stringent than previous legal safeguards, and the

problem is lack of respecting patients' rights to forgo treatments that prolong the dying process. In place are laws which protect patients from assault and battery. Unfortunately the patients who are inflicted with unwanted and inefficacious treatment are not around to press their cases in court, since they inevitably die. The vitalist position that caused them grief in their dying, perhaps espoused by professionals or by family, is alive and thriving.

34. *Directives*, 60.

35. John Paul II, *Veritatis Splendor*, 86.

36. Nuland, *How We Die*, 153.

37. See Immanuel Kant, "Suicide," in Mappes and DeGrazia, *Biomedical Ethics*, 375–78.

38. Karl, Barth, *Church Dogmatics*, vol III, no. 4, ed. G. W. Bromley and T. F. Torrance, trans. A. T. Mackay, et al. (Edinburgh: T. & T. Clark, 1960), 404.

39. Richard Selzer, *Up from Troy: A Doctor Comes of Age* (New York: William Morrow and Company, 1992), 282–96. The story appears also as "A Question of Mercy," *New York Times Magazine*, September 22, 1991, 32–38.

40. Selzer, *Up from Troy*, 295.

41. Selzer, *Up from Troy*, 296.

42. Campbell, "Religious Ethics and Assisted Suicide," 267–58.

43. John F. Kavanaugh, *Who Count as Persons?: Human Identity and the Ethics of Killing* (Washington, D.C.: Georgetown University Press, 2001), 134.

44. Christopher P. Vogt, "Practicing Patience, Compassion and Hope at the End of Life: Mining the Passion of Jesus in Luke for a Christian Model of Dying Well" (paper delivered at the annual meeting of the Society of Christian Ethics, Pittsburgh, Pennsylvania, January 11, 2003), 1.

45. Vogt, "Practicing Patience," 6.

46. This account was reprised in Peter J. Bernardi, "The Hidden Engines of the Suicide Rights Movement," *America* 172, no. 16 (May 6, 1995): 16. The original story appeared in *The Santa Rosa* (California) *Press Democrat* (September 14, 1993).

47. Gregory E. Pence, *Re-Creating Medicine: Ethical Issues at the Frontiers of Medicine* (Lanham:Rowman & Littlefield Publishers, 2000), 165.

48. Quoted in Paul Wilkes, "The Next Pro-Lifers," *New York Times Magazine*, July 5, 1996, 25.

49. See Edmund D. Pellegrino and David C. Thomasma, *Helping and Healing* (Washington, D.C.: Georgetown University Press, 1997), 54–66.

50. James L. Hallenbeck, "Terminal Sedation: Ethical Implications in Different Situations," *Journal of Palliative Medicine* 3, no. 3 (fall 2002): 314.

51. Lynn A. Jansen and Daniel P. Sulmasy, "Sedation, Alimentation, Hydration, and Equivocation: Careful Conversation about Care at the End of Life," *Annals of Internal Medicine* 136, no. 11 (June 4, 2002): 845.

52. The problem of people "starving" if they are terminally sedated has been raised. (See discussion in Hallenback, "Terminal Sedation," 318.) From the Catholic perspective this should not be an issue. That artificially supplying nutrition and hydration in some cases may be extraordinary and therefore not morally obligatory has been discussed in chapter 7.

53. *Directives, 61.*

54. For a more thorough discussion, see Paul C. Rousseau, "Palliative Sedation," *American Journal of Hospice and Palliative Care* 19, no. 5 (September/October 2002): 296. Rousseau offers guidelines for patients whose pain is "existential" as well as physical.

55. Jansen and Sulmasy, "Sedation," 845.

56. The complete case and discussion is found in Hallenback, "Terminal Sedation," 314.

57. See Candace Cummins Gauthier, "Active Voluntary Euthanasia, Terminal Sedation, and Assisted Suicide," *Journal of Clinical Ethics* 12, no. 1 (spring 2001): 43–45. While active euthanasia is prohibited by law, terminal sedation is not.

58. The term is used by Timothy Quill to describe the caring doctor's response to patients who request assisted suicide.

59. Margaret A. Farley, "Issues in Contemporary Christian Ethics: The Choice of Death in a Medical Context," *The Santa Clara Lectures* 1, no. 3 (May 1, 1995): 14.

60. Farley, "Issues," 13.

61. Ron Hamel, of the Catholic Health Association, has been among Catholic ethicists who have endorsed terminal sedation for the imminently dying and raised serious cautions for its use as an "acceptable" form of euthanasia.

62. Ron Hamel, presentation given at a conference, *Recovering Our Tradition: A Catholic Perspective on End-of-Life Care of the Dying,* Tucson, Arizona, January 23, 2002.

63. Barth, *Church Dogmatics*, 405.

Chapter Nine

Final Gifts: Interpersonal Dimensions of Dying

"Mamma's gonna buy you a mocking bird. And if that mocking bird don't sing, mamma's gonna buy you a diamond ring."[1]

"People who need people are the luckiest people in the world."[2]

Giving gifts is one of the more pleasurable of human activities. We watch our children and grandchildren smile or squeal in glee as they open a wonderful Christmas present. We enjoy the surprise on the face of a friend as she opens the "something special" that we brought back for her from a trip. All of us want to be givers as the perennial folk song suggests, "Momma's gonna buy you," because love begets giving. Most of us are at least a little uncomfortable with being on the receiving end. "Oh, you shouldn't have." "Oh, dear, I didn't get *you* anything." Gift giving is not only important when life is young, it has meaning at life's end. What does this look like to the dying and to those who care for them?

THE GIFT OF RECEIVING

The first gift that is part of the end-of-life concerns strengthening of the essential ties of relationship. It is an affirmation of the lines from the song, "People who need people are the luckiest people in the world." The illusion of individuality is burst by the vision of the human person presented by the Catholic tradition. None of us is born alone nor can we function without others. To say otherwise is to live in a dream. We are dependent on God, who knit us in the womb (Ps. 139:13) and who knew us before we were born. We are dependent on each other not only for the material stuff and staff of life but for the very language and culture on which we build our unique and autonomous identities. As we ready ourselves for the last stage of life, we need others more than ever. The dying need to continue social, family, and other interactions. The caricature of someone being abandoned in the far room of the hospital, while sometimes true in practice, does not describe what we have come to see as the "good death" nor what is adequate for the last months and days of human persons.

The good death may be a cliché, but it is not an easy task. Often the vision we have of how we would like to die is swept away by the real. So too can the demands of caring for the dying be overwhelming for family members, friends, or even for paid caregivers. The romantic extended family of *Little House on the Prairie* or *Leave It to Beaver*, showing many happy hands making work light, or the starched nurse, white and compassionate, who never tires but sits for hours with the dying do not exist in modern America. Families are scattered, jobs demand many hours away from the home, modern medicine truncates the personalized caring that characterized a former, more intimate culture.

For many the inability to care for loved ones at home and the need to find alternatives can result in guilt for the would-be caregiver. Donna expressed it this way, "I had to put Dad in a nursing home. As an only child who must continue to work, going to his house each day, washing sheets and changing beds, making sure he took his medicine—it was eating me up. Now I am sure my mother is looking down from heaven with disapproving eyes. I feel so guilty!" For Donna there were few good choices. While she *experiences* guilt, what she was able to do for her dad had been done and *no moral blame* is due her. It is important to separate how we *feel* about what we do and the *real possibilities* that are available in concrete situations. Finding a good nursing home for her dad was Donna's only reasonable alternative.

Feelings of guilt play a part in most dying. We think that there must have been more that could have been done. As we replay the event in the calm present of our minds, we do not remember the anxiety, the fear, the haste with which decisions had to be made. To separate the choices that were possible at the time from an idealized and rested revisit of the event is essential. It is important that we move on.

There is a marvelous image from the movie *The Mission*, which pictures a reformed mercenary soldier carrying his armor (symbolic of his reprobate past) lashed to his body. Because of its weight, the man has difficulty maneuvering up the steep mountain path. Wisely, one of the native guides takes a knife and cuts the armor free. No one should have to continue to carry a heavy burden from the past. To move on in peace is good mental health.

Nevertheless, are there ways to make dying better? Can the idealized care of connectedness be realized in a "good" death? First, we must not generalize in such a way as to assume that everyone has the same picture of what this means. Many have a vision of a warm and peopled death—family and friends together at home and at the bedside. Some conjure an end that is solitary, un-intruded by the grief and solicitation of others. Most of us will find the reality does not match the vision.

For those whose medical condition or whose personal preference warrant companionship on the journey, one contemporary solution is hospice. Originally, when I first taught a course on end-of-life issues, I assumed that everyone knew about hospice and that there was little need to discuss this option in class. My students quickly dispelled that error.

The hospice movement affords a professional and pervasive support service to those near death and to their caregivers. There are over 3,000 hospice centers in the United States. As a booklet published by the National Hospice Organization states: "Hospice is not an end to treatment—It is a shift to intensive palliative care that focuses on helping the patient to live his or her life to the fullest."[3] Its primary function is to alleviate unpleasant and painful symptoms in the dying, but hospice offers other services. These include educational information about the process of death and its palliation, counseling and other social services to address the emotional and spiritual aspects of coping with terminal illness, as well as grief counseling.

Sometimes the greatest loneliness comes to those who outlive the caring for a loved one. If there has been an intense period of involvement with a dying person—washing and moving the failing body, giving medicine, waiting, watching—there will be a period of intense grieving. Caregivers experience their own range of conflicting emotions: anger and guilt; sadness and laughter; the satisfaction of being a giver and the frustration over an overwhelming task. They see their time consumed with caring for life that slips away, while their own living is put on hold. Hospice offers help for families and care givers during and even *after* the event of death.

The services of hospice can be utilized even when the patient dies at home. This is true whether there are caregivers available or in some cases even if the person lives alone. Patients who reside in long-term or other residential facility or even patients in tertiary care hospitals can take advantage of hospice services. The hospice team can adjust to the needs of any of these situations and help make arrangements for added care giving if needed. Not only does hospice provide regular visits to the location of the patient, but nurses are on call twenty-four hours a day to deal with concerns, to give advice, to listen, or to contact the patient's physician if needed.

There are several misunderstandings about hospice. Referral is seen as a banner signaling defeat, the end of the fight against the ultimate enemy, death. The American culture avoids death. Physicians, who may have their own problems with facing this ultimate symbol of failure for their healing efforts, are sometimes reluctant to recommend their patients for hospice. Many people think it is a service to be used only in the last few days of life. All tend to collude in the dance of keeping death a secret from the dying and from themselves; and while they dance, the clock ticks toward midnight. The illusion turns into a pumpkin and the hopes scurry into the dark night of death.

The fact is that hospice *is* for the dying. Referral is generally recommended within the last six months of life, but it can be used with patients who rally for significantly longer periods. Diseases such as cancer manifest their final stages in somewhat predictable temporal terms, but hospice can be effective for many terminal conditions that have a gradual trajectory toward the final days. *Proximity to the time of death* rather than the type of illness is what dictates when hospice should be called. A diagnosis of a terminal illness, a likely venue for denial of death, is a good time to plan for adequate care, symptom control, and distribution of time to attend to whatever "last things" a person wishes to address. Hospice can supply the help and opportunity.

Another myth about hospice is that it is expensive and that most insurance plans do not pay for it. More than 80 percent of people eligible for hospice under Medicare do not know that they qualify for benefits.[4] Hospice treatment is available and paid for by Medicare, Medicaid, and many other insurance plans. While what is covered will vary, it is likely that some form of care, particularly in the patient's own home, will be reimbursed. Eligibility can be renewed on a periodic basis if the patient's projected life span is greater than the six months' period usually stipulated.

Hospice embodies an approach to death congruent with the Christian vision. It frankly recognizes that all persons die and that all deserve a death with dignity and with aggressive alleviation of painful and discomforting symptoms. It allows the dying to exercise substantial control or choice about *where* they will die and *under what conditions*. It affirms the communal nature of human living and of human dying as well as the basic interdependence of persons.

Its services extend beyond the needs of the dying to the needs of the living who care for them. One of the most fearful aspects of proximity to death is our discomfort with this foreign visitor. The body, in its dying, is not something with which modern human beings are comfortable. One of the more important services offered by hospice is to address questions about what to expect when someone dies. Knowing what to expect, caregivers can more readily give themselves over to care than to their own anxieties.

THE LEGACY OF THE DYING

At the end of life giving is framed in terms of the generosity of caregivers. But there are gifts that can by given by the dying themselves. The last days and moments of life provide an opportunity to provide for members of the family as well as to the larger community. It is an opportunity to contribute to the common good.

Although death removes our bodily symbol from the presence of those we love, there is much of ourselves that we can bequeath. It is important that we mend fences and repair bridges that connect us to others. No one wants to leave a legacy of guilt, anger, and regret. Who do I need to talk with before I go? What do I need to say to them?[5]

Acknowledgment that the hours before passage into death are few provides a unique opportunity for all to do what they never have had time to do before. It is a bit like being under a deadline: I have to clean the house before my mother-in-law comes; I have known about this report for weeks, but now it is due—tomorrow. Nothing like pressure to produce results.

What might an end-of-life conversation look like? It can be opportunity to have the dying person tell his story as well as a time for the family to receive and cherish the story. Who am I? What do I value? What are the things I have accomplished in my life? What have I yet that I wish to accomplish? These questions can be the flesh on the bones of a biography, an important "work" for the dying person but also invaluable to those who love them. Open-ended questions help the conversation to achieve a richness and texture.

Not everyone likes to have conversations that go beyond the trivial. Some will fill an entire lifetime with talk of sports, potty training, or the latest shows on TV. Unspoken is the principle: "Do not go beyond the mundane." Once I tried to have a conversation with my father about God, religion, and meaning in life. His response—remember this was the man who called a cemetery a golf course—was a one sentence, "I have worked that out myself." End of conversation.

Hospice speaks of five things needed for relationship completion. Ira Byock, who has written extensively on these issues, offered a quick checklist of these phrases to a man dying of COPD (chronic obstructive pulmonary disease). From all accounts, Steve was an unlikely candidate for a warm and fuzzy growth experience of communication as he died. Yet Byok's scribbled list: "I forgive you"; "Forgive me"; "Thank you"; "I love you"; and "Good-bye" provided Steve what he needed to bring some closure to his relationships. "He didn't set out thinking of his illness or impending death as an opportunity to grow as a person—indeed, the idea would have seemed ludicrous to him when he was well—but the prospect of dying so scared him that he was willing to try anything that might relieve the terror." As he died, notes Byock, Steve "changed in remarkable ways."[6] He died at peace.

We often wish to retrieve what time and death have lost. Don't I wish I had Mom's wonderful recipe for pumpkin pie? What was it Dad used to use to clean metal doorknobs? I wonder what my sister remembered from our childhood days that she cherished? Several weeks ago I began an e-mail conversation with a high school friend. We have laughed about our teachers, the naïvité of those years, and remembered electronically the anecdotes of yesterday. What a precious exchange! What a shame it would be to have lost it!

Last times offer an opportunity to sort meaning. The dying person carries in her failing body precious memories and stories of the past. How many of us has wished to know how Uncle Charlie moved to Kansas or whether there was really a gypsy in our family tree. If not told, some one-of-a-kind family stories will be buried with the corpse. Last times offer the chance to express past joys and past sorrows, a chance to share the former and rejoice and to heal the latter.

Mary, the person with the lymphoma whose family had difficulty making a decision about whether to treat her cancer, lived a year beyond the diagnosis. The extra time allowed her to rejoice in the birth of her first local grandchild, born before she became too ill. More importantly, as she lay dying in her own home with her daughters caring for her (with the help of hospice), many occasions presented themselves for the siblings to retrieve the good things about their own growing up. The day Mary died was one of sorrow, but the sorrow was mitigated by the wonderful together times the process afforded the family. All the daughters felt a sense of peacefulness and closure. This story presents such a contrasting picture to the sterile scene of death in the ICU.

Even those with no close relationships may have an urgent need to share such information and feelings. Deathbed "confessions," although the stuff of melodrama, may be the important legacy many dying persons wish to impart before time runs out. Caregivers should be attentive to the opportunity to bring such questions to the fore.

There is a way to leave our physical presence as well. Bodily organs and tissue have potential to offer health and even the life to others. Most of us who drive have the opportunity to indicate on the drivers' license that we are willing to donate one or more of our organs for use in another's body long after we are no longer alive. The family of a deceased may donate organs as well. Up until very recently a family decision to deny donation took legal precedent over the expressed wishes of the dead person. Now the wishes of the patient concerning the disposition of the body have stronger legal stance, similar to what they enjoy with regard to advance directives.[7]

Every year thousands of people whose lives could be saved by donor organs die.[8] Every year the techniques for transplant and the ability to suppress the immune systems of those receiving organs so they do not attack the foreign biological tissue is improved. Every year lives are saved because of the generosity of dying persons and/or their families. Yet even with such compelling data many are reluctant to donate organs. This has been true in the Catholic culture, among others.

In the past the Catholic *principle of totality* taught that "mutilation" of the body for other than the health of the patient's own body is wrong. As late as the middle of the last century Catholics were cautioned against such things as kidney donation to save the life of a relative.[9] Behind the principle was the belief that one could not attack (mutilate) the biological integrity of the human body except to cure it (removing a gangrenous limb, cutting out a tumor). Cunningham extended the principle to include not only the good of the patient but the good of humankind, suggesting that donation of an organ to another was a contribution to the good of the totality of humanity. With this new perspective, persons were encouraged to donate a part of their own living bodies even at tremendous sacrifice to themselves.

Pius XII cautioned that, since the human body is "the abode of a spiritual and immortal soul," and "is destined of resurrection and eternal life,"[10] it must not be treated as a thing nor may its integrity be compromised. Although the pope goes on to affirm the efficacy of donating one's body for good reasons to the causes of science (cadaverous organ transplants were not yet done in the 1950s, so the pope's remarks had to do with donation of bodies to medical schools), he sets certain guidelines for its proper care.

Catholics believe in the resurrection. For many this has been understood as a reassembling of the buried body from its grave. In the past the emphasis on teaching about resurrection has been on the saving of the individual soul. The Catechism with which many now elderly Catholics grew up asks: "Why did God make me?" The answer: "To show forth [God's] goodness and to share with me the everlasting happiness of heaven." *My* salvation was key, and it was envisioned as a reunion of body and soul in the beatific vision.

Modern Catholic reticence to donate body organs after death may stem from this construct of resurrection from earlier times. A more contemporary theology of resurrection, not unlike that found in Paul, does not see resurrection in that vein. Paul speaks of the resurrected body as different from the physical body. He is not altogether clear, however, on what that means or in what way the resurrected body is different from the body of the alive person.[11] What is clear, however, is that resurrection is NOT the same as resuscitation.

Modern eschatology (a study of the last things: death, judgment, heaven, and hell) emphasizes not only a future heavenly reality—about which we really know very little—but the present earthly reality. This focus calls us to make things just and good in the here and now, in the only world that we can currently know. Life after life is a continuum. And the activities of the now—concern for others, working for justice, making the world a better place—count in what we refer to as "resurrection."

Included in this new vision is a retrieval of a neglected Hebrew scripture image of resurrection. In the graphic passage from Ezekiel (37:1–14), it is not the "dry bones" of an individual that are raised, it is the whole people of Israel. They are brought back, animated by God's spirit, and returned to their land. "Heaven," as Zachary Hayes notes, "is not simply a question of individual salvation. The relational and corporate nature of humanity remains even here where all human relations are brought to a new depth of fulfillment in the final relationship with God."[12] Resurrection is not a prescription for individual salvation but one of *personal* fulfillment in the Catholic vision of person as radically connected to one another and to the world. It is a prescription to make the world better. At the end of life, it is the wonder drug which holds the promise of a better death.

As we return to the question from which this digression on Christian eschatology began, part of the answer to how a realized eschatology (a focus on the God in our midst rather than only on a future fulfillment) may take the form of organ donation. Today the posthumous gift of organs by Catholics is strongly encouraged. John Paul II calls it an "act of self-giving, that sincere gift of self which expresses our constitutive calling to love and communion."[13] It offers the dying person a final opportunity to give literally of himself for the good of others. Are we not called, like Jesus, to have our deaths bring life? Is not the broken bread of Eucharist rent precisely to vivify those come to the table? This is the picture dramatized in the modern French movie *Jesus of Montreal*, where the contemporary actor who plays Jesus is killed. The final scene shows his various organs being life-flighted for transplantation into the dying bodies of others. The donation of the body, which is integral to personhood and through which we have expressed and experienced our relatedness in life, is a final gift of love.

There is a marvelous story told by Richard Selzer about a woman who wanted to listen to her husband's heart once more, the heart which she had donated after he was killed in an accident. After contacting the man who had received the organ, Hannah's persistent wish to hear her husband's heart once more was reluctantly granted by the recipient. She went to visit him. For several minutes she bent over the man's chest, listening to the regular and familiar beat. "At last Hannah opened her eyes and raised her head. Never had she felt such a sense of consolation."[14] For one woman the knowledge, and indeed the experience of the gift she had given, was solace for her loss.

There are some difficulties with the donation of organs that must be addressed. First, following from the inviolability of personal freedom, no one should ever be coerced to donate organs or to pressure loved ones to do so. A gift is a free and generous donation. In the highly stressed situation that surrounds death, the compromise of freedom is easily made.

Second, the proposal that organs could be bought and sold is not consistent with a Catholic perspective. While the shortage of organs has prompted the entertainment of commerce of bodily parts,[15] such activity makes of the human body a commodity. It frames the choice in utilitarian terms rather than in terms that respect the dignity of human beings in all their aspects, including their bodily reality. Even the bodies of the dead are still human bodies. The *Catholic Directives* are most clear on both points, "Further, the freedom of the donor must be respected, and economic advantages should not accrue to the donor."[16]

Third, the question of when a living human being, whose body is sacrosanct, turns into a corpse, whose parts may be disbursed for others' good has been the subject of heated debate. The old criterion which saw death as the termination of the heartbeat has given way to use of brain death as a criterion for a final pronouncement of life's end. Hearts can be kept beating, which keeps organs functionally alive until such time as they can be removed for transplant. Catholic teaching has insisted that death must occur before organs may be removed for transplant. It is not appropriate to invade the body to prepare it for transplant before death (whole brain death) has occurred. It would not be appropriate, then, to use the organs of a person in PVS or those of an anencephalic *until and unless* that person's total brain has stopped functioning. This is a decision completely separate from whether or not continued *treatment* in such a case is warranted.

As we die, what responsibility have we to the common good in decisions we make about our end-of-life care? When is it appropriate to utilize expensive and scarce treatments and equipment? Although the impact on others—the common good—may not be readily apparent ("After all, my insurance pays") what I choose in the narrowness of my hospital room has repercussions well beyond its walls. The desk of the dying always bears the weight of unfinished business. There are things we are unable to say; there are people we cannot join with any longer, either because the grace to do so is not ours or they are incapable of overcoming the breach between us. That is all right. As Christians we trust that God will make up for us what we cannot do ourselves. The limits of the human person are not only physical limits—I still yearn for the unattainable WNBA contract—but the limits of our own psyche and the grace that is given us. That's why there is God. As we lay dying, we must come to grips with these limits, forgive ourselves and others, and embrace the mercy of the divine.

As my mother went through the dying process, the family experienced a number of months before the actual day of death arrived. During that time Mom would not eat, content to wait for death in a passive stance.[17] I had read books about final words and final intimate conversations. I so wanted to talk with my mother in ways that expressed my love and would assure her that dying was OK and that she could talk with me about anything she wanted. Nevertheless I was still her little girl who longed to rest my head on her shoulder and cry, because my mother was dying. I was unable to deliver the meaningful words and have the wonderful conversations that gestated my expectant imagination.

Since the dying process had taken a number of months, my family and I took a weekend off, leaving Mom in the care of a competent nurse. About two hours before we arrived home, my mother died. It had been her "plan" that we would not be with her for the final passage, since she wished to spare us what she thought would be a difficult experience. The execution of her plan meant that I would never be able to frame the "good" conversations that my romantic imagination had constructed.

Later I discovered that she had the "important" conversation about death several times, but not with me. The parish priest, who had visited her a number of times during her final illness, provided the nonthreatening ear that the daughter had been unable to give. I had wanted to give the gift. I had wanted to share the intimate "final words" with her. I had wanted to control the last minutes of my mother's life. I had wanted to be with her, saying all those good things that people wish they would have said. It was not to be. Mom had recognized my psychological "shortness" and realized that I was unable to play in the NBA of human interaction where the final "game" would be conversations about important things and about death itself. She, with utter graciousness, gave her final gift by respecting my limits.

Do I regret this? Certainly. Do I wish it could be undone? Of course. But I must realize, as she did, that things are as they are. As I write these words, tears come. They are tears no longer of regret, but of gratitude for the love of a mother. Like the God she respected and served, she knew how to stay in the background and allow what is to be. She understood and respected her own autonomy and the limitations of others.

Why do I share this story? Probably to some degree to revisit my own history, to assure myself twenty years later that there wasn't really more I was capable of doing at the time. But most importantly, it is an illustration of the messiness of human life, the inability of us all to orchestrate how each moment will play out. The sovereignty of God ultimately charts the course of our lives. The final exit for human beings is through the doors of death into the waiting arms of the divine.

The human person lives her life. She does what she can to create herself. Now how does she end her life? A good death is the continuation of the awesome mystery of a good life, not necessarily a great life, but a life adequate to the call of God to us.

Ultimately, each experience of death is unique. As each human person comes into life a one-only version of the spark of God. Each person builds a life of wonder and hope that only he or she can live. At life's end, each hopes for an experience of dying that is congruent with the person's chosen life path. For all, however, this path is companioned by the footsteps of others. The parousia is a celebration of personal uniqueness and of communal interdependence. It is a party where gifts are exchanged and life is celebrated.

QUESTIONS FOR DISCUSSION

1. What is hospice? What services does it provide? When should it be suggested to patients and families?
2. What patients could benefit from hospice care?
3. How can dying persons and their loved ones bring closure in the mutual giving of gifts?

NOTES

1. Anonymous, "Hush, Little Baby," *The Fireside Book of Children's Songs*, ed. Marie Winn (New York: Simon & Schuster, 1966), 12.

2. Bob Merrill and Jule Styne, "People," *Great Songs of Broadway* (New York: Quadrangle, 1973), 260.

3. *Hospice Care: A Physician's Guide* (Arlington, Va.: National Hospice Organization, 1998), 12. This small book is a user-friendly guide which would be helpful not only to its intended audience of physicians but to families of the dying. Interested care-givers might call the office at 703/243-5900 or visit the organization online at http://www.nho.org.

4. "Hospice: A Service That Satisfies—But Is Unavailable to Many Dying Americans," *State Initiatives in End-of-Life Care* 17 (November 2002): 2.

5. See appendixes for ideas on how to approach these questions.

6. Ira Byock, *Dying Well: Peace and Possibilities at the End of Life* (New York: Riverhead Books, 1997), 140.

7. The new law took effect in June 2002. Any written instructions *before* that date do not override familial preference. If people wish to be sure that their wishes to donate organs are honored, it would be wise for them to update their instructions.

8. Pence, *Recreating*, 39. Statistics from 1988–1998 indicate a growing number of deaths each year by those awaiting major organs such as hearts, lungs, kidneys, and livers.

9. David Kelly discusses this piece of Catholic history, citing Bert Cunningham's work on organ transplants in the mid 1940s. See *Emergence*, 267–69.

10. Pius XII, "Tissue Transplantation" (May 14, 1956), *The Human Body: Papal Teachings*, 380–83, reprinted in Kevin D. O'Rourke and Philip Boyle, *Medical Ethics: Sources of Catholic Teachings*, 2nd ed. (Washington, D.C.: Georgetown University Press, 1993), 218.

11. I Cor. 15:35–49. Paul's stream of consciousness midrash leaves the reader puzzled as to what the difference between the physical body and that beyond the grave. Maybe puzzlement is what he had in mind.

12. Zachary Hayes, *Visions of a Future: A Study of Christian Eschatology* (Wilmington, Del.: Michael Glazier, 1989), 198.

13. John Paul II, "Many Ethical, Legal, and Social Questions Must Be Examined in Greater Depth" (June 20, 1991), *Dolentium Hominum,* Vatican Press 1992, n. 3, 12–13; reprinted in O'Rourke and Boyle, *Sources*, 220.

14. Richard Selzer, "Whither Thou Goest," *The Doctor Stories* (New York: Picador, 1998), 81.

15. Pence, *Recreating*, 42, argues that monetary incentives actually create choices for people, and that objections to exchanging money for body parts is "more of an aesthetic objecion than a moral one."

16. *Directives, 30.*

17. Contrary to common understanding that persons who refuse food die quickly, my mother lived for nearly six months with little more than a few sips of water and a few spoonfuls of cereal each day. Every time anyone tried to introduce solid food, she would remove it from her mouth with a tissue.

Chapter Ten

The Final Blessing: Religious and Pastoral Dimensions of Dying

"Go in peace to love and serve the Lord."

Catholics with any degree of liturgical awareness recognize the last words they hear before they leave Sunday Mass: "Go in peace to love and serve the Lord." As they shuffle to retrieve coats or canes, children, or wayward Cheerios on the church floor, the words linger into the music of the processional hymn. Although likely the words are not often interpreted in this way, they are an appropriate send off to those who die.

Human beings have always sought out ritual as an expression of meaning and a celebration of life's important events. Several thousand years before Abraham lived, human communities were burying their dead with care and with ceremony. The familiar movements and words that comprise liturgical observance ground us in the real and connect us to one another as well as to the transcendent. Ritual can be ordinary, the peek-a-boo games of childhood, or very special, the high holy days of Lent to Easter. In contemporary life and in the Catholic context we need rituals to help us face the illogical realities we name sickness and death.

The human condition causes us all to seek for meaning: to search out answers for why life happens as it does and for whether there is anything logical or just to blunt the pain and suffering that we all experience. Within the Catholic tradition there are two rituals, sacraments, which are designed to address illness and dying. They offer solace as well as an answer to the questions of what life is about.

The first is called Anointing of the Sick. As early as the ninth century, church communities celebrated anointing of the infirm to heal physical illness and to strengthen the spirit. Especially in cultures that did not understand the

171

biological origins of sickness, it was important to make sense of it in some way. Later (about the twelfth century), the focus shifted from healing and consolation to the forgiveness of sin, an extension of the biblical admonition to forgive sinners.[1] As time went on, the sacrament's occasion of celebration got pushed closer and closer to the time of death. Before the Second Vatican Council families generally waited until a dying person's last breath to call the priest. Likely this delay reflected a denial of death or a fear that the summoning of the priest amounted to admitting human defeat. Further, it was believed that dying persons should be the last to know their terminal condition. To call the priest was to admit to the patient as well as to the family that death was imminent. In this extreme context it was the priest's function to perform the "last rites" over the body. Somehow, the perceived magic actions of the priest brought comfort to the sad space of grief. Nevertheless the ceremonies often did little to comfort the patient, who likely was beyond cognizance of what was going on. In any case, the sacrament was not often a celebration for the dying; it became the first of two celebrated for the dead.

In the post-Vatican church the elements of the sacrament which emphasize healing of body and spirit have been retrieved. The new rite for the sacrament of anointing underlines the importance of its efficacy for the sick as well as those who care for them. It remembers body and spirit, providing a ritual that addresses the integral whole of the human person as well as the place of the sick within the community.[2]

Joseph Martos has pointed out the retrieved communal dimension of the sacrament, that "relatives and friends, nurse and doctors, are invited to take part in the sacramental ministry of the priest by praying with him when he comes for his visit."[3] Hopefully the "visit" occurs periodically during a serious or terminal illness. It is inappropriate to delay the celebration of the sacrament until moments before death. It is recommended that it not be "saved" for a one-time event but celebrated whenever serious illness is present.

For caregivers and sick persons alike, such ritual has many benefits. First, sacramental celebration brings the community together in a frank appreciation of God's action in human lives, God's constant love and care. Second, the use of physical elements—in this case the oil or the bread and wine of Eucharist—make connections between the things of Earth and the things of God. To have the sick touched for reasons other than taking blood pressure, turning to keep bed sores at bay, inserting needles, and other necessary medical interventions is to remind them that they are more than simply a dying body. Oil is soothing, the sign of king-making,[4] the lubrication used for body massage, the mark on the athlete of old as he began a race. It is the promise of greatness, the reminder of vitality, a sign of human bodily connection. How fitting for honoring the body at any time. How particularly important as the body faces its own decay.

Several years ago I delivered a series of lectures at a retreat for ministers. The organizers had put together a prayer service in which all the participants were to gather in a circle and each in turn was to anoint the person next to them. As it happened, I was placed next to an older man who lived alone and whose only outside contact was his ministry in the parish. After the service and after I had anointed him—completely by chance since he happened to be next to me in the circle—he remarked that this was the first time he had been touched in a long time. No one ever touched him. Since he lived a solitary life and had no relatives, there was little opportunity for him to experience any physical human contact. The soothing touch of a contrived ceremony offered him something not available to him in another context. The experience was a sacramental moment both for him and for me.

Although many who are sick and close to death are likely touched, since they require medical and comfort care, it is likely that they are rarely touched in other ways—as human beings on an equal footing with their caregivers. The sacrament of the anointing allows that opportunity. It reminds the dying that they are more than an ailing biological organism; they have a unique dignity in God's image.

The third element in the sacrament of the anointing is that of reconciliation. We talked in the last chapter about closure, the need for human intersection that brings forgiveness of self and of others, that says "I am sorry." Sometimes we limited human beings do not have the psychological "right stuff" to do this well or even to do this at all. Steve, the quiet man who learned to take the five things of relationship completion and integrate them into his dying, may be the exception rather than the rule of people who find it difficult to forgive in life. Kubler-Ross has remarked that people live as they die: passive or pugnacious; communal or individualistic. Sacramental celebrations remind us that God can and does make up what we lack. God forgives us when we cannot forgive ourselves; God builds bridges which we are too weak, either physically or psychologically, to complete. The sacrament can raise human ordinariness to a new dimension. The saving action we name "sacrament" effects what our limited selves may be incapable of doing. Its effect, notes Martos, "should be a personal encounter with God as a transcendent source of strength and power, and a trusting cooperation with the grace of inner and outer healing."[5]

Fourth, the sacrament of the dying includes the sacred meal of Eucharist. We speak of communion as "bread of life" and "cup of salvation." In the sacrament of the sick the elements of nourishment, often for persons who no longer can take pleasure or receive benefit from ordinary food and drink, perform the function of pointing to the divine and of communication with those present in a real "banquet," food for the journey—as the scripture tells us. Is it not this life to which the rest of life points?

The second ritual is not listed among the seven of the church. It occurs immediately after the passing of the person into new life. There may be tears, undoubtedly there is sorrow. There may be a last touching of the still-warm corpse and the disbelief that death really has taken someone loved. There may be the mixture of emotion: sadness, anger, regret, even relief that the ordeal is done. There may be the need to process new feelings. "The dying body and the dead body acquire terrifying qualities. These bodies render visible the processes which are denied in the pursuit of an ideal which rests upon the control of bodily boundaries," observes Hallam and her coauthors.[6] Seeing death in another brings us to face it for ourselves. It is not an easy event. The hardship is more pronounced when the deceased is a young person or a child.

The rubrics are predictable. The body is removed. The empty room stands as mute testimony to life departed. After the sickroom has been stripped of its central character, the sheets have been torn away, the other reminders of death to life have been removed. The cross is empty. Calls are made to relatives and friends, announcing the passing. Perhaps the priest is called and final prayers are said above the corpse. The family is consoled. The body is transported, cleaned, dressed, and prepared by the funeral home for its final social hour. Papers are signed certifying that what was witnessed has indeed occurred. Sorting between the atmosphere of shock and sadness the family prepares final tidbits of news for the obituary and begins to think about the funeral service.

These rituals of the ordinary tie those of us left both to the deceased and to the realness of the life that is left. It is important that we give ourselves over to them. The Benedictines have a motto: *Ora et labora* (pray and work). We are beings that need the dirty dishes—or soiled bed linens—of life as well as the peak moments of prayer that point to the afterlife. The rituals of cleaning up after the death, the preparations for the funeral, all are important elements in the process of grieving. For those who assist the grieving, for those who do pastoral work with families of the dying, it is important not to swoop in and perform tasks which those who are in sorrow may need to heal their own hurt. It is not only the "*ora*" which heals, it is also the "*labora*."

The final ritual for Catholics is the celebration of the funeral liturgy and the burial. Ordinarily the body is brought to church, covered with a white cloth symbolizing resurrection, and incensed with respect. Today, since the church allows Catholics the option of cremation if they prefer, a memorial service may be substituted. The familiar actions and songs, motions and words of Eucharist draw us in and anoint us with healing. If the family wishes, they may have a part in planning the liturgy. Pastoral ministers should help in this task, guiding the planners to appropriate readings and songs. The central focus of any sacrament is the saving action of God. Even a funeral liturgy should not be primarily a maudlin tribute to the dead but should concentrate on the joy of God's love and the conquest by that love of death and sin. While some few words remembering the life celebrated may be spoken, they should not be the central focus of the ritual.

Religion and religious ritual are not simply an attempt to keep the wrath of God at bay as we obey the rules and offer to God the pains of living. Not simply a quick fix—when we have exhausted our other alternatives, let's plead with the divine to fix it. Rather, religious practice is the entering into a relationship with love, and with the God who loves.

For Christians the gospel is the narrative of birth, life, and the passage through death. It is the story not only of the Jesus of history and the Christ of faith, it is the story for all persons who claim kinship with the Son of God. We are called by God to come into life for a few years. During those years we are called to create ourselves in our relationships with our bodily selves, with others, with the earth, and in all of these with God.

This book has been at attempt to celebrate life and to make the dying process better for those who face it themselves and those who accompany the dying. Many of the stories related here are the life and the death dramas of real people, at whose death bed I have stood and cried and at whose funerals I have sung and been healed.

May we all die in the arms of friends. May we leave a legacy of ourselves in love, forgiveness, and stories of our own wonderful, unique lives lived out in pursuit of relationship with God and therefore with one another. We are fallible; we are limited; we see these wounds in the diseases that affect our bodies and distress our spirits.

The gospels and epistles of John remind us of the need to become young as we die. We are God's "little children," beloved disciples (learners) as we explore our unique path of life. We are asked, like the disciples, to "come and see," to taste the bread of life. Having dined at the royal banquet of the liturgy, having passed through the darkness of death we come alive again in a sacred time and sacred space which "eye has not seen nor ear heard (1 Cor. 2:9). May we all die with the taste of chocolate on our tongues, a fitting foretaste of eternal life. May we all go in peace to love and serve the Lord!

QUESTIONS FOR DISCUSSION

1. Describe the two official rituals in Catholic tradition that can ease the process of grieving. What can be done to make these rituals more effective for the community of the bereaved?
2. Describe the "rituals of the ordinary" that accompany death. What is their value?

NOTES

1. In the first several centuries of Christianity it was not clear what happened with those who, after having been baptized, turned away from Christ by serious sin (adultery, murder, apostasy) and now wanted to return to the Christian community. One solution was to put off Baptism until death was imminent. This practice probably was the genesis of a sacrament of forgiveness that many old Catholics would recognize (Extreme Unction).

2. Modern sacramental theology emphasizes the communal nature of divine mediation of God's saving acts (the sacraments). A former theology tended to interpret sacramental action in a much narrower and individualistic, almost magical manner.

3. Joseph Martos, *Doors to the Sacred: A Historical Introduction to Sacraments in the Catholic Church* (Tarrytown: Triumph Books, 1981), 339.

4. The term we use for Jesus, "messiah," means anointed one.

5. Martos, *Doors*, 339.

6. Hallam (1999), *Beyond the Body*, 21.

Appendix One

Composing a Personal Advance Directive

What is the ideal picture I have of the last days of my life.

Where would I like to be? (Inside? Outside? At home? In a hospital? At some other location?)

What would I be doing?

Who would be with me? Do I wish to be touched or held?

What would I like to eat or drink?

How would I like to be?

Awake? Asleep?

Treated aggressively by medical means?

Comfortable (with symptoms controlled by medication)?

Suffering naturally (short of breath, in pain, worried)?

What would I need to feel spiritually prepared?

Priest (to talk with, to celebrate final sacraments, just for comfort)?

Solitude (to make peace with myself)?

Last conversation with particular people?

Do I feel that I am already spiritually ready for death?

How many days would I want to prepare for death? Would I prefer to die suddenly?

What else would accompany my ideal death (music, readings, special objects)?

Appendix Two

Creating a Personal Autobiography

The Past:

What are my favorite stories?

What are my most cherished memories?

What friends have enriched my life?

What hurts do I bear that I want healed before I die?

The Present:

Who am I now?

What do I value?

What can I still do now?

What unfinished business remains in my life?

The Future:

What do I want to do before I leave life?

Who would I like to see?

Where would I like to go?

What is my ultimate concern (what gives my life its meaning and motivates me)?

GLOSSARY

Active euthanasia—the direct and intentional ending of the life of another with or without that person's consent

Advance directives—Documents by which people indicate their wishes regarding health care in the event that they are temporarily or permanently unable to speak for themselves. Such documents take legal form as living wills or durable powers of attorney for health care. While verbal advance directives do not enjoy the legal standing of written documents, they should be taken seriously from a moral perspective and honored by those charged with making decisions for care. Living wills may not have legal status until or unless the person is in a terminal condition.

Anencephaly—congenital absence of all or a major part of the brain and bones of the skull. The condition is incompatible with life for more than a few hours.

Anthropology—the study of the characteristics of human persons

Aortic balloon—an inflatable device inserted into the major artery (aorta) to supplement the normal pumping action of the heart, when that organ's pumping is insufficient to supply needed blood to the rest of the body

Artificial feeding—nourishment by temporary or permanent tubes inserted intervenously or into the intestinal tract and through which nutrients and water can be administered

Assisted suicide—the act of helping others to die by their own hands

Autonomy—self-governance or self-determination. Autonomy includes the concepts of freedom of choice and freedom of action as well as whatever is needed for effective deliberation of choices. In the Catholic tradition freedom and knowledge are prerequisites for moral agency.

Basic goods—a list of human-worthy values which are never to be acted against in moral decision-making

Beneficence—the principle of medical ethics that states that persons have a duty to help others

Best interest standard—decisions about treatment made in the absence of any knowledge of patient preference or values

Brain death—the final cessation of activities in the central nervous system, especially as indicated by a flat electroencephalogram for a predetermined length of time; cessation of cerebral (upper cognitive area of brain) and brain stem (lower area, which regulates breathing and other noncognitive activities) function. A person who is brain dead has no respiratory activity, no spontaneous breaths, and no response to stimuli. Spinal reflexes may persist; no movements may be seen. Cardiovascular activity may persist, sometimes for as long as two weeks, but usually there is cardiovascular collapse within several days.

Cardiopulmonary resuscitation—external compression of chest and blowing of air into lungs used to replace normal heart action and breathing

Catholic Directives—*Ethical and Religious Directives for Catholic Health Care Services*, a publication of the National Conference of Catholic Bishops meant to reaffirm ethical standards of health care that flow from Catholic teaching and to provide guidance on certain moral issues facing Catholic health care

Central line—tube places in one of the larger veins (blood vessels which travel to the heart) to administer fluids, medication, and/or nutrition

Cerebrum—the largest and most highly developed portion of the brain, the cerebral hemispheres; the seat of conscious, voluntary, and intellectual human functioning

Coma—A state of pathological unconsciousness in which patients are unaware of their environment and are unarousable. Patients in coma may progress to a vegetative state, although this is not associated with an improvement in their overall functional outcome.

Common good—the idea that all persons are entitled to a participation in benefits of the goods of society. Common good demands the protection of the dignity and human rights of all.

Competence—a legal term that judges that persons have the mental capacity to carry on their own affairs

Do not resuscitate order (DNR)—a written order that must be signed by the physician that instructs the medical team not to initiate measures to restart a heart that has stopped beating

Double Effect Principle—a tool for decision-making in cases where an anticipated action has more than one effect and not all the effects are in themselves good. The agent satisfies the principle if he or she, with a good intention, purposely aims at the good effect or consequences; and the evil effect is not greater than the good that is done (due proportion of good over evil).

Durable power of attorney for health care (DPAHC)—the person or the legal document which names that person to make decisions for another, when that other is no longer able to make decisions for themselves. The powers of the DPAHC may be limited by particular states laws, specifically in the areas of removal of life support or artificial nutrition and hydration, unless the principle has specified in writing what is wished.

Endotrachial tube—a tube placed within the trachea (the major tube through which one breathes) to directly inflate the lungs

Eschatology—The branch of theological study which considers the "last things," namely death, judgment, heaven, hell

Euthanasia—in Greek, "good death." Usually refers to the taking of the life of another with benevolent reasons, with or without their consent. The term is used in the Netherlands to refer to sanctioned physician-assisted suicide.

Extraordinary means—In medicine any means to a medical end in which the burden to the patient, and from the point of view of the patient, is greater than the benefit expected. Such evaluations are always case specific. They are not a judgment of the extraordinariness of the *medical* intervention but rather of the *moral* considerations of how burdensome the considered intervention is to this particular patient. The Catholic moral tradition sees anything that is considered extraordinary not to be morally obligatory.

Futile treatment—a medical intervention that will not achieve its goal. Treatment can be deemed futile in cases where the patient's values indicate that the benefit does not outweigh the benefit, even if the medical standards for futility are not met.

Gaudium et Spes (The Church in the Modern World)—one of the documents from the Second Vatican Council

Hidden agenda—those things beneath the level of human consciousness which may influence our behavior

Hospice—a concept and an organized method of caring for the dying and for their caregivers. The goal of hospice is the best quality of life for as long as the patient lives. Hospice can include nursing care, palliation, and other kinds of therapy and services aimed at the psychological and spiritual needs of patients and families.

Impediments—anything that lessens a person's freedom or knowledge either preceding or during moral action. Impediments may lessen or eliminate a person's moral responsibility.

Informed consent—the notion that for medical treatment and procedures the patient must understand the risks and benefits of the anticipated intervention and give assent

Intended and foreseen consequences—terms used in moral theology to distinguish between results of a particular actions that are the aim of the agent (intended consequences) and those which the agent knows will happen but which are unavoidable (foreseen consequences) but not directly intended. *Bad* foreseen consequences always must be proportionately less in their evil than the good that is intended, and to be regretted by the agent; if they are to be considered part of a morally good moral decision.

Intensive Care Unit (ICU)—a specialized area of the hospital in which sophisticated technology and intervention are used to resuscitate, maintain, or improve the condition of a seriously ill patient

IV (intervenous tube)—a tube inserted into the vein

Living Will—a legal document that specifies in writing the wishes of a person regarding medical treatment should that person not be able to indicate preferences. Living wills generally are used to specify whether a person wishes such treatments as respirator support or artificial feeding in the event that there is a terminal medical condition.

Lou Gehrigs' disease (amyotrophic lateral sclerosis)—a disease of the nervous system characterized by progressive weakness, until the patient is no longer strong enough to breathe and/or swallow

Moral evil—actions, freely chosen, which counteract a value; sin. E.g., murder, stealing

Morphine—an opiode, one of a group of powerful pain-killing medications

Nasogastric tube—a plastic tube inserted through the nose, down the esophagus, and into the stomach for the purpose of feeding or removal of fluids

Neocortical death—the irreversible loss of function of the "upper" brain (cerebrum, not brain stem)

Nonmaleficence—the principle of bioethics that states that people have an obligation not to harm others

Ontic evil—physical, nonmoral, or premoral evil, that is, any reality that has a negative impact on human persons but is not freely and deliberately chosen. E.g., sickness, natural disasters, accidents

Ordinary (and extraordinary means)—in the Catholic tradition those interventions which are effective and/or carry with them only a proportionate burden are called "ordinary." (Interventions which either are not effective or, if effective, carry with them a disproportionate burden are called "extraordinary." Such classifications are always case-specific and cannot be applied based on the generally accepted simplicity, availability, or low cost of the intervention.)

Palliative care—relief of symptoms which cause suffering, including but not limited to control of pain. Palliative care does not aim to cure but to provide all the necessary relief to patients and families, including assistance with decision-making, psychological, spiritual, and financial issues.

Passive euthanasia—in the Catholic tradition the noninitiation or the removal of life-sustaining technologies or interventions when it is determined that they are futile

Patient Self-Determination Act (PSDA)—federal law passed in 1991 which requires that patients entering hospitals or nursing homes be asked if they have or wish to have advance directives

Percutaneous endoscopic gastrostomy (PEG tube)—a tube placed through the abdominal wall or stomach wall to provide a way of administering fluids, nutrients, and/or medication

Persistent Vegetative State (PVS)—A state of eyes-open unconsciousness with sleep-wake cycles in which the patients are not aware of themselves or their environment. The condition of persons in a subset of patients who suffer server anoxic brain injury and progress to an enduring state of wakefulness without awareness

Personalism—the philosophy, popularized in the earlier part of the twentieth century in Europe, which places the human person and human acts at the center of the moral project

Portable DNR—legal document by which a patient can indicate a wish not to be resuscitated in the event that the heart or breathing stops. The document must be signed by a medical doctor and does not require that the patient be in a terminal condition.

Proportion—assessment of nonmoral good and evil which will be part of the overall consequences of an action. Actions with proportion will have more good in the total consequences than evil. Such actions are, by proportionate standards, morally right actions.

Proportionate reason—in Catholic moral theology the assessment that the good in the consequences outweigh the evil. It does not refer to a logical or good reason as the basis for doing an action that would otherwise be immoral.

Reasonable person standard—a decision-maker should be given the amount of information necessary for a "reasonable" person to make a decision; the reasonable person standard is not a judgment about how reasonable the decision itself may be

Relativism—a moral position that holds that anyone's values and moral perspective is equally as good as another's; choice of one's perspective is arbitrary

Respirator—an apparatus for administrating artificial respiration in cases of respiratory failure.

Resuscitation—all interventions that may be done in an attempt to maintain life. Resuscitation includes such things as IV fluids, medications, compressions of the chest, and ventilation.

Subjective standard—the wishes of competent patients (subjects) about the sort of medical intervention they want; the previously expressed written or oral wishes for treatment of patients who now is unable to express preferences for treatment. Such preferences should be applied as the "standard" of care for these patients.

Substituted judgment—decisions are made by a surrogate, whose decision takes the place of the decision of a person who is unable to decide fore themselves. Substituted judgment should be based on the values and/or known wishes of the patient, rather than on those of the proxy or surrogate.

Suicide—the intentional and direct taking of one's own life

Terminal condition—the judgment that a person has a disease or illness which will likely take result in death within a short period of time, sometimes as long as six months

Terminal sedation—a term used to indicate the use of medication sufficient to relieve pain in the dying which may cause the dying person to lose consciousness and remain unable to communicate

Totality, principle of—the good of the part may be sacrificed for the whole, such as the removal of a diseased organ to preserve the entire body's health

Vasopressors—a medicine which stimulates a contraction of the blood vessels and produces a desirable rise in blood pressure

Vatican II (Second Vatican Council)—a meeting with representation from the whole church held in Rome between1962–1965. It was the twenty-third general council of the Catholic Church.

Ventilator—equipment used to maintain a flow of air into and out of the lungs of a patient who is unable to breathe normally

Vitalism—the belief that all life, even vegetative life, should be aggressively preserved

Whole brain death—the condition in which both the upper (cerebrum) and lower (brain stem) portions of the brain have ceased to function

Bibliography

Ackerman, Terrence F. "The Moral Implication of Medical Uncertainty: Tube Feeding Demented Patients." *Journal of the American Geriatrics Society* 44, no. 10 (1996): 1265–67.

American Bishops. *The Challenge of Peace: God's Promise and Our Response.* Washington, D.C.: United States Catholic Conference, 1983.

American Medical Association. "Principles of Medical Ethics (1980)." In *Biomedical Ethics*, edited by Thomas A. Mappes and Jane S. Zembaty. 3rd ed., 54. New York: McGraw-Hill, 1991.

Angell, Marcia. "The Case of Helga Wanglie." *The New England Journal of Medicine* 325, no. 7 (April 15, 1991): 511–12.

Ashley, Benedict. "Dominion or Stewardship: Theological Reflections." in *Birth, Suffering, and Death*, edited by Kevin W. Wildes et al., 85–106. Boston: Kluwer Academic Publishers, 1992.

Barth, Karl. *Church Dogmatics.* Vol III, no. 4, edited by G. W. Bromley and T. F. Torrance, translated by A. T. Mackay, et al. Edinburgh: T. & T. Clark, 1960.

Bascom, Paul B., and Susan W. Tolle. "Responding to Requests for Physician-Assisted Suicide." *Journal of the American Medical Association* 288, no. 1 (July 3, 2002): 91–98.

Becker, Ernest. *Denial of Death.* New York: The Free Press, 1973.

Bernardi, Peter J. "The Hidden Engines of the Suicide Rights Movement." *America* 172, no. 16 (May 6, 1995):14–17.

Bernardin, Joseph. *Consistent Ethic of Life.* Kansas City, Mo.: Sheed and Ward, 1988.

Boer, Theo A. "After the Slippery Slope: An Evaluation of the Dutch Experiences on Regulating Active Euthanasia." Paper presented at the annual meeting of the Society of Christian Ethics, Pittsburgh, Pennsylvania, January 10, 2003.

Bohr, David. *Catholic Moral Tradition.* Huntington, Ill.: Our Sunday Visitor, 1999.

Borthwick, Chris. "The Proof of the Vegetable: A Commentary on Medical Futility." *Journal of Medical Ethics* 21, no. 4 (August 1995): 205–208.

Bresnahan, James F. "Killing and Letting Die: A Moral Distinction Before the Courts." *America* 17, no. 3 (February 1, 1997): 8–16.

———. "Palliative Care or Assisted Suicide?" *America* 178, no. 8 (March 14, 1998): 16–21.

Brody, Howard. "The Physician's Role in Determining Futility." *Journal of the American Geriatrics Society* 42 (August 1994): 875–78.

Bruera, Eduardo, and Neil MacDonald. "To Hydrate or Not to Hydrate: How Should It Be?" *Journal of Clinical Oncology* 18, no. 5 (March 2000): 1156–58.

Byock, Ira. *Dying Well: Peace and Possibilities at the End of Life.* New York: Riverhead Books, 1997.

Califano, Joseph A. "Physician-Assisted Living." *America* 179, no. 15 (November 14, 1998): 10–12.

Callahan, Daniel. *The Troubled Dream of Life: Living with Mortality.* New York: Simon & Schuster, 1993.

———. "On Feeding the Dying." *Hastings Center Report* 13, no. 5 (October 1983): 22.

———. "When Self-Determination Runs Amok." *Hastings Center Report* 22, no. 2 (March/April 1992): 52–55.

Campbell, Courtney. "Religious Ethics and Assisted Suicide in a Pluralistic Society." *Kennedy Institute of Ethics* 2, no. 3 (1992): 253–58.

Carter, Stephen L. "Rush to a Lethal Judgment." *New York Times Magazine,* July 21, 1996, 28–29.

Christie, Dolores L. *Adequately Considered: An American Perspective on Louis Janssens' Personalist Morals.* Louvain: Peeters Press, 1990.

———. "Relativizing the Absolute: Belief and Bioethics in the Foxholes of Technology." In *Notes from a Narrow Ridge: Religion and Bioethics,* edited by Dena S. Davis and Laurie Zoloth, 87–111. Hagerstown, Md.: University Publishing Group, 1999.

———. "This Is My Body: A Good Friday Reflection." *Emmanuel* 102, no. 3 (April 1996): 152–55.

Cohen-Almagor, Raphael. "A Concise Rebuttal." *Journal of Law, Medicine, and Ethics* 28, no. 3 (fall 2000): 285–86.

Committee for Pro-Life Activities. "Guidelines for Legislation on Life-Sustaining Treatment." Washington, D.C.: National Council of Catholic Bishops, 1984.

Congregation for the Doctrine of the Faith. *Declaration on Euthanasia.* Washington, D.C.: United States Catholic Conference, 1980.

Connors, Russell B. "U.S. Catholic Bishops on Nutrition and Hydration: A Second Opinion." *Journal of Clinical Ethics* 4, no. 3 (fall 1993): 253–55.

Cranford, Ronald E. "The Persistent Vegetative State: the Medical Reality (Getting the Facts Straight)." *Hastings Center Report* 18, no. 1 (February/March 1988): 27–32.

Crigger, Betty-Jane. "Where Do Moral Decisions Come From?" *Hastings Center Report* 26, no. 1 (January/February 1996): 33–38.

Culver, Charles M., and Bernard Gert. "The Definition and Criterion of Death." In *Biomedical Ethics,* edited by Thomas A. Mappes and David DeGrazia. 4th ed., 312–15. New York: McGraw-Hill, Inc., 1996.

Curran, Charles E. *The Catholic Moral Tradition.* Washington, D.C.: Georgetown University Press, 1999.

Davis, Dena S. "Rational Suicide and Predictive Genetic Testing." Unpublished draft. January 15, 1997.

Dekkers, Wim J. M. "Autonomy and Dependence: Chronic Physical Illness and Decision-Making." *Medicine, Health Care and Philosophy* 4, no. 2 (2001): 185–92.

Diem, Susan J., et al. "Cardiopulmonary Resuscitation on Television: Miracles and Misinformation." *The New England Journal of Medicine* 334, no. 24 (June 13, 1996): 1578–82.

Dietzen, John "Are Living Wills Appropriate for Catholics?" *Catholic Universe Bulletin,* February 7, 1997, 9.

Dixon, Nicholas. "On the Difference between Physician-Assisted Suicide and Active Euthanasia." *Hastings Center Report* 28, no. 5 (September/October 1998): 25–29.

Drane, James F. *Clinical Bioethics: Theory and Practice in Medical-Ethical Decision Making.* Kansas City, Mo.: Sheed and Ward, 1994.

Dresser, Rebecca. "Advance Directives: Implications for Policy." *Hastings Center Report* 24, no. 6 (November/December 1994): S 2–S 5.

———. "An Alert and Incompetent Self: The Irrelevance of Advance Directives: Commentary." *Hastings Center Report* 28, no. 1 (February 1998): 28–30.

———. "The Irrelevancy of Advance Directives: Commentary." *Hastings Center Report* 28, no. 1 (January/February 1998): 28–29.

Edson, Margaret. *W;t.* New York: Faber and Faber, 1999.

Emanuel, Ezekiel J., and Linda L. Emanuel. "Living Wills: Past, Present, and Future." *Journal of Clinical Ethics* 1, no. 1 (spring 1990): 9–19.

Emanuel, Linda. "Advance Directives: What Have We Learned So Far?" *Journal of Clinical Ethics* 4, no. 1 (spring 1993): 8–16.

Farley, Margaret A. "Issues in Contemporary Christian Ethics: The Choice of Death in a Medical Context." *The Santa Clara Lectures* 1, no. 3 (May 1, 1995).

Foreman, D. M. "The Family Rule: A Framework for Obtaining Ethical Consent for Medical Interventions from Children." *Journal of Medical Ethics* 25, no. 6 (December 1999): 491–96.

Frankena, William. *Ethics.* Englewood Cliffs, N.J.: Prentice-Hall, 1963.

Fuller, Jon. "Physician-Assisted Suicide: An Unnecessary Crisis." *America* 177, no. 2 (July 19, 1997): 9–12.

Garrow, Andrew, et al. "Anoxic Brain Injury: Assessment and Prognosis." *UpToDate,* 2002 <http://www.utdol.com/application/topic/topicText.asp?file=cc medi/22605> (Sept. 22, 2002).

Gaudium et Spes. The Documents of Vatican II, edited by Walter M. Abbott. New York: America, 1966.

Gauthier, Candace Cummins. "Active Voluntary Euthanasia, Terminal Sedation, and Assisted Suicide." *Journal of Clinical Ethics* 12, no. 1 (spring 2001): 43–50.

Gelineau, Louis. "On Removing Nutrition and Water from Comatose Woman." *Origins* 17, no. 32 (January 21, 1988): 545, 547.

Goold, Door, et al. "Conflicts Regarding Decisions to Limit Treament: A Differential Diagnosis." *Journal of the American Medical Association* 283, no. 7 (February 16, 2000): 909–14.

Grant, Mark D., et al. "Gastrostomy Placement and Mortality Among Hospitalized Medicare Beneficiaries." *Journal of the American Medical Association* 279, no. 24 (January 24, 1988): 1973–76.

Grisez, Germain. *Christian Moral Principles, The Way of the Lord Jesus.* Vol. One. Chicago: Christian Herald Press, 1983.

Guglielmo, Wayne J. "Assisted Suicide? Pain Control? Where's the Line?" *Medical Economics* (October 11, 2002): 48–59.

Gula, Richard M. *Reason Informed by Faith: Foundations of Catholic Morality*. New York: Paulist Press, 1989.

———. *What Are They Saying About Euthanasia?* New York: Paulist Press, 1986.

Hallam, Elizabeth Jenny Hockey, and Glennys Howarth. *Beyond the Body: Death and Social Identity*. New York: Routledge, 1999.

Hallenbeck, James L. "Terminal Sedation: Ethical Implications in Different Situations." *Journal of Palliative Medicine* 3, no. 3 (fall 2002): 313–20.

Hamel, Ron. Paper presented at "Recovering Our Traditions: A Catholic Perspective on End-of-Life Care." Conference sponsored by the Supportive Care of the Dying, Tucson, Arizona, January 23, 2002.

Hanson, Mark J. "Religious Voices in Biotechnology: The Case of Gene Patenting." *Hastings Center Report Special Supplement* 27, no. 6 (November/December 1997): 1–19.

Hardon, John A. *Modern Catholic Dictionary*. Garden City, N.J.: Doubleday and Company, 1980.

Hayes, Zachary. *Visions of a Future: A Study of Christian Eschatology*. Wilmington, Del.: Michael Glazier, 1989.

Hospice Care: A Physician's Guide. Arlington, Va.: National Hospice Organization, 1998.

Howe, Edmund G. "The Vagaries of Patients' and Families' Discussing Advance Directives." *Journal of Clinical Ethics* 4, no. 1 (1993): 3–7.

Jansen, Lynn A., and Daniel P. Sulmasy. "Sedation, Alimentation, Hydration, and Equivocation: Careful Conversation About Care at the End of Life." *Annals of Internal Medicine* 136, no. 11 (June 4, 2002): 845–49.

Janssens, Louis. "Ontic Good and Moral Evil." *Louvain Studies* 4 (1972–1973): 115–56.

———. "Ontic Good and Evil: Premoral Values and Disvalues." *Louvain Studies* 12 (1987): 62–82.

John Paul II. *The Gospel of Life*. Boston: St. Paul's Books and Media, 1995.

———. *Veritatis Splendor*. Washington, D.C.: United States Catholic Conference, 1993.

———. "Many Ethical, Legal, and Social Questions Must Be Examined in Greater Depth." In *Medical Ethics: Sources of Catholic Teachings*, edited by Kevin D. O'Rourke and Philip Boyle. 2nd ed., 220–22. Washington, D.C.: Georgetown University Press, 1993.

Jonas, Hans. "Not Compassion Alone: On Euthanasia and Ethics." (Interview) *Hastings Center Report* 25, no. 7 (Special Issue 1995): 44–50.

Kant, Immanuel. "Suicide." In *Biomedical Ethics*, edited by Thomas A. Mappes and Jane S. Zembaty. 3rd ed., 316–19. New York: McGraw-Hill, 1991.

Kavanaugh, John F. "Killing and Letting Die." *America* 183, no. 8 (September 23, 2000): 23.

———. *Who Count As Persons? Human Identity and the Ethics of Killing*. Washington, D.C.: Georgetown University Press, 2001.

Kaveny, M. Cathleen. "Assisted Suicide, Euthanasia, and the Law." *Theological Studies* 58, no. 1 (March 1997): 124–48.

Keenan, James F. "The Case for Physician-Assisted Suicide?" *America* 179, no. 15 (November 14, 1998): 14–19.

Kelly, David F. *Critical Care Ethics.* Kansas City, Mo.: Sheed and Ward, 1991.

———. *The Emergence of Roman Catholic Ethics in North America.* New York: Edwin Mellen Press, 1979.

Knauer, Peter. "The Hermeneutic Function of the Principle of Double Effect." In *Readings in Moral Theology No. 1: Moral Norms and Catholic Tradition*, edited by Charles E. Curran and Richard A. McCormick, 1–39. New York: Paulist Press, 1979.

Kubler-Ross, Elisabeth. *On Death and Dying.* New York: MacMillan Publishing Company, 1969.

Lantos, John D. "Futility Assessments and the Doctor-Patient Relationship." *Journal of the American Geriatrics Society* 42, no. 8 (August 1994): 868–70.

Lynn, Joanne, and James F. Childress. "Must Patients Always Be Given Food and Water?" *Hastings Center Report* 13, no. 5 (October 1983): 17–21.

Malcolm, Andrew H. "The Ultimate Decision." *The New York Times*, December 3, 1989, 38.

Martos, Joseph. *Doors to the Sacred: A Historical Introduction to Sacraments in the Catholic Church.* Tarrytown: Triumph Books, 1981.

May, William E. *Catholic Bioethics and the Gift of Human Life.* Huntington, Ill.: Our Sunday Visitor, 2000.

May, William E., et al. "Feeding and Hydrating the Permanently Unconscious and Other Vulnerable Persons." *Issues in Law and Medicine* 3, no. 3 (1987): 203–17.

Mayo, David J., and Martin Gunderson. "Vitalism Revitalized." *Hastings Center Report* 32, no. 4 (July/August 2002): 14–21.

McCormick, Richard A. "Bioethics: A Moral Vacuum?" *America* 180, no. 15 (May 1, 1999): 8–12.

———. "'Moral Considerations' Ill Considered." *America* 166, no. 9 (March 14, 1992): 210–14.

———. "To Save or Let Die: The Dilemma of Modern Medicine." In *How Brave a New World? Dilemmas in Bioethics*, 339–51. Garden City, N.J.: Doubleday and Company, 1981.

———. "Vive la Difference! Killing and Allowing to Die," *America* 177, no. 18 (December 6, 1997): 9.

Meier, Diane E. "Palliative Care: What Patients and Families Need to Know." Paper presented in Cleveland, Ohio, April 14, 2001.

Meilaender, Gilbert. "On Removing Food and Water: Against the Stream." *Hastings Center Report* 14, no. 6 (December 1984): 11–13.

Miles, S. H. "Informed Demand for 'Nonbeneficial' Medical Treatment." *New England Journal of Medicine* 325, no. 7 (August 15, 1991): 512–15.

Mouton, Charles P. "Cultural and Religious Issues for African Americans." In *Cutural Issues in End-of-Life Decision Making*, edited by Kathryn L. Braun, James H. Pietsch, and Patricia L. Blanchette, 71–82. Thousand Oaks, Calif.: Sage Publications, 2000.

Murray, Thomas H. "Individualism and Community: The Contested Terrain of Autonomy." *Hastings Center Report* 24, no. 3 (May–June 1994): 32–33.

National Conference of Catholic Bishops. *Ethical and Religious Directives for Catholic Health Care Services*. Washington, D.C.: United States Catholic Conference, 1995.

Nelson, James Lindemann. "Families and Futility." *Journal of the American Geriatrics Society* 42, no. 8 (August 1994): 879–82.

New Jersey State Catholic Conference. "Providing Food and Fluids to Severely Brain Damaged Patients." *Origins* 16 no. 32 (January 22, 1987): 582–84.

New York State Task Force. *When Death Is Sought: Assisted Suicide and Euthanasia in the Medical Context*. New York State Task Force on Life and the Law, 1994.

Nuland, Sherwin B. *How We Die: Reflections on Life's Final Chapter*. New York: Vintage Books, 1995.

O'Connell, Timothy E. *Principles for a Catholic Morality*. Revised edition. New York: Harper & Row, 1990.

O'Rourke, Kevin D. "Evolution of Church Teaching on Prolonging Life." *Health Progress* 69, no. 1 (January/February 1988): 28–35.

———. *A Primer for Health Care Ethics: Essays for a Pluralistic Society*. 2nd ed. Washington, D.C.: Georgetown University Press, 2000.

O'Rourke, Kevin D., and Philip Boyle. *Medical Ethics: Sources of Catholic Teaching*. 2nd. ed. Washington, D.C.: Georgetown University Press, 1993.

Overberg, Kenneth R. *Mercy or Murder*. Kansas City, Mo.: Sheed and Ward, 1993.

Panicola, Michael. "Catholic Teaching on Prolonging Life: Setting the Record Straight." *Hastings Center Report* 31, no. 6 (November/December 2001): 14–25.

Paris, John J., and Richard A. McCormick. "The Catholic Tradition on the Use of Nutrition and Fluids." *America* 156, no. 17 (May 2, 1987): 356–61.

Parry, Richard D. "Death, Dignity and Morality." *America* 179, no. 15 (November 14, 1998): 20–21.

Pellegrino, Edmund D. "The Metamorphosis of Medical Ethics: A 30-Year Retrospective." *Journal of the American Medical Society* 269, no. 9 (March 3, 1993): 1158–62.

Pellegrino, Edmund D., and David C. Thomasma. *Helping and Healing* (Washington, D.C.: Georgetown University Press, 1997.

Pence, Gregory E. *Recreating Medicine: Ethical Issues at the Frontiers of Medicine*. Lanham, Md.: Rowman & Littlefield Publishers, 2000.

Pietsch, James H., and Kathryn L. Braun. "Automony, Advance Directives, and the Patient Self-Determination Act." In *Cultural Issues in End-of-Life Decision Making*, edited by Kathyrn L. Braun, James H. Pietsch, and Patricia L. Blanchette, 37–54. Thousand Oaks, Calif.: Sage Publications, 2000.

Pius XII. "The Intangibility of the Human Person." In *Medical Ethics: Sources of Catholic Teachings*, edited by Kevin D. O'Rourke and Philip Boyle. 2nd ed., 326–28. Washington, D.C.: Georgetown University Press, 1993.

———. "Tissue Transplantation." In *Medical Ethics: Sources of Catholic Teachings*, edited by Kevin D. O'Rourke and Philip Boyle. 2nd ed., 218–19. Washington, D.C.: Georgetown University Press, 1993.

Poorman, Mark L. "The Family in End-of-Life Decisions." *America* 171, no. 12 (October 22, 1994): 12–15.

Quill, Timothy E. "Death and Dignity: A Case of Individualized Decision Making." *The New England Journal of Medicine* 324, no. 10 (March 7, 1991): 691–94.

———. *Midwifing Through the Dying Process*. Baltimore: The Johns Hopkins University Press, 1996.

Rabow, Michael W., and Amy J. Markowitz. "Responding to Requests for Physician-Assisted Suicide 'These Are Uncharted Waters for Both of Us . . .'" *Journal of the American Medical Association* 288, no. 18 (November 13, 2002): 2332.

Rachels, James. "Active and Passive Euthanasia." In *Biomedical Ethics*, edited by Thomas A. Mappes and Jane S. Zembaty. 3rd ed., 367–70. New York: McGraw-Hill, 1991.

Rousseau, Paul C. "Aggressive Treatment in the Terminally Ill: Right or Wrong?" *Journal of Palliative Medicine* 5, no. 5 (October 2002): 657–58.

———. "Palliative Sedation." *American Journal of Hospice and Palliative Care* 19, no. 5 (September/October 2002): 295–97.

Schneiderman, Lawrence J. "Exile and PVS." *Hastings Center Report* 20, no. 3 (May/June 1990): 5.

———. "The Futility Debate: Effective Versus Beneficial Intervention." *Journal of the American Geriatrics Society* 42, no. 8 (August 1994): 883–86.

Schneiderman, Lawrence J., and Nancy S. Jecker. *Wrong Medicine*. Baltimore: The Johns Hopkins University Press, 1995.

Schneiderman, Lawrence, et al. "Medical Futility: Its Meaning and Ethical Implications." *Annals of Internal Medicine* 112, no. 12 (1990): 949–54.

Schotsmans, Paul. "When the Dying Person Looks Me in the Face: An Ethics of Responsibility for Dealing with the Problem of the Patient in a Persistent Vegetative State. In *Birth, Suffering, and Death: Catholic Perspectives at the Edges of Life*, edited by Kevin W. Wildes et al., 127–44. Boston: Kluwer Academic Publishers, 1992.

Selzer, Richard. *The Doctor Stories*. New York: Picador, 1998.

———. "A Question of Mercy," *New York Times Magazine*, September 22, 1991, 32–38.

———. *Up from Troy: A Doctor Comes of Age*. New York: William Morrow and Company, 1992.

Shannon, Thomas A., and James J. Walter. "The PVS Patient and the Forgoing/Withdrawing of Medical Nutrition and Hydration." *Theological Studies* 49, no. 4 (December 1988): 623–47.

Sheehan, Myles H. "Feeding Tubes: Sorting Out the Issues: Efficacy of Artificial Nutrition and Hydration Is Determined by Several Clinical Factors." *Health Progress* 82, no. 8 (November/December 2001): 22–27.

Storey, Porte. "Artificial Feeding and Hydration in Advanced Illness." In *Birth, Suffering and Death: Catholic Perspectives at the Edges of Life*, edited by Kevin W. Wildes et al. Boston: Kluwer Academic Publisers, 1992.

SUPPORT investigators. "A Controlled Study to Improve Care for Seriously Ill Hospitalized Patients (SUPPORT)." *Journal of the American Medical Association* 245, no. 20 (1995): 1591–98.

Teno, Joan M., et al. "Advance Directives for Seriously Ill Hospitalized Patients: Effectiveness with the Patient Self-Determination Act and the SUPPORT Intervention." *Journal of the American Geriatrics Society* 45, no. 4 (April 1997): 500–507.

————. "Do Advance Directives Provide Instructions That Direct Care?" *Journal of the American Geriatrics Society* 45, no. 4 (April 1997): 508–12.

Van der Feen, Julie R., and Michael S. Jellinek. "Consultation to End-of-Life Treatment Decisions in Children. In *End-of-Life Decisions: A Psychosocial Perspective*, edited by Maurice D. Steinberg and Stuart J. Youngner, 137–77. Washington, D.C.: American Psychiatric Press, 1998.

Vogt, Christopher P. "Practicing Patience, Compassion and Hope at the End of Life: Mining the Passion of Jesus in Luke for a Christian Model of Dying Well." Paper presented at the annual meeting of the Society of Christian Ethics, Pittsburgh, Pennsylvania, January 11, 2003.

Vollmann, J. "Advance Directives in Patients with Alzheimer's Disease: Ethical and Clinical Considerations." *Medicine, Health Care and Philosophy* 4, no. 2 (2001): 161–67.

Weijer, Charles. "Cardiopulmonary Resuscitation for Patients in a Persistent Vegetative State: Futile or Acceptable?" *Canadian Medical Journal* 158, no. 4 (February 24, 1998): 491–93.

Weissman, David E. "The Syndrome of Imminent Death." *Fast Facts and Concepts # 3.* <http://www.eperc.mew.edu>.

Welie, Joseph V. M. "Living Wills and Substituted Judgments: A Critical Analysis." *Medicine, Health Care, and Philosophy* 4, no. 2 (2001): 169–83.

Welie, Joseph V. M., and Sander P. K. Welie. "Is Incompetence the Exception or the Rule?" *Medicine, Health Care and Philosophy* 4, no. 2 (2001): 125–26.

————. "Patient Decision-Making Competence: Outlines of a Conceptual Analysis." *Medicine, Health Care and Philosophy* 4, no. 2 (2001): 127–38.

Wildes, Kevin W. "Life as a Good and Our Obligation to Persistently Vegetative Patients." In *Birth, Suffering, and Death*, edited by Kevin W. Wildes et al., 145–54. Boston: Kluwer Academic Publishers, 1992.

————. *Moral Aquaintances: Methodology in Bioethics.* Notre Dame, Ind.: University of Notre Dame Press, 2000.

————. Ordinary and Extraordinary Means and the Quality of Life." *Theological Studies* 57, no. 3 (1996): 500–512.

Wilkes, Paul. "The Next Pro-Lifers." *New York Times Magazine*, July 21, 1996, 22–27, 42, 43, 50–51.

Wojtyla, Karol. "The Person: Subject and Community." In *Person and Community: Selected Essays*, translated by Theresa Sandok. *Catholic Thought From Lublin,* Vol. 4, edited by Andrew N. Woznicki, 219–62. New York: Peter Lang, 1993.

Youngner, Stuart J. "Two Times What? Quantity and Quality of Life in Tube Feeding Decisions." *Journal of General Internal Medicine* 12, no. 2 (February 1997): 134–35.

Additional Resources

Catholic Sources:

Catholic Perspectives: The Right to Die. Chicago: Thomas More, 1980.

Congregation for the Doctrine of the Faith. *Declaration on Euthanasia*. Washington, D.C.: United States Catholic Conference, 1980. Also in *Origins* 10 (August 10, 1980): 16.

John Paul II. *On the Christian Meaning of Human Suffering*. Washington D.C.: United States Catholic Conference, 1984.

———. *The Gospel of Life (Evangelium vitae)*. Washington D.C.: United States Catholic Conference, 1995.

National Conference of Catholic Bishops. *Ethical and Religious Directives for Catholic Health Care Services*. Washington D.C.: United States Catholic Conference, 1995.

———. Committee for Pro Life Activities. *Guidelines for Legislation on Life-Sustaining Treatment*. Washington D.C.: United States Catholic Conference, 1984.

———. Committee for Pro Life Activities. *Nutrition and Hydration: Moral and Pastoral Reflections*. Washington D.C.: United States Catholic Conference, 1992.

New Jersey State Catholic Conference. "Providing Food and Fluids to Severely Brain Damaged Patients." *Origins* 16 (January 22, 1987): 583.

Oregon and Washington Bishops. "Living and Dying Well." *Origins* 21, no. 22 (November 7, 1991): 345–52.

Other Helpful Sources:

"Aging with Dignity: Five Wishes." P.O. Box 1661. Tallahassee, Florida 32302–1661. www.agingwithdignity.org. (This is a lengthy pamphlet on which persons can express their wishes about end-of-life treatments and care.)

Advance Directives, Surrogacy, Competency, and Futility. From EPEC Project Participant Handbook. American Medical Association, 1999.

Buckman, R. *How to Break Bad News: A Guide for Healthcare Professionals*. London: Macmillan Medical, 1993.

"Dying Well: Colloquy on Euthanasia and Assisted Suicide." *Hastings Center Report* 22, no. 2 (March/April 1992).

Emanuel, E. J., and Linda Emanuel. *Why Now? In Regulating How We Die*. Cambridge, Mass.: Harvard University Press, 1998.

Hospice Care: A Physician's Guide. National Hospice Organization, 1901 North Moore Street, Suite 901, Arlington, Virginia 22209 ((703) 243-5900/ http://www.nho.org/ e-mail: drsnho@cais.com)

Jennings, Bruce, et al. *Access to Hospice Care: Expanding Boundaries, Overcoming Barriers*. Special supplement to *Hastings Center Report*. March–April 2003.

Lynn, Joanne. *Handbook for Mortals: Guidance for People Facing Serious Illness*. New York: Oxford University Press, 1999.

Morris, Virginia. *Talking About Death Won't Kill You*. New York: Workman Publishing, 2001.

Preston, Thomas A. *Final Victory: Facing Death on Your Own Terms*. Roseville: Prima Publishing, 2000.

Schneiderman, Lawrence J., and Nancy S. Jecker. "Beyond Futility to an Ethic of Care." *American Journal of Medicine* 96: 110–14.

Webb, Marilyn. *The Good Death*. New York: Bantam Books, 1997.

Websites: General Gateways to Pain and Palliative Care Information:

www.epere.mew.edu
www.growthhouse.org.

Index

About the Author

Dr. Dolores Christie is executive director of the Catholic Theological Society of America with national offices at John Carroll University. Retired from a planned career in biology to raise a family, the author 'unretired' to do pastoral work and to attend graduate school in theology. A master's degree, a weekly commute from Cleveland to Duquesne University in Pittsburgh for a Ph.D. in Catholic Theology, and twenty years of college teaching later, she retired again.

An experienced clinical ethicist, she serves on the ethics committees of a tertiary care hospital, a long-term care facility, and on the Ohio Solid Organ Transplant Consortium ethics and patient selection committees. In her current retirement she does part-time college teaching, which leaves time to play with her ten grandchildren and to bake sticky buns "from scratch" for family celebrations when the six grown children and their families come home.

She is the author of *Adequately Considered: An American Approach to Louis Janssens' Personalist Morals* (Peeters 1990) as well as several book chapters and articles and many reviews. Her article, "This Is My Body: A Good Friday Reflection" (*Emmanuel Magazine*), won the 1997 Catholic Press Journalism Award for Best Magazine Article.

She lives in Cleveland with her physician husband of forty-three years, Richard Christie.